THE

VOLUME 5

Albert Outler

Edited by Leroy Howe

LIBRARY

PASTORAL

PSYCHOLOGY

The Pastoral Psychology of Albert C. Outler

Edited by Leroy Howe

Published by Bristol Books, an imprint of Bristol House, Ltd.

First Edition, January 1997

ISBN: 1-885224-11-7

Printed in the United States of America

Bristol House, Ltd.
P.O. Box 4020
Anderson, Indiana 46013-4020

To order call: 1-800-451-READ (7323)

The Pastoral Psychology of Albert C. Outler

Edited by

Leroy T. Howe

Table of Contents

Foreword

When I talked with Albert Outler in the spring of 1989 about the scholar who I felt should be invited to edit his pastoral psychology papers, he was pleased. We agreed that Leroy Howe had the credentials and experience to bring together the papers into book form, along with comment that would help the reader get into the working thesis of the paper at hand.

Howe has the rare ability to hear what a person is saying, traffic in that person's reasoning, and dialogue in words that are familiar to the one who converses with him. I know this from firsthand experience. Howe chaired my doctoral committee when I earned a Doctor of Ministry degree (*Biblical Preaching and the Use of Humor*) at Perkins School of Theology. The thesis dealt with the ontology of humor. During the orals I discovered that two of the three professors did not have the foggiest notion of what I was talking about. Only Leroy Howe comprehended the ontic insight to the workings of humor. I related this uncanny ability of Howe's to Outler (who also quite readily latched onto the ontology of humor). He acknowledged that he too had witnessed this particular competence in Howe.

In this book Howe hears what Outler is saying and in his Preface and introductory comments to each paper relates this to the reader in language easy to understand.

Howe and Outler discovered their agreement on issues in pastoral psychology shortly after Howe joined the Perkins faculty in 1969. Howe's Ph.D. in philosophical theology at Yale initially landed him a position teaching philosophical and systematic theology at Perkins. Then in 1979, at the invitation of the dean, Howe changed teaching fields to concentrate on theology in the practice of pastoral care and counseling. And he continued post-doctoral training in psychotherapy and supervision to broaden his support base in this relatively new field. Throughout this period Outler was supportive of Howe. In the Preface to this book Howe writes of the men's common interest in theological anthropology. The two had many long talks during the 1970s about how pastoral care as a discipline had slipped from its theological moorings to become tossed to and fro on the winds of the latest fads in psychotherapy. Outler strongly encouraged Howe's change of teaching field and often expressed the hope that Howe would help to restore theological reflection to the church's ministry of pastoral care and counseling. That longing expressed by Outler was forthrightly addressed by Howe in his 1995 Abingdon book, *The Image of God: a Theology for Pastoral Care and Counseling.* He plans a sequel to set forth a theology for marriage and family counseling in pastoral contexts.

Outler's pastoral psychology has been and will continue to be a theological grounding for caring pastors' reflections on theories of psychology, and for psychotherapists who care to know more about humanity's spiritual moorings. Howe outlines this book in a manner that presents the humanity of Jesus Christ as "the way and the truth" coming to grips with the various psychologies floating around in any given time in history. In no way does this mean that one is called to integrate each new theory of psychology into one's Christology. Rather, any particular psychological theory is to be judged by the illuminating paradoxical truths revealed in Jesus Christ (fully divine; fully human). Which is to say that any psychological *theory* is to be tested against *revelatory* faith experience, grounded in Scripture, and lived out in the tradition of the church. Then, where positive test results will allow, age-old Christian truths may perhaps discover a new language to get their message of salvation across to persons in modern times.

That "new language" does not necessarily come only from psychological theories. It can come from Scripture itself. So much of our understandings of salvation is expressed through the forensic metaphors of Scripture. The vivid pictures of the courtroom scene, i.e., the judge, the defendant, the jury (God's wrathful but righteous judgment against guilty sinners), etc., penetrate guilt-ridden consciences as few paradigms can. But Outler alerts us to the weakness of that metaphor in a modern society that senses no guilt. For these moderns there are other healing metaphors in Scripture that lend themselves to pastoral and therapeutic care. For example, there is nothing forensic about loving one's neighbor, about Jesus' "I am" statements (the door, the vine, the light, the bread, the good shepherd, the way, the truth, the life), the numerous parables Jesus used in speaking to people's particular situations, etc. But there is much healing offered in those Scriptures, a source that both pastors and psychotherapists should tap and use.

This written word reveals the living Word, Jesus Christ, who, Outler reminds us, is "our high priest and brother," who has "identified himself with the total range of our human upreach and downfall." The mystery of Jesus' humanity is the mystery of our humanity. All the more reason we need to study the Scriptures even as we study psychological theories, and accept the Chalcedon tradition of Jesus Christ (fully divine and fully human) as we encounter new insights into human behavior; and all of this under the illuminating Spirit of Truth as we faith our ways through human quandaries.

Through Leroy Howe's work in bringing these Outler papers together in book form, the disciplines of theology and psychology have a bridge over which both might traffic, meet and greet each other, and in conversation come to experience a common humanity in Jesus Christ and what Howe describes as the essence of Outler's pastoral psychology: "happiness, holiness, and hallowing."

Bob Parrott
General Editor
The Albert Outler Library

Preface

Those who know of Albert Outler's scholarly work during the later periods of his life are likely to think of him primarily as an ecumenist and as a historian of the Methodist tradition. There are good reasons for so regarding him. Outler was profoundly affected by the Second Vatican Council of the Roman Catholic Church, at which sessions he was an official observer on behalf of The Methodist Church, and well before the conclusion of the Council in 1965 he began provoking both his Protestant and his new-found Roman Catholic colleagues to reflect on the contributions of Vatican II in dialogue with one another. His entrance into the very heart of Roman Catholicism's efforts to re-vision itself, combined with lively involvement in the major theological discussions of the World Council of Churches' Faith and Order Commission, put Outler on the frontlines of most of this half-century's struggles to bring about unity, in some form, across a perilously divided Christendom whose fratricidal conflicts still threaten to undermine the integrity and the effectiveness of its evangelical witness.

Shortly before he immersed himself in the sessions of Vatican II, Outler had embarked on a serious and summative effort to bring scholarly discussion of Methodism's founder, John Wesley, to a new level. A one-volume introduction to Wesley's writings as a whole[1] became something of a preface to the project of preparing a new, multi-volume edition of Wesley's *Standard Sermons*,[2] work on which Outler continued well into the 1980s. Though the overall picture of Wesley that emerges in Outler's editing and in his commentary is not one with which every Wesley scholar is congenial—it should come as no surprise that Outler's Wesley is preeminently an "ecumenical" Wesley—hardly anyone is likely to dispute the quality of Outler's Wesley scholarship; it sets a standard that future generations of scholars will have difficulty emulating. Outler's background as a historical theologian, his ecumenical involvements, and his sensitivity to the pastoral dimensions of Wesley's life and work are all brought to bear on the Wesley project impressively and to lasting effect.

The breadth and depth of Albert Outler's contributions as an ecumenist and as a historian of Methodism can obscure the fact that these areas of interest were not the ones of greatest importance to him. What mattered most, instead, were the issues of pastoral theology and how they might best be addressed in a sustained dialogue with the theorists and practitioners of the modern psychotherapies. Early in his seminary student days at the Candler School of Theology of Emory University, Outler developed the enthusiasm that lasted a lifetime for integrating the wisdom of the modern sciences of the *soul* with the classical Christian understanding of the *humanum* in its transcendent dimension. (It is both fateful and tragic that *psyche* continues to be rendered as "mind" in our society and that even the venerable American *Psyche-atric* Association continues to compound the confusion with its frequently revised manuals of *mental* disorders.) So taken was Outler with the possibilities for integration that he wrote his Bachelor of Divinity thesis on the subject, sought eagerly in his pastoral practice for ways clergy might bring the insights of modern psychology to bear on their pastoral care and counseling, and finally opted for further graduate study expressly for the purpose of pursuing these issues further.

Given the passion generating Outler's trek to Yale, it might seem curious that, once there, he pursued a course of study in historical theology instead. The reasons were pragmatic only: He had the resources for only a limited time of study for his Ph.D; the faculty member who would be his principal advisor was on sabbatical during Outler's first year; and his background in classics, he was advised, would make it possible for him to complete a degree in historical theology before the money ran out! (One of Outler's most fetching stories of himself is with Carla, his young wife and most committed supporter, parked across the way from the Yale Divinity School complex on the day of registering for courses, debating their unanticipated situation in the front seat of their car, and his becoming a historical rather than a pastoral theologian as if in the blink of an eye.)

When Outler returned to Yale as a faculty member in the mid-1940s, he pursued in earnest his commitment to historical scholarship, but with a significant investment of time and energy now devoted explicitly to pastoral interests. He pastored a small congregation not far from the university, and became something of a commuter to New York City in order to study and train in psychotherapy at a leading psychoanalytic institute. The results of these labors are amply exhibited in his 1954 book, *Psychotherapy and the Christian Message,*[3] a seminal examination of human existence and experience from the perspectives of both the classical Christian tradition and psychodynamically oriented psychotherapy. Though Outler's career, from 1951 centered at the Perkins School of Theology of Southern Methodist University, quickly moved to embrace the ecumenical and historical interests described previously, he never let the issues with which he struggled in the *Psychotherapy . . .* book drift very far from his attention, as the material in this book should make plain.

In the Outler Archives of Perkins' Bridwell Library are over 1500 pages of previously unpublished materials written by Outler across his scholarly career on the various topics pertaining to sustaining dialogue among pastors, pastoral theologians and counselors, and psychotherapy researchers and clinicians on the structure, dynamics, and possibilities of human nature. A good bit of this material is in the form of lectures and informal presentations on several occasions. Some consist of notes and drafts of lectures never given and essays never published. An especially significant collection of material was presented in a course Outler taught at Perkins in his last year of full-time teaching before retirement. From this rather large body of material on a subject clearly dear to him from the outset, I have selected for inclusion in this volume a sampling that I consider representative of the whole and demonstrative of the importance he placed throughout his

career on maintaining an ongoing dialogue on psychotherapeutic and religious understandings of being human.
For Outler, such a dialogue held considerable promise for
enlivening the fields of both psychotherapeutic and pastoral practice, as pastors learn to respect what the human
sciences have to contribute to the care of souls and as
psychotherapists gain at least a glimpse of that transcendent horizon on which the true Healer of the soul arises in
and for human consciousness.

The editing of Outler's own contributions to this dialogue has consisted largely in agonizing over what to
include and what to leave out; in compiling a sample that
spans his academic lifetime, including his student years; in
modest abbreviations for the sake of gaining precious
space to include other selections; in rendering some of his
uses of pronouns more congenial to current preoccupations with inclusive language (when doing so leaves the
substance of his points intact); and smoothing out an
expression or two here and there. (Most who have ever
attempted editing anything by Albert Outler learn sooner
rather than later that he was his own best editor, and as
one colleague once remarked, a man seemingly incapable
of an infelicitous phrase.) At the beginning of each selection, and as a beginning to the whole course of lectures
mentioned above, I offer a brief introduction defining the
context and in some cases previewing the issue or issues
to be discussed. I hope these introductions will prove
modestly helpful and never intrusive. In the next few
paragraphs of this general introduction to the book, I want
to offer a few general considerations of Outler's pastoral
psychology by way of critical reflection on its contribution to
our own pastoral work today.

From the very first essay included in this volume, it
should become apparent how strongly Albert Outler felt
about the power of a Christian vision of the world to shape
a positive response to life's vicissitudes, challenges,
disappointments, and joys. That form of trust that a grace-
bestowed faith sustains opens out onto a comprehensive
perspective on the world as a created order in which
human beings, bearing the Creator's own image, have

preeminent meaning and share a common destiny. Over against human beings' willful resistance to, defiance toward, and outright rejection of God's gift of creation and sustenance in an order of things congenial to their highest, most worthy aspirations, the power, persistence, presence, and prevenience of our all-sovereign Creator, Sustainer, and Redeemer remain our unfailing and true source of hope and of being itself, eternally. In Jesus Christ, fully and truly God and man, the Christian vision itself focuses with unmistakable clarity, and the power to sustain it is bestowed freely and lovingly by the One who intends far more for each of us than we both can and dare imagine.

Outler believed it crucial that some such vision of the whole of things remain ever-present in both pastoral and clinical work on behalf of suffering human beings, and he was especially concerned to make a convincing case for such a transcendent orientation to "secular" psychotherapists. But he believed just as strongly that all creation bears its own eloquent witness to the Logos who the world's Creator also is, and that the human encounter with that Logos must be by way of the rationality, freedom, and discursiveness that are the hallmarks of humanity bearing the divine image and called to incarnate the divine likeness that was fully manifest in Christ. Otherwise expressed: the world in which we exist and the "nature" that we bear as human creatures are amenable to discovery and understanding through rational scientific inquiry, and even the most exclusively "humanistic" forms of such inquiry can yield wisdom about the human condition that is worthy of attention, respect, deliberation, and criticism on both scientific and *theo*-"logical" grounds. Most important for sustained encounter with the Logos of creation is the willingness of both religionists and scientists to respect each other's distinctive presuppositions, methodology, field-specific travails, and commitment to truth. With such mutual respectfulness in place, participants in the dialogue then can move on to the real intellectual effort, always self-involving, of determining what each can bring to the other in a common search for better ways of applying knowledge to the betterment of the human condition (to the extent, at least, that finite mortal beings can better their condition by their own efforts at all.) As Outler engaged both the scientific and the theological/religionist side of the discussions over the years, he seemed to regard his principal work with scientists as that of endeavoring to create a climate of openness even to hear what a religious tradition might have to contribute to our understanding of the human psyche. By contrast, pastors and pastoral counselors seemed to him both giddy to learn from the scientists and desultory about contributing something to the discussion from the perspective of a distinctively Christian anthropology forged by earnest and prayerful theological reflection that is serious and ongoing. Both kinds of attitude, Outler saw, undermine even the possibility of genuine dialogue. In general, Outler's efforts to create a context for a continuing dialogue between theologians and psychotherapists had greater impact on the latter than on the former. For this reason, I intend to focus the remainder of this introduction on redressing at least some of the inequity, as best I can, given the worrisome state of pastoral care and counseling theory and practice today.

For all the vaunted attempts during the 1980s to rediscover the roots of pastoral care in the churchs' historic practices, most especially those having to do with the fostering of spirituality, the care of souls in the churches still threatens to be overwhelmed by the mental health professions in general and their blatantly heteronomous attempts to gain and maintain control over all the accepted and acceptable norms for helping and healing people. Practitioners of these professions appear mesmerized by the soothing sounds of alluring voices pitching the lures of psychopharmacological, family systems, solution-oriented, group, narrative, desensitization, and even eye-movement therapies (to mention only a few), hinting not so subtly that they contain within themselves (somewhere) our final redemption from misery, satiation of narcissistic neediness, securing of entitlements, reconciliation of alienated relationships, happy accommodation to reality, and the promise of at least momentary interludes of untrammeled bliss. Not incidentally, all these therapies (and many others besides) now are heavily subsidized, criticized, and digitalized by the solons of managed care. Therefore, now even more than in Outler's time there is a desperate need for informed, intelligent, and inspired voices sounding a deeply pastoral understanding of the human condition whose base is a critically reflected and empathically appropriated theological anthropology expressive of the Christian tradition's best insights into the transcendent origin and destiny of the *humanum*. Instead, however, what most often passes for pastoral counseling in and beyond the churches is a slavish doling out of apprentice-level training in the latest psychotherapeutic fad, with pastoral care all too often reduced to the skillful reconnoitering of mental health professionals who can "really" help distressed parishioners. What bothered Outler most about the pastoral practice he knew was not only its inattentiveness to its own theological foundations, but its adulation of secular practitioners who knew even less about the theoretical foundations of and justification for their own interventions.

In the selections to follow, Outler articulates from a number of perspectives and at different times in his career what he regards as the indispensable foundations of a sound theological anthropology, as that anthropology is brought to bear on soul-care. Whatever may be the reactions to the specifics of Outler's formulation, his most important point of all should not be missed: pastoral care and counseling, from first to last, depends upon some well-formed view of human nature from the perspective of Christian faith, and it is a primary responsibility of every pastoral caregiver to come to terms with the task of formulating and reevaluating constantly his and her grasp of the subject as a necessary condition for faithful and effective caregiving. For Outler, what is central to a theological anthropology is a strong doctrine of creation, including especially a firm grasp of God's prevenient grace; Christology without apology, and with the person of Jesus Christ presented as the paradigm for human existence on earth; and an appreciation of the dialectical intertwining of the experiences of anxiety and guilt with the reality of grace. In another volume in this series, Outler's work on Christology is given extended consideration. Here, I will confine my comment to a single point: the deep reflection Outler has given Christological questions, from the perspective of classical Christian thinking, is especially evident in the strikingly nuanced way he lifts up the humanness of Jesus Christ as a paradigm for the "ideal outcome" of all pastoral care and counseling without becoming mired in the morass of our peculiar contemporary "quest for the historical Jesus." (Julian Hartt, a Yale theologian well known to Outler and appreciated by him, once seditiously and deliciously called this genre of theologizing "the hysterical quest for a new Jesus.")

A bit more extended consideration is due Outler's dialectical point on anxiety, guilt, and grace. Perhaps the most difficult struggle Outler faced in showing the power of a classically Christian perspective on the *humanum* for contemporary pastoral practice came from his growing perception of a certain kind of transformation in modern consciousness that he believed would compound the difficulties many people will have in developing even a rudimentary understanding of Christian claims about the human condition. In specific, Outler argued that classical Christianity depends upon the possibility of human beings' recognizing and taking with utmost seriousness their condition of sinfulness, a condition signaled by feelings of guilt that shape the context for receiving and appropriating the Christian message as, first and finally, a message of grace. Another way of stating the premise is that the capacity for feeling remorse and for expressing contrition is a touchstone for the communication and reception of the gospel of God's mighty acts of salvation in Jesus Christ. But, Outler goes on to argue, it is just such an assessment of guilt in human experience that modern consciousness, aided and abetted by the so-called "Freudian Revolution," has called radically into question. Today, most guilt feelings are regarded as simply neurotic, that is, purely internal in nature and without an objective basis; those feelings that *are* reality-based are properly dealt with by means of acknowledging acts of genuine offense or harm to another, of accepting forgiveness and/or making recompense, and of living out of the reconciliation effected rather than guilt feelings further harbored. Guilt is dealt with on the plain of action among humans only; there is no human *condition* signified by the word, and certainly it has nothing to do with the quality of our relationship to any transcendent Being.

Outler's *apologia* for the Christian tradition on this subject is intriguing. Basically, he accepts the contemporary critique at face value and shifts our attention to another aspect of our sinful, "fallen" condition to which he believes the Christian message still speaks: our sense of hopelessness. If we no longer are particularly anxious about coming punishment for our sins and in our sin-filled condition, Outler writes, we still are vulnerable to a kind of anxiety that none of the modern utopias, tried and promised, can possibly assuage: the anxiety that all of our hopes, dreams, strivings, and successes not only will come to naught but have no meaning in their very essence. The narcissistic rage and sense of entitlement Outler saw as epidemic in modern life is for him the principal outward sign (and sigh) of how deep our hopelessness lies in the center of both the conscious and unconscious psyche, and of the intensity of our readiness to see our situation from a transcendent perspective bathed in grace that calls us to a kind of hope whose power of actualization lies beyond ourselves, but is made available by divine grace.

Outler's willingness to bracket this important part of the Christian tradition could easily be misconstrued as the typical kind of apologetic move facile "liberal" theologians make unabashedly for the sake of rendering the gospel credible to contemporary sensibility at whatever cost to the integrity of biblical faith. What would be missed in such a superficial analysis is the subtlety by which he brings together psychodynamic theories' fundamental conviction that at the heart of human unhappiness is the mismanagement of anxiety with the Christian tradition's affirmation that anxiety is endemic to the condition of fallenness and the one effect first addressed in God's saving advent (". . . Fear not, for I bring you good tidings . . ."). Having said this, it must be acknowledged also that anxiety-oriented theories of soul-care reflect the continuing influences of psychodynamically oriented psychotherapies and of existential theologies no longer at the forefront of their respective fields. One can only imagine the twinkle in Outler's eye, however, as he contemplated assessing the worth of a theoretical orientation in terms of whether a particular generation of scholars liked it or not. Certainly in the field of psychotherapy, declining interest in psychodynamic foundations is little more than a sign of a weakness of will to deal with theory altogether, and the tragic result is the reduction of much that is called therapy to interventions based solely on the whim of the therapist, drawing praise precisely for their mysteriousness and imperviousness to careful examination. Without careful attention to theoretical foundations, Outler knew well, therapists become little more than mechanics of the soul, their offices little more than fix-it garages, and their work little more than experimentation conducted at their patients' expense.

In today's climate of opinion, the pastoral issue is not so much the eclipse of guilt in modern consciousness, but the rise of shamelessness and the attending conviction that just as a former generation may have banished the burden of excessive guilt, people now must be liberated not only from the destructive consequences of being abused by others' shaming behavior, but from anything that might contribute to anyone's feeling uncomfortable in any way about himself or herself at any time. Our current sensitivity to shame-based distresses in the psyche and in relationships may make possible a fuller appreciation of what the Christian tradition actually has said about the primary manifestation of the sense of fallenness in human consciousness: anxiety about the condemnation not of one's acts of omission or commission, but about one's very being, to its very core. To those who may be feeling the burden of such shame, the Christian witness of faith is not so much a word of forgiveness but rather one of assurance that the image of God by which we are constituted as human beings never is lost, and that its power to lead us into a new life is indeed fully restored in Christ. In many respects, Outler's discussion of guilt seems actually to be about just those experiences of shame to which we are becoming increasingly attuned, sometimes exquisitely.

Outler's attachment to psychoanalytically oriented psychotherapies, then, pervades a great deal of his pastoral psychology, but without taking control of it. Faithful to the tradition he represented as a theologian, he did not hesitate to criticize severely the failures of psychoanalysis to be open to the transcendental horizons of human existence (Oskar Pfister to the contrary notwithstanding) and to question whether its proponents possessed the intellectual wherewithal to analyze the human psyche deeply enough to discover its transcendent ground and aim. In his later years, Outler seemed to look more to Jungian theory to supply the needed lenses with which to see the genuinely transcendent possibilities in the human spirit. More recent developments within the psychoanalytic movement itself, however, may well offer that for which Outler inquired in vain of those who stood more stolidly on Freudian footings. Within object-relations theory, for instance, important new work is emerging that casts religion in a more positive light, not only for the contribution it can make to the process of maturation, but for the very truth value of its images, concepts, and convictions. Outler surely would be pleased with the prospect of a wholly new dialogue advancing at the frontiers of the very orientation he considered in many ways inimical to religious belief.

But now, it is time to conclude this introduction and to let Albert Outler speak for himself. I am very grateful to Dr. Bob Parrott for the opportunity to offer this labor of love on behalf of the memory of a dear colleague and friend. Dean Robin Lovin of the Perkins School of Theology has afforded me the opportunity to complete the project as one part of a research leave during the fall semester, 1995; I am appreciative to him in many ways for his continued support of my scholarly work. Christopher Heard provided invaluable technical assistance organizing the materials for my editing and offering salient comments about their contents.

Leroy T. Howe
Editor

PART 1

Albert Outler as Pastoral Psychologist

Introduction

Albert Outler's capacity for sustained and honest self-reflection is delightfully manifest throughout all his writing, exhibiting in many important ways how the self-awareness of the healer is indispensable to all care-giving. The following essay offers a glimpse of this capacity in its early stages of development. It is an autobiographical contribution written for a course taught by Hugh Hartshorne, Outler's principal mentor in pastoral theology during his graduate student days at Yale. Here, Outler also sounds out two themes with striking clarity: his conviction about the pervasiveness of human sinfulness, and his optimism about the power of Christology for the ordering of ministry.

In all of his subsequent striving for an inclusive theological vision from which to greet modern psychology's variegated understandings of the human condition and its prospects, these two themes together serve as a kind of compass facilitating the navigation of cognitive terrain often so complex as to make many feel that they are on the verge of intellectual shipwreck. They provide an early definition of the foundation for Outler's understanding of himself as anchored by and in "classical Christianity."

CHAPTER

1

A Brief Statement of Religious Experience and Belief

A ccounts of religious experience and belief are notoriously unsatisfactory. For one thing, they rarely have the same meaning for the reader that they have had for the author; it would be a miracle if they set in motion the same reintegrations for two minds of varied backgrounds and development. In the second place, genuine religious experience or belief is the most difficult human response to communicate adequately. Thought is at least one step removed from "the real" that that thought seeks to express. Language is, likewise, another step removed from thought, since one can never with completeness or clarity say all he thinks. Thus, if religion is the supreme effort to apprehend and come into relationship with Reality (God, to me), any effort to express the results of that quest must be three steps removed from the ultimate Reality. With the reader amply forewarned, then, I shall describe briefly what seem, in retrospect, the important events in my own religious development and then try to sum up the substance of my present religious faith.

I was born into a Methodist parsonage in South Georgia and was reared "in the lap of religion" of a fundamentalistic, but warmhearted, joyous sort. I got my taste for the prose of the Authorized Version from hearing my father each morning read the Psalms and poetical passages from the prophets at the breakfast table. My earliest definite recollection of a religious experience is of a sermon, preached in our church when I was five, on the misadventures of the prophet Jonah. The thing that impressed me most was not the fish story, but the greatness and resourcefulness of God, and his ways with recalcitrant servants. With it came a definite feeling of awe, but not of cringing fear, for that springs out of the feeling that the object feared is capricious and incalculable. I had been taught that God was thoroughly reliable, and I imagined him like my father, who never descended on one in a fury, but whose advice and orders commanded a healthy respect. I have never had a hysteric fear of hell or divine punishment, but rather was early taught that though God's dealings are inexorable, yet "all things [somehow] work together for good," if you loved him and expressed that love in obedience.

Life rocked along as might be expected under the circumstances until the age of twelve. I became deeply interested in a revival being carried on in our church and underwent an experience of contrition and acceptance that can be set down as my *first* conversion. It was three years later that I had another experience, of a similar sort, which I regard as "my call to preach." There was no theophany, of course; it was simply that it dawned on me that the deepest need in my life was to know God and to search out his will for myself and others. From that, the obligation to communicate that Will, as I came to know it, became inevitable. This basic conviction has never left me.

In college the intellectual struggle about religion began. It was the typical tumult, first about the authenticity of the Bible and then about the possibility of determining an absolute, as opposed to a relative, standard of conduct by which I could measure and guide my life. I was saved, as I suppose most are, more by the evident faith and integrity of one of my professors, whom I greatly admired, than by all the lectures I heard or the books I read, *pro fide.* My third conversion or crisis occurred about this time, for after a sermon by a visiting theological professor (during religious emphasis week), I went out into the woods and faced out the problem as far as I could go. This was the conclusion: God must be real, even if I cannot comprehend him; Jesus Christ was all that I could conceive of love and goodness, and therefore all I could know of God and all I needed to know. In his way of living was all that I could ask of meaning, dignity, and heroism. All the alternatives were lesser ones, leading to a materialistic and vulgar code of values and conduct, however glossed with worldly prestige. Until, therefore, it was clearly proved that Christianity was wrong, and that there was a better way for human striving, I should follow on after Christ, no matter if it were "afar off." I suspect now that a lot of this ratiocination was directed at the goal of staying within the general religious culture pattern; I am a born conformist, stirred to nonconformity here and there by a restless, though timid, search for truth. I can claim a great admiration for religious living, with its abandon and daring and leaving "all for thy sake"; it ought to be confessed in the same breath that I've actually done but very little of it.

Immediately after graduation I had the opportunity to test my fledgling wings. The job was superintendency of a rural high school in Appling County Georgia. There were two country churches thrown in for weekend ministry. At school, I had been keenly interested in psychological problems; and soon after I came to Baxley, I became acquainted with an interesting couple. Mrs. ——'s condition challenged me to seek to find what abnormal psychology could do to interpret and help a case of mental maladjustment and struggle, and she became my first "patient." Her first book was the occupational therapy that helped pull her out of the doldrums, and her second proclaimed her complete recovery. This naturally reinforced my interest in psychotherapy. Meanwhile, the work out in the country was causing acute tension. The plain, uncultured backwoodsmen were not impressed by tentative speculations about God and life, and I came to see how fruitless is a preaching that ends lamely, with a "perhaps" or a speculation, however dogmatically stated. Two years out there gave me a love for the soil and the men who work it; I learned that influencing human behavior was not a matter of imparting knowledge, but of moving emotions, stirring up loyalties that would then root themselves in habit and life. It was here that another crisis developed that involved an either/or decision, and the decision came, with great emotional stirrings, along the line of my second conversion: my destiny was to preach and teach religion.

From Baxley I was moved up the state to a circuit in the cotton country, there to preach to landowners, some of whom were practicing virtual peonage. It was there that I tried my hand at reform and found out why the prophets accomplished so little, in the matter of tangible results. While serving this circuit, I entered the theological seminary to carry on the two enterprises at the same time. I found at school almost no opportunity to carry on my study in psychotherapy. I wanted to be trained in a method of helping people in distress to find release and reintegration that would be more adequate than revivalism and at the same time more real than the glib futilities of religious education, as I knew it. I had seen both tried in a variety of situations and fail to fulfill their bright promises. Failing to find what I wanted, I plunged into the conventional courses and gained what I now regard as an invaluable background in biblical literature, theology, and church history. The chief service of my seminary days was to offer intellectual clarification about beliefs and problems that I had been holding suspended, waiting for a solution. From my professors I gained a new viewpoint of the social responsibility of Christianity that considerably broadened my horizon of interest and effort. On the side, and with unsystematic help from various sources I worked at abnormal psychology and psychotherapy. Finally, over the protest of some of the more staid professors, I handed in a thesis on the subject, embodying all that I had learned from a rather meager experience and what I could get out of books.

During seminary days, I had married, and a new angle developed in my religious life. Being religious by yourself and among men is one thing; the intimacy of marriage, stripping away all pretense and reserve, is quite another. My wife was an Episcopalian and so was I, only of the Methodist variety. Marriage has done a great thing for my religious life: it has objectified it to a certain degree and provided a lively forum in which to test ideas and conduct.

Our first appointment after graduation from seminary was to a small town in Middle Georgia. Here again I was worried by the wide gap that lay between the chill perfection of the religion of the seminary and the need and urgency of the religious problems of real people in real "life-situations." Here my work in psychotherapy, however crudely done, bore much fruit. This is no disparagement of our educational program or my sermons; it seems to me that they fit most naturally together. Three years among these plain people gave rise to considerable rethinking, brought a realness in prayer, hitherto undiscovered, and demonstrated the power of the gospel of Christ, even in these times, to touch and change individuals and groups.

From Gordon, I was moved into Macon, as assistant pastor and educational director of the largest church in our Conference. After the glamor wore away, I began to perceive the difficulties in running a huge church, in which an overwhelming majority of the members were but very mildly interested in Christianity. Our church school was "one of the most modern and best-equipped in the entire connection," but the contrast between the amount of activity and results was disheartening. The total result of that year was disillusionment about the chances of the modern church to disentangle itself from "the world" and thereby accomplish its mission. As Reinhold Niebuhr put it, what is possible in such situations is inadequate and what would be adequate was, apparently, quite impossible. And so I came to Yale!

Now about my religious beliefs: they are an awful hodgepodge. I have been in turn a fundamentalist, then a radical, then a "social gospeler," an exponent of religion by nurture and education; and each of these has left its trace in the complex of my beliefs. In addition, the approach of psychology has led me to an interpretation of motivation and personality that gives color to all the rest. However confused, and a little proud to be without label or party, I am still convinced of the authenticity of my earlier vision: to follow Jesus, as I can see him, so long as my faith holds.

What I am trying to do, as far as my rational efforts are concerned, is to find an intelligible fusion between the truths of the two most effective contemporary religious movements, Barthianism and Buchmanism. At the same time, I must understand personality in the terms in which psychology has presented it.

Barth's emphasis on a transcendent God, and a humanity that can be saved only by grace, finds an echoing chord in my own belief, although it seems obvious that Barth has pushed the matter to the extreme. The religion of the immanentists, such as Coe and the humanists, seems to me to lack vitality to reproduce itself in the lives of the common man. It seems to me to be a religion for sophisticated moralists, but since their number is so small in comparison to the rest of humanity, it fails to leaven the whole lump. The essential note of the Buchmanites, life-changing for individuals, is characteristic of the best tradition of the church, especially in those eras where she was most alive. It is but half of the picture, but it is the more important half, prerequisite to any other religious advance.

It seems clear to me, on the basis of my present experience and observation, that the springs of human life lie deep in the unconscious and emotional phases of our being, and are acted upon by our rational concepts only partially and usually *ex post facto*. The task of religion, then, is to do something that education, as such, rarely does, namely, appeal to and sublimate, as far as possible, the emotional and aesthetic impulses of people. Hence, I believe in a religion of vital symbols and a frank recognition of the irrational and incalculable drives of folks, particularly when in groups.

The fact of human sin, it seems to me, is inescapable; it is upon this problem, as Brunner has observed, that all religions of immanence break up, as a ship crashes against a submerged rock. Salvation from sin is something that man cannot accomplish alone; somewhere in the process help must come from beyond one, and it is to the source of that help that human beings' faith and loyalty will naturally turn. Sin can be overcome by suffering love; the proof of this is Christ on the cross. The theology of the religious culture into which I was born was largely centered around a substitutionary theory of the Atonement; I broke away from the legalism of that as soon as I saw how contrary it was to the spirit of Christ. I took refuge then in the theory of moral example (viz., of Abélard), until I perceived how thin and sterile such a theory was to grapple with the ravages of sin in the human heart. Now, I believe in the atonement as a ransom, not to the devil or *to* anyone, but rather that the Cross was what it cost God to prove his goodness and love that would bring people to repentance. All this sounds old-fashioned, to be sure. But I was driven to it, not because I didn't want to be up-to-date and "liberal," but because in my seven years of pastoral experience, it has been the only thing that has really worked.

God is both real and personal to me; he is at one and the same time the perfection of values toward which life strives and, standing apart from life, because greater than the world he has made, he becomes the judge of the relative values of living. Salvation is of grace by faith, and not of my own merit, save as one appropriates and utilizes the grace of God. This is classical Christianity, as I understand it, and none of the blind alleys into which I have nosed have demonstrated the clarity, potency, or wonder that such a faith brings to life.

It follows from the above that I practise the traditional methods of private religious living. Prayer is a genuine reality and I pray to God as wholly Other, with whom I may cooperate, but never coerce. I like to read the Bible as devotional literature; to biographies of the saints and the histories of vital religious movements do I owe more than I can express for example and insight. But most of all, in Jesus Christ, as divine, I find literally "the way, the truth, and the life."

My social hopes take their form almost exclusively from Jesus' concept of the kingdom of God. That that kingdom shall come in at the end of a process of social reform, I strongly doubt. Indeed, the kingdom is not of this world; it is the rule of God to which we submit and enter thereby a loyal relation as children of God and brothers and sisters to each other. The moral standard of my faith is perfection; no matter how imperfect or faulty my quest has been so far, I will not accept as final, for myself or for society, anything less than the highest and best as we know it in Christ.

"I believe in . . . the life everlasting." I don't know very much about it, but it follows as a very close corollary of my belief in God as both great and good, and in human personality as intrinsically worthful. The pearly gates and golden streets seem rather ornate and crass to me; it is enough to believe that "where he is, there I may be also."

I have not yet succeeded in fusing my religious faith and scientific interests in the realm of metaphysics, although I have no particular difficulty living with both together. Science has and ought, or so it seems to me, to depend for its philosophical basis upon a frank nominalism, which will keep it concerned with concrete particulars and guard it against intangible speculation. Experimental science is, in the nature of the case, materialistic. Religion, conversely, depends upon idealism for its foundation; indeed, it is idealism expressed in aspiration and behavior. That this is a paradox I do not deny. Where it may lead I do not know; so far it has not required an either/or decision.

The substance of this paper has been stated dogmatically, not because it is believed to be infallible, but simply because my purpose at the outset was to state, rather than to defend, my religious faith. From the changes it has already undergone, I have no notion that it will remain static. I do intend, however, that the main lines of its future development shall stay as close as possible to the core of what has been the Great Tradition in Christianity. When I can no longer do that, I shall feel duty-bound to renounce religion as an illusion and make friends with the mammon of unrighteousness.

Editor's Note

The only comment Professor Hartshorne seems to have made on this rather remarkable effort of his young graduate student is on the essay's very last sentence. Hartshorne suggested that it was neither a logical inference nor an emotional consequence of what went before, and that, as such, it seemed merely "superimposed on an otherwise intelligible and attractive structure." On the returned paper, Outler wrote, "One is inclined to agree with Hartshorne's comment."

In retrospect, this little interchange portends much. It hints that even from his earliest writings, Outler exhibited a curious predilection for undue self-deprecation that became well-known to his colleagues and friends, and that almost invariably appeared incongruous with the quality of achievement of the very writing in which it appeared.

Introduction

On March 21, 1972, Outler presented the following address, originally untitled, to the Dallas Society for Religion and Mental Health. Its early paragraphs offer a series of self-reflections from the vantage point not of a graduate student embarking on his first systematic thinking about his personal experiences and beliefs, but of a mature scholar at the height of his powers viewing with some degree of alarm the tumultuous changes occurring in the world he has sought to influence.

The paragraphs are especially valuable for their positioning of Outler's own contribution to the religion-psychotherapy dialogue in the 1950s alongside the work of his two most significant partners in the enterprise, David E. Roberts and Rollo May. His analysis of what our Enlightenment-born culture has come to, shared in different ways in many different papers over many years, here seems uncommonly prescient of reactions and feelings a quarter of a century later.

CHAPTER

2

Forty Years Later: Some Personal Reflections on Religion and Mental Health

Seen from the outside, my career must appear even to a friendly observer as spread much too widely and too thin over a jumble of interests and inquiries: history, theology, ecumenism, psychology, sociology, philosophy. As we all know, versatility exacts its price: inexpertness and distractedness, despite one's diligence and eagerness. And, as I begin to set my life and work in retrospect, all of this is all too obvious. Yet I keep hoping that somebody might notice a more coherent pattern in all this diversity that suggests something more integrated and integrating in it than random curiosity.

Ever since I can remember, my career has actually been focused (from an inner perspective) on the twin problems of crisis and development. On the one hand, what is it that perdures in and through radical change—in history and in personal existence? And, on the other hand, how are we to understand the paradox of freedom and disorder that dominates all crises? Both of these two questions focus on the *humanum*—the nature of human nature. The first question points to an intersection of theology and history; the second to an intersection of theology and psychology. And every main inquiry on my life's agenda has been related to one or the other of these questions—or both together. Thus, I am and have been a theologian, first and last, using the methodologies of critical history and depth psychology as well as I could to illuminate the human possibility, the human tragedy, the human mystery.

It was forty years ago that I discovered psychotherapy as a resource for theological insight and pastoral care of *some* sort—and in close connection with an old-fashioned Kraepelin-school psychiatrist in a medical school dedicated to the nineteenth-century credo: "All psychiatric disorders have a somatic base." There was nobody in pastoral care on the seminary faculty, but the man in Christian Education had read Henry Yellowlees and had some fairly primitive notions of endopsychic conflict. My resulting thesis was itself fairly primitive, with no precedents that we knew of at the time, and I wouldn't recall it now except as it may help you see the line of development that I'm trying to suggest. In the course of my research, I discovered Freud and Adler and Jung, and then Franz Alexander and the Menningers and, finally, Harry Stack Sullivan. But I also discovered that the psychiatrists of that epoch could scarcely have cared less about theology, or even a transcendentalistic anthropology, that their main concern in any possible collaboration with pastors and rabbis was to reduce the unwitting harm they tended to wreak in the field of mental health. Thus, when Dave Roberts and Rollo May and I got to know each other, we set about quite consciously to develop a dialogue between theology and depth psychology at the level of theory, of clashing and consilient concepts. Roberts took direct aim at the anthropological problem in his *Psychotherapy and a Christian View of Man;*[1] Rollo May went all the way into psychotherapy (with only remnants of his original theological interests).[2] I tried to carry Roberts' dialogical program one step further in my little *Psychotherapy and the Christian Message.* What we hoped for at the time was that the psychotherapists (and, more particularly, the psychiatrists and scientific students of personality) would take us up on our proposal that the human condition has to be understood transcendentally (i.e., theologically); or else, at the very least, they might be persuaded to grapple with the dimension of human tragedy on some other ground than their knee-jerk, Enlightenment rationalism. In this, we largely failed.

Depth psychology and modern psychiatry have gone on developing, past Freud and the classical orthodoxies of psychoanalysis and psychosomatic medicine; on to new preoccupations with chemotherapy, on the one hand, with such labels as "biopsychologist" and "psychochemist," and transactional or value analysis, on the other. But there has been very little serious or profound reflection within the so-called sciences of man upon the anthropological clues and claims of the Judaeo-Christian tradition.

Concurrently, the pastoral care movement went on developing largely as a sort of paramedical and paratheological enterprise, with most of its science *and* theology on loan, for purposes of practical paraphrase and adaptation. The harvest of genuinely new and creative theoretical insights from this endeavor has, in my own view, been meager and disappointing: a host of relatively capable practitioners of an essentially static theory.

Meanwhile, in these four decades, the whole human scene has changed in ways that we can scarcely comprehend, much less cope with. We are plunged into two concurrent and interactive crises of a mutation in the human psyche, on the one hand, and of the loss and recovery of the sense of transcendence, on the other. Without presuming to cover all of the operating dynamisms in the crisis and without attempting to develop any one of them fully, here and now, I'd like, for our reflections tonight, to comment on some of the more evident and interesting aspects of our current situation as I see them and as they affect our mutual interests in religion and mental health.

1. The first, of course, is the great basic mutation of the concepts and patterns of authority in our time: the real and the hollow victories of freedom. My childhood was spent in the last age in the history of Western civilization in which authoritarian values were still acceptable and partially enforceable in what was still called "polite society"—the reign of customary morality, of effective taboos of behavior, with religious (or at least transcendental) overtones. Freud's equation of anxiety and guilt seemed self-evident, the superego was very real and very tyrannous (and religion was often its ally!). In my lifetime, I've seen

the mutation—and I'm inclined to stress the term because I am convinced that this is more than a surface change, or linear development, in Western society (and its cultural spin-offs)—the mutation of the moral-demand systems by which the young are socialized, politicized, humanized. What we have to deal with is a radical shift from anxiety-guilt to anxiety-aggressiveness, from self-denigration to self-acclaim and self-righteousness, from the notion that life's untowardness is probably deserved to a universal, and nearly paranoid, sense of victimization (everybody and his sister feel themselves victims of unmerited and intolerable treatment by "them"), the shift from boot-strapping as a way of life to scapegoating. There are no intrinsic, absolute, unappealable authorities left, no taboos inviolate, no sanctions that are sacred. "Elite" is a dirty word, egalitarianism is our new myth—the classical notion of "superiority" (which fueled the classical concepts of virtue) is generally rejected, the so-called Puritan work ethic (thrift, industry, sobriety) ridiculed. And the new alternatives, including the new quests for instant salvation, are all self-justifying, self-warranting.

One of the ironies of this situation is that it confounds the tasks of the psychotherapist and religionist in a rather special way. Since Kant and Freud, our job has been "human liberation" from the external slaveries of an authoritarian society and from the subjective slaveries of sin and/or neurosis. Our gospel has been liberation (from inauthentic self-understanding of every sort and social injustices of nearly every sort). And now we are tasting the real and yet also the hollow victories of our gospel, even as we are also beginning to sense the tragic anomalies of freedom, such as the sense of randomness and a disorder in human experience generally. We are at the end of "The Age of Reason," yet we are mostly ill-prepared to serve as advocates of any alternative concept of social order.

2. Concomitantly with the radical societal and moral revolution, psychology itself has been experiencing its own protracted crisis: of a "science" without an identifiable object—the psyche. One of the great triumphs of our time has been the general discrediting of the age-old mind-body dualisms. But now, we have no plausible or even intelligible theories of psychophysical monism that explain either the phenomena of "experience" or of

the experiencing of subject. Thus we keep on working on behav ior, with little or no acknowledgment that we are dealing with a real and urgent mystery with averted or blinded eyes. The nature of the psyche is not just a problem but a real mystery—and yet the average psyche-ologist has, quite ironically, disqualified himself from even considering the anomaly of a logos with an indefinable subject or object.

3. A third major development affecting the very possibility of authentic human self-understanding is the complex of nonpsychological agents of psychological change that loom so large as oppressive portents to the young: technology, overpopulation, pollution, the breakdown of the melting-pot process in European and American life, the passing of Western dominance and of white supremacy, computerization, the eclipse of the Gutenberg Galaxy, etc.

4. With this, I think I also see the first signs of the waning of the current mystique of "humanity" and "the perfectibility of human society," the eclipse of utopia, and a spreading disenchantment with the hopes and dreams of the human enterprise. The two dominant notions of the epoch that now, I think, is winding down (after two centuries) were invention and progress. Both were functions of a new confidence in what man could make of (1) his world (by invention) and (2) what he could make of himself (by progress). The result was the most expansive and creative outburst (over a full two-century span) of any epoch in human history. Its successes reinforced its humanistic premise: that people can, and should, take charge of their destinies, since, indeed, there are no other comparable resources available for their fulfillment, natural or divine. Thus it was that the *humanum* was divinized and the mystique of humanity generated. And this mystique fueled the dreams and policies of almost every society on the planet: capitalist, Marxist, and now Maoist. Religion survived, but marginally, almost always at the mercy of science and ideology—chiefly as a secondary reinforcement to utopian hopes and expectations.

And now we've come to the end of that epoch: discontent with the quality of life our inventions have provided and with the radical ambivalence of all, or most, of what we have called "progress." The cry against technology is really a loss of our

enchantments with what machines can do for our human fulfillment; the self-hatred that is spreading through developed coun-
tries is really a frustration with what development has brought
with it, as far as human happiness is concerned. Along with
these disenchantments, the mystique of humanity (the nerve and
genius of the Enlightenment) begins to dissolve. The eruptions
of the 1960s were desperate attempts at forcing the millennium;
the relative apathy of the past two years is the fruit of the discovery that millennia cannot be forced. And now, I suppose, we are
entering an epoch of increased political irascibility and cynicism. For we are losing our confidence in the human achievement of human perfectibility without recovering the older grounds
of faith, hope, and love that upheld the hopes of Western man
before the Enlightenment.

5. Yet another sign of this new epoch we are entering is the
insistence of many of our symbol manipulators that we can and
must re-mythify our human perceptions of reality. The people
who have done most to expose and dissipate the myths and symbols of our older traditions are now proposing the creation of
new myths and symbols. And this I regard as an ominous self-
deception. For what they mean by myths and symbols (what
anybody has ever meant by "myth," "symbols," and cognate
notions, however conceived) is that composite of worldviews,
world pictures, values, imperatives, and sanctions that command,
direct, control the always uneasy balance between personal freedom and social order. But, as all the monotheisms have argued,
the controls that human beings create to control themselves are
creatures of their creators, which is to say, idols. And people
have never been able to worship or be controlled by idols as
idols—i.e., as their own handiwork. And anything consciously
created by us—myths, symbols, rituals, celebrations—can only
remain a fake "absolute," always in peril of skepticism and cynicism. The result of this sort of thing, thus far in human history,
has been chaos followed by tyrannies of one sort or another.

Thus, I view all of the various attempts at the conscious
renewal of moral intentionality in human behavior and the planned
recovery of social order with frank dubiety—so long as they are
based on humanist and secularist premises. And my doubts are
rooted in a very simple premise: human aspirations are incontinent and infinite (or at the very least they point to, and presup-

pose, the infinite), yet the human condition is finite, inescapably and without recourse. Everything it takes to be fully and truly human (identity, freedom, and love) is infinite, in presupposition and import. Yet every dimension of human existence is finite: limited by the particularities of space, time, and death—for every individual without exception.

6. This means that death becomes the focus of the human problem all over again, as it did in ancient Greece and Israel. But we are condemned to a new realism about death, for one of the strictest implications of any psychophysical monism is that there is no survival of death by a part of psychophysical entity. We have denied ourselves the luxuries of belief in ghosts, spooks, and *animae*. In this connection, the most interesting day I've had in a long time was with James Hillman of the Jung Institute in New York. Hillman (in this country for the Terry Lectures at Yale) was announcing his break from Jung and Freud on the crucial point of *dream interpretation*. For seventy years, depth psychologies have understood dreams as "messages," from the unconscious, or from the world of archetypes, or from some inner sending center: coded messages, phantasmic messages, etc., but messages that, decoded, might yield some wisdom about life and its quandaries.

Hillman now proposes—with an impressive array of Jungian-type evidence, from comparative mythology, classical literature, etc.—that dreams are more adequately to be understood as rehearsals of death, that the essential passivity and impotence of the ego in dreams is a prehumous reminder of death. (He points to the close connection between dreams and the "underworld" in classical mythology and chthonian religion, etc.) Just as sleep itself is an analogue of death and *vice versa*—in common speech and psychological symptoms—so also sleep-phantasizing (dreaming) is a way of facing death in advance and as a sort of stimulus to insight, before death, as to life's meaning and its inescapable finitude.

I was not altogether convinced by Hillman's arguments and evidence. But on the face of it, this is a brilliant and stimulating notion, with all sorts of implications for psychotherapy in theory and practice. These can be developed, and doubtless will be—amidst indignant protests from orthodox Freudians and Jungians (as happened at the New York meeting). But the main point for me is that this could be the threshold of a whole new problematic about life and death and, therefore, a whole new way of drawing our modern disenchanted human back to a serious consideration of the meanings of life and death, in the context of a newly recovered sense of transcendence—of the truly ultimate.

For the love about which we have grown so glib in our brave, despairing rhetoric is simply not available on demand, or by wishing or willing—or sexual exercise in any quantity whatsoever. St. Paul's triptych of faith, hope, and love are linked in a strange complex of contingency. Love depends upon hope, which implies a future and a continuity from the here and now into that future. This, of course, is why orgasm is not a sufficient sign of love and why hope and death are mortal enemies. Hope and expectation are as elemental and primitive in experience as pain, pleasure, and dread. Hope, however, depends on faith, which is an act of accepting and depending on the transcendent, the transhuman, the infinite. The greatest of these is, indeed, love. But love can never flourish or survive apart from the hope that rests on faith.

7. So I come back around to the point you might have expected, but I hope with some fresh angles of interpretation: the future of humanity lies with our capacities for religious faith, which is in order to hope, which is in order to love, which are in order to human fulfillment. In a way, of course, this is a pessimistic comment, since the future of religious faith is in dire jeopardy in our time, as witnessed in our religious institutions of all sorts. Yet when the half-gods go, it may be that we shall turn again to the encompassing Mystery in which we live and move and have our being, and see again the face of love and truth and find again the better way of 1 Corinthians 13—not just of love alone (that way lies delusion) but of faith, hope, and love: in religion and in mental health.

PART 2

On the Mystery of Being Human

Introduction

Central to Albert Outler's conception of pastoral theology is the necessity for its grounding in as full an understanding of the human condition as the resources of the natural and human sciences, in dialogue with classical Christian thought, will make possible. His principal complaint about most approaches both to psychotherapy and to pastoral care and counseling was their indifference to foundational thinking at this level: integration is the key, and integration cannot be accomplished without at least an attempt to master elements of the discussion on both sides of the inquiry, the secular and the theological. Particularly tragic for Outler was the conspicuous inattentiveness of the pastoral counseling discipline to the rich resources of the Christian tradition and to making this tradition available for clarifying the transcendental dimensions of human existence in the world. Bereft of meaningful associations to classical Christian thinking about the subject, pastoral counselors can only become caught up in the winds of secular doctrine about the *humanum,* rendered silent about any contributions the Spirit of all Truth might have to make to contemporary understanding.

In the following three selections, a modestly abbreviated version of the Earl Lectures, which he delivered at the Pacific School of Religion, Berkeley, California, in February 1969, Outler offers one of his most engaging efforts to supply the needed theoretical foundations by carefully considering what the Christian faith has to say about being human. At this time of his scholarly work, Outler was demonstrating considerable interest in revisionary forms of Thomistic thought, and felt the work of Bernard Lonergan to be especially worthy of serious study. Lonergan's influence is strong in these lectures.

CHAPTER

3

The *Humanum*: Crux and Crunch in Contemporary Theology

There is a foolhardiness in an uptight, aging square from Texas approaching the *numen tremendum* of our West Coast civilization as it is apotheosized here in the Bay Area. Here, we are assured, is where the myths of our metro-American future are being engendered, here the convergence of the continuing "gold rush" and the new humanity. And here I come, loaded with liabilities: hoary, a WASP, a Southerner, a traditionalist (of sorts), a rationalist (of sorts), enshrouded in my gray-flannel suit, diffident and mildly impudent. This latter springs largely from a lively bias against sacred cows, and by "sacred cow" I mean *any* object of knee-jerk reverence, *any* pattern of uncritical enthusiasm, even in good causes. My warrant for such irreverence will appear, I hope, in these lectures. Whatever the *humanum* is, it is not reflex behavior; knee-jerks in any direction (against the establishment, for the enraged, or even on behalf of pathological moderation) are infrahuman. Moreover, "sacred cows" are often only modern replacements for ancient idols, and idolatry has a doubtful record in the service of true humanity.

But my real audacity in trying to make this particular scene, and in asking for your irreverent attention, is my choice of topics. Start talking about human nature and suddenly *all* your hear-

…s are professionals, with expert testimony to offer and to refute. Besides, what more is there to say about the *humanum* after three millennia of incessant conversation on just this topic? Well, this much at least: man is what's happening now, everywhere and all over. The problem of humanity's prospects and possibilities has suddenly become newly urgent to everyone, filling up the theological horizons. We are caught up in a protracted spasm of self-concern—a sour mix of hope and frustration, a muddle of insights (scientific, political, religious), a baffling confusion of self-confidence, self-righteousness, anxiety, and self-loathing.

In the Genesis myths, the order of interest runs: "In the beginning, God." And thence, from Creator to creation and finally to human beings as crown of creation. I intend to reaffirm that order in these lectures, but not quite in the old way and not without awareness that its reversal has become the chief premise of modernity. The *humanum* is the ruling passion in our epoch, God having been superannuated or exiled. New visions stir us: the new humanity, man on his own in the human amphitheater, as tribunal of last resort. Yet, despite this new-found self-possession, we are deeply troubled and beset. Having cut our leading strings to heaven, we have failed to find a solid footing on earth. Until recently our species existed in relatively tight, closed societies with predictable ranges of agony and glory. Now a new rate and range of change has upset all that. Human values have been magnified (not to say absolutized); the revolution of rising expectations has given us a glimpse of a secular Eden. At the same time, the frustrations of our hopes increase and this reinforces a spreading, deepening mood of chronic outrage. Healthy wild primates rarely fight within their own species; animal behavior in general is stabilized by autonomic and social controls. But man turns out to be more destructive than all the other primates put together—and this as a function of the aggressions of overcrowding and alienation, the rage-generating pressures of multitude and immensity. We are free and mobile as no generation ever was, and yet bound and badgered as none was either. We have maneuvered ourselves into the intolerable spot of trying to avoid anarchy or holocaust by suppressing or sublimating imperative animal impulses, with the choice of anarchy or holocaust increasingly attractive to the increasingly desperate. Traditional moral demand systems have been strained past the breaking point. The most poignant aspect of this revolution is the paradox of its soaring idealism and its human callousness, the utopian dreams that fuel its fury and the partisan conflicts it has spawned. The past is under assault, the future is being hailed, even if the promise of that future has nowhere been fulfilled.

The church is involved in this crisis of self-tormented man—deeply—and is even less ready for effective response this time than in some of her earlier upheavals. For one thing, we are confronted by a massive shift away from ancient moralisms to a new antinomianism in which the gospel of God's unmerited forgiveness (justification by faith) seems more and more psychologically irrelevant. Humankind is more anxious than ever but far less equally guilt-ridden; Romans 7 has a different ending and Romans 8 has been dropped from the canon. Then, again, there is the growing alienation between church and "the new bourgeoisie." They're dropping away in droves from what they regard as a pseudo-prophetic ministry that has used them long enough as a golden goose and whipping boy. We lost the intelligentsia in the Enlightenment, labor in the Industrial Revolution, the rural proletariat in the agricultural revolution, and now it has come suburbia's turn to reject our ill-concealed contempt. Curse Constantine and his avatars if you like, but when we have finished scuttling the institutional church, we will discover that sectarian Christianity (which is what will be left) can provide islands of light in a darkling sea but will no longer deeply affect the social and political destiny of what remains to the secular city.

An older generation might remember Reinhold Niebuhr's once-familiar aphorism, "Man has always been his own most vexing problem." But the young are experiencing the old problem in new tonalities. Human destiny has fallen into human hands, so they say. We can have whatever future we *really* want, so we keep telling ourselves. Meanwhile, our living spaces decay, the good earth looks better from outer space than up close, bigotry blooms, reason flees the Academy, faith falters and the odds rise that our nuclear eschaton will be triggered not by villains but by good people in desperate befuddlement. It is, therefore, in order to ask what sort of creature it is that has worked himself up to such a brink. Our powers of conceptual thought and communication allow us to dominate the natural environment (including our animal congeners) and yet not really to control it. Our powers of self-understanding and self-transcendence generate behavior that is, as Plato said, ec-centric (an organism with its organizing center not entirely self-centered). We know more about ourselves as mechanisms and organisms than any one ever did before; yet less, or at least no more, about ourselves as persons.

This suggests that man is more than a self-vexing problem; he is also a self-concealing mystery. This is not a way of referring to what we don't yet understand but instead to what we cannot and never will understand, in terms that would satisfy any canon of direct verification. By "problem" I mean any sort of perplexity that, in some sense or other, is soluble in principle. By "mystery" I mean an undeniable reality that nevertheless defies definition or management by technical reason. The *humanum* is such a mystery. One finds an impressive unanimity on this point among people who differ widely in their interpretations. All that human beings know about themselves is transcended by their aspirations, by their human hungers, by their unaccountability. One of the subtlest and most ominous of all our self-deceptions is the notion that the human mystery can finally be reduced to the human problem, because those who deny their self-transcendence deform their own humanity. This, obviously, is a polar notion: a problem and a mystery, a biological organism and a self-transcending subject, etc., etc.

An illuminating angle of vision on the polarity may be found in what Bernard Lonergan calls "horizon-analysis"—or in a well-meaning adaptation of it as I understand its application to the *humanum*. "A horizon," says Lonergan, "is a maximum field of vision from a determinate viewpoint,"[1] which sounds a bit like Husserl's notion of a *Blickrichtung* ("an intentional line of sight"), except that Lonergan means to give equal stress to what is out there to be seen and to the epistemic biases of the viewer. This means an object pole (phenomena as they swing across the horizon line) and a subject pole ("the possibilities of intentionality— meaning possessed by the subject"—affecting and being affected by his specific noetic disposition at any given time). Horizons shift, viewpoints are "converted"; and this explains why theories and their verifications generate an endless process of inquiry. "Conversions" of our subjective viewpoints occur at several levels, says Lonergan—conceptual, moral, religious, Christian; and these obviously do not exclude each other in their interaction. In the case of the human horizon, however, the difference between, say, behaviorism and dualism at the conceptual level makes a difference in the intentionality-meanings of all assessments of the data in sight. Again, at the level of moral concern, one's assumptions about the dignity and worth of persons affect the range of options in one's objective evaluation. The viewpoint of determinism "converted" to an acknowledgment of self-transcendence opens up new options otherwise closed. And the specifically Christian perspective on man generates an even more specific horizon shift.

Now, in some ways, it is a threadbare commonplace to note that what is knowable is not constructed by the knower, even though the knower's biases affect the range and quality of his and her knowledge. And yet this particular way of thinking about thought helps a little to bridge the subject-object chasm that has been cried up by the existentialists; it could aid in the dialogue between those who still take seriously Pope's motto about "the proper study of mankind [being] man." In this way, we can consider man as an animal with entire seriousness, with dire consequences for the classical body-mind, body-soul dualisms but with hopeful prospects for other models that take their partial clues from Christian claims about Jesus of Nazareth. Such a viewpoint has a consonant moral perspective: "the world" as human beings' "home," human dignity as our prime value, the hope of becoming *fully* human. And I think of it as a reasonable way of talking about the mystery at the heart of the *humanum*.

Humanity's animal origin is old stuff by now and need not be belabored. At least three aspects of this problem, however, are worth repeated mention, since they may illuminate my main point. The first is that though the biological evolution of *homo sapiens* has been negligible, his human evolution has been, quite literally, extraordinary. Why so little advance beyond the simian in one way, so much in another? So far, references to the slight amplifications of cortical convolutions in the human brain case fail to flip the light switch in my mind. Whatever the *humanum* is and may be, it is *not* a simple function of organic evolution. But if not that, what then?

A second notable fact about the human mystery is the strange dissymmetry between some of our hominid and our human traits.

As far as technical intelligence, behavioral adaptability, fabrication, individualization, socialization, etc., are concerned, it is plain that we share these traits with other animals in greater and less degree. *Homines faber, loquens et ludens* are really not all that different from chimpanzees and bottle-nosed dolphins. But when it comes to speech, moral anxiety, cumulative cultural development, self-consciousness and conceptual judgment, we are on a decisively different level of behavior and experience. And these are the traits that have made the human "scene."

A third point may be the most significant of all. It's a commonplace that the human infant is the most radically unfinished of all animal young; the human maturation span is the most elongated. We know that this means a protracted crisis of dependence utterly decisive for personal development. And we know that this dependence is fearfully complex and precarious: food, shelter and herding do not suffice to mature a human being. Human young require freedom *and* discipline, but in the interest of their own responsible use of freedom. They require teaching, but in the interest of their own capacities for self-directed learning. They require love (unconditional love), but in the interest of their becoming loving persons. And all this requires the human analog of grace and faith: infants' environments must be trustworthy and loving and they must learn to trust and love, or else their human growth is deformed. Freud spoke of infantile sexuality and taught us to recognize the omnipresence of love. We might speak of infantile religion and ponder the omnipresence of faith, hope, and love ("these three; but the greatest of them is love").

Even on his animal horizon, therefore, man is both problem and mystery, despite the obsession of most people against any explicit mention of the mystery bit. Mortimer Adler has proposed a verification-wager for the crucial point: if something like a "Turing machine" is developed in which both hominids and humans can communicate conceptual thoughts to each other and a third human, the human problem will then be "solved"—in that we will know that human beings differ from other animals only in degree—and the notion of mystery can be discarded. Until then, says he, we are stuck with a probable difference in kind and can give no rational explanation of it. For my part, I should think that even a Turing machine would be a distinctively human development, with some startling theoretical questions left flapping loose in the psychological breeze. In any case, the human mystery, as mystery, remains in all its lure and horror, and it deserves more urgent reflection than it's been getting, even in a narcissist age.

There are, of course, alternative human horizons whose expositions have exercised thoughtful people for millennia. They all begin with the difference between the human and the rest of animate nature and then proceed to ponder the differences. Generally, though, they have agreed on one version or another of body-soul, body-mind dualism: the human as some extra thing, some sort of spirit, soul, mind, or whatever, inserted, infused, or integrated in a "body," "flesh" or *re extensa*. This tradition of dualism, in its varieties, is ancient and massive and has so long and honorable a connection with Christian thought that most people have supposed it to be an essential part of Christian orthodoxy. More people can take the death of God more calmly than they do the more cogent denial of the existence of the human self as a hypostatic being separable from the body. Neurologists as eminent as Sir Charles Sherrington and John Eccles could never quite shake off the dualistic nuances in their models of personality. Nor can we. All ordinary language has been built to distinguish between bodily and mental dimensions in our behavior, feelings, and psychic states. Animism is the matrix of all religion; dualism is a "natural" perspective. There's no time here to lay out its virtues and faults. But most moderns have already agreed that its faults are fatal: psychophysical monism or integrity is as nearly a universal consensus as one can point to in contemporary horizon analysis today, however inconclusive its final import. It strikes me, then, that both the biologists and the philosophers might take more seriously than they have the notion of radical mystery at the heart of the *humanum*. One gets the impression, however, that even the bare notion of mystery offends the secular spirit.

In the course of prolonged puzzling about all this, the most helpful line of sight I've come upon is in the Thomist dictum that the soul is the form of the body, the body is the matter of the soul—neither identified with nor separable from the other. And it has occurred to me that this perspective (this sort of horizon analysis) has real significance for fruitful dialogue between life-science people and philosophers and theologians, since it has the conscious intent of bringing natural science and biblical revelation into intelligent interaction. In such a horizon analysis, we might well begin with the neglected evidence that man, as animal, is an incontinent animal, not merely in degree but also in kind. All of our distinctively human interests tend to be unrestricted. Our inbuilt biological controls are hopelessly inadequate, chiefly because of these predispositions to human excess, in all directions. Our hungers are insatiable, our yearnings and hopes are literally boundless. This tendency to moral and spiritual extravagance looks both ways: human perversions, cruelty, and misery, etc., are wrongly called "beastly"; at the spectrum's other end, we still never make "angel." In both directions, what we recognize as distinctively human experience and interest argues self-transcendence, but transcendence in, toward, and from what? All animals need freedom; yet human freedom is something different in scope, quality, and effect. All animals are curious (at least prehensive). But human curiosity and mental activity is oriented to infinite regress and infinite progress. We question our questions and all our answers open up new questions; our impulse to inquiry and desire to know is forever open-ended. All animals are moved by love and hate, at one or another level of meaning: man is the animal whose loves and hates are both incontinent. We are the sexiest of all primates; sex is incessantly available; copulation face to face makes sex more "personal" and therefore freighted with meanings that always include more than orgasm and procreation. Yet human love also reaches upward and forward in friendship, spiritual refinement, community, and communion in ways that are not merely extrapolations of *libido.* It is, therefore, self-transcending, but, again, toward and from what?

The shadow side of this human incontinence is equally transcendent and tragic. Freedom, intelligence, and love are each and all regularly perverted into tyranny, bigotry, and inhumanity. Arthur Koestler has wondered whether this ghastly paradox reflects some pathological quirk in the evolutionary process that might be remedied by some sort of chemical humanizers. We might even speak of *homo simul sapiens et maniacus,* and then ponder the prospect of a new priesthood of chemists and pharmacists not taking their pills while feeding them to the rest of us.

Man, obviously, is a self-tormented and tormenting animal: mangled in his manhood, dwarfed in his humanity; predatory and deadly. Good and evil flow from the same potencies of self-transcendence. Man makes himself and unmakes himself and his world! In such ways the *humanum* defies logical definition, classification or correlation, without remainder, within the realm of animate nature. That he is an animal is obvious; that he is only animal is not obvious at all. The *humanum* is not a hypostatic entity ("soul" or "a little man in the head"—or guts); it is not preexistent; it is not separable from bodily process; it is not differentiated by race, class, culture, or piety. As an entity, it simply does not exist—in space, time, or causal nexus.

Ah so! And then what? What *is* the human proprium? How are we to understand ourselves as human, in a crisis where it is precisely what is human that twitches the fearful balance of history? How can we ever become fully human unless we understand what it is to have been human at all? How is the whelming tide of inhumanity ever to be reversed or redeemed save by some sort of authentic humanization? What is the final horizon of our infinite strivings and aspirations? These questions are as urgent as any of the others now agonizing human beings and nations. They point to our root dilemma beneath our visible and tangible concerns. And it is no better than high-minded triviality to argue that these are specious questions simply because they imply a mysterious dimension in the *humanum.* It is a mere prejudice that dismisses mystery on the ground that it cannot be dealt with in terms of verifiable propositions or controlling knowledge. The demand for fruitful insight grows more imperious as we recognize the decisive moral conversions that are actually in process in contemporary human horizon-analyses. How else would you account for the rise of a universal moral passion for the human possibility whatever it is judged to be? Whatever the *humanum,* it has come finally to be regarded as a supreme value by more people than ever before in human history. The sense of human dignity and the hope of becoming fully human are the effective fuels of current revolutions, the valid premise of the new politics, the moral substance of the new utopianism. But, equally, this is also the source of the disenchantments of those who feel denied their honest expectations. Hence the bitter outrage of those who have to settle for the secular city in place of paradise?

Anyway you take it, the human mystery, the human haecceity, is unfathomable by any horizontal probing we can reach. Personal reality exceeds all attempted definitions of "person"—Boethius', Strawson's, or whoever. Man is *selfed* but not fully self-possessed. Man is value-oriented—bound to discriminate between some option of right and wrong—but never, really, self-justified (i.e., successful in being self-righteous). Always, our utmost need is "to grow and grow, until we arrive at the utmost limits of ourselves." And so we come at last to a ridiculous thesis that I hesitate to mention, especially in a Christian church amongst sophisticated clerics. It's a bleached bone of a notion, biblical and pre-scientific. Its classical expression comes in *I, i,* of *The Confessions* of an ancient African bishop, St. Augustine, and once it was a Christian commonplace. Pardon my paraphrase: "You, O God, made us on purpose for co-existence and communion with you; and deep in our hearts [the human mystery] we are restless and rootless until we come, at last, to a new rest and rootage [security and self-fulfillment] in your constant care and pro-vidence." Here, the view is clear that the heart of the human mystery is rather more an appointment and inspiration of God, however it may also be related to natural process.

My courage to talk in this vein nowadays, in the face of its flip rejection by the *nouveau avant* as "traditional," comes partly from my conviction that it "has reason" (as the French say), partly from some interesting new sounds in the old chorus of the secularists (has Peter Berger heard something the rest of us will soon be hearing, again?), and partly from the still-mounting evidence that human nature is tragically misunderstood when it is taken by itself as the limiting notion of our finite knowledge. The chief casualty in the "death of God" episode is its unintended sequel: the death of the *humanum.* Moderns have lost their awe of the infinite: the results are god-awful. We have tried to banish the sacral from our secular city; the secular city is by way of thwarting our true humanity.

Now all this has been for naught if you've concluded that what I'm trying to do is to sneak a god of the gaps back onto the human scene and thus inflate the human enterprise with piety. If I am a dualist in disguise, I have disguised it from myself. If there is an ampler way of honoring all we know about the *humanum*—all of it—and of enhancing the human prospect, I'm eager to serve on the welcoming committee. But none of the accountings that ignore or discard the postulation of humanity's divine environment comes even close to honoring the human mystery in its full actuality. And it is irrational to levy an antitheological veto as to the terms in which such a mystery might be pondered. For we already know what happens when that is done: utopianism displaces Christian realism, human aspirations turn into enchantments, and the agony and glory of existence is transformed into tragedy that may be noble or squalid, but stark in either case.

There is a Christian analysis of this human horizon that assumes that human beings can be both human and holy, both fully humanized and truly divinized (i.e., truly participant in God's grace and perfections). This view denies that humankind is God's puppet or artifice and affirms, instead, that God is responsible for us—for our potency to become human—and that we are responsible to God—for the reception and use of God's gifts and pro-vidence. This Christian way of appraising the *humanum* starts from a special clue that comes from a special instance of very real humanity that amounts to its authentic revelation. This clue is found in Jesus of Nazareth, a man of God's own choosing who was made to be both Lord and Christ, hinge of our history and pioneer of our salvation (i.e., our full humanity). That he is also confessed as the authentic revelation of the very mystery of God is not a contradiction. It is, rather, a crucial integral in the total Christian vision of God and humans in their entire relationship. It is to this Christian clue that we turn in the next lecture, and after that, to such insights a perspective like this may provide in our own gropings for self-understanding and in our own adventure in passing from barely human to truly human to fully human.

Introduction

The earliest statement from Outler included in this volume, from his graduate student days at Yale, winsomely exposed the importance that Christology would have for his developing theology and for the maturing faith that would provide the foundation for his ministry as pastor, scholar, and teacher. Here, the subject of Christology is discussed in somewhat technical terms and without apology, in a way that reveals the vital center of Outler's deepest and most personal reflection across a lifetime. In this lecture, Outler also connects Christology with theological anthropology in such a way as to make their bond inseparable. The import for pastoral psychology is profound: The only horizon from which someone who purports to offer *pastoral* care and counseling as something distinguishable from, and distinctive in relation to, all other forms of psychotherapy and caregiving, is that which has been shaped by the God-intended and graciously sustained life, ministry, death, and resurrection of Jesus Christ. Growth into a humanness whose measure is *this* man is the goal, end, and "optimal outcome" of all pastoral ministry.

CHAPTER

4

The Christian Clue

Over and beyond the obvious problems ingredient in our study of man, there is a genuine mystery at the heart of the *humanum*. This mystery must be posited since it cannot be identified or understood solely in terms of our animal origins or their evolutionary mutations. The relevance of this focus is the fact that the *humanum* has become the horizon-filling problem in contemporary theology and yet, so far, all our wrestling with the human problem has shed precious little light on the human mystery itself—except to discredit the dualistic perspective in which it has traditionally been viewed. From all this it follows, I think, that a religious view of the human condition provides an ampler horizon for probing the depths of human experience and perplexity than those delimited by a secular perspective.

Now, anyone who will go this far is ready for the next step: to consider the special clue Christians have believed they have in Jesus of Nazareth as a disclosure of this mystery, *par excellence.* Such a notion is, of course, no better than a Christian commonplace, but it has been all too easily misunderstood as Christian moralism (*In His Steps* or *What Would Jesus Do?*), or else misconstrued in terms of one or another of the dualistic traditions that have dominated Christian anthropology and Christology almost from the beginning. It strikes me as a marvel that the biblical witness to the human mystery in Jesus Christ, together with its relevance for our self-understanding, has survived its successive deformations in heresy, orthodoxy, and modern Christianity.

It seems worth noting early on that the biblical people were agonizingly concerned about human nature and history and the meaning of human existence, yet they never devoted much more than marginal interest to the theoretical problems of human beings' place in nature. God and man—that was their endless fascination: history and tragedy, redemption and hope. The human escapade is constantly in view because of their interest in God's experiment with this covenant community in which human beings are called to become fully human in themselves and fully humane to each other. This is why Deutero-Isaiah's messianic vision comes so close to the apex of human aspiration: a peaceable kingdom, a joy-filled society in which justice and love are habitual virtues, where none shall "hurt or destroy in all my holy mountain, says the LORD" (Isaiah 65:25). Even so, we never are offered an integrated theory about the *humanum*. The rich metaphor of the *imago Dei* remains curiously underdeveloped in the Old Testament, and in its infrequent usage in the New Testament its reference is Christological. The pinched nerve in the Old Testament was the lingering threat of graven images and other manifestations of human beings' demonic tendency to deify some thing or somebody.

It was to have been expected, therefore, that when a small band of renegade Jews began preaching a hot gospel about messianic visions and hopes stirred by the ministrations of an unauthorized Galilean rabbi who was then denounced by the Sanhedrin, crucified as a zealot, and resurrected as Israel's Lord and Christ, the reflex verdict was scandalous (i.e., the rejection of the new faith as a serious threat to monotheistic faith). It was, at best, fanaticism; at worst, idolatry! "We preach Christ crucified" (says Paul), "a *skandalon* to the Jews and a *morian* to the Gentiles" (1 Corinthians 1:23)—and no wonder. To any orthodox Jew, this preaching amounted to a crass betrayal of their hard-won faith in *one* God; to the religious Gentile (in the Levantine motley called "Greek" only as a misleading grab-bag label) the Christian slogan, "Jesus is Lord," was blatant nonsense. If I told you that I had two brothers, that one of them was an only child, your instant reaction would be "nonsense"—or worse. But this is the way it sounded in gentile ears to say that a man really was "Lord and Savior," "the power of God and the wisdom of God," "the fullness of the Godhead bodily." It could mean only that the Christian preachers did not understand their own key terms ("God," "man") and their relational implications.

As it turned out, however, the Christians managed to hang on to the Christological compound of the New Testament: viz., that in Jesus, we have to do with the living God (no less!) yet also with one of us ("in every respect like us, yet without sinning" [Hebrews 4:15]). The catholic tradition was confronted by a succession of attractive alternatives to the compound as it appears in the New Testament—psilanthropism (Jesus as prophet), Gnosticism (Jesus as spook), Arianism (Jesus as part-God/part-man). At Nicea, they finally found a formula, awkward on many counts but valuable in the main essential: the Christian conviction that Jesus shared fully the mystery of the God-Father; for *this* is what the *homoousion to patri* was meant to mean. *Ousia* denoted many things to Greek-speaking Gentiles, all of them entitative: "being," "essence," "substance." Yet none of these notions would serve as appropriate designatum of God, who was generally understood by the Christians as quite beyond accessible being or logical definition. God is ultimate, encompassing *mystery,* and Jesus shares that mystery fully: the same *ousia,* the same *mysterium tremendum.* Thus, the Christians understood themselves to be speaking of God and Jesus without implying ditheism; rather, they were pointing to a single shared mystery of the *Deus absconditus et revelatus.* Then, by way of identifying the triplex self-manifestations of this shared mystery, the Christians borrowed the Greek term *hypostasis* and gave it a Christian twist and used it to refer to those personal activities of God in creation, history, and community, already designated by the biblical metaphors—Father, Son and Holy Spirit, one God in three distinctive activities of personal presence.

Jesus, then, is *homoousion to patri:* the human agent of God's meaning-giving activity in the world (i.e., *ho Logos tou theou*). This, as anyone not blinded by those perverse clichés about static

Greek metaphysics can see, is a highly dynamic conception of God's absence from and presence in history. But just because it focused so specifically on Jesus of Nazareth it raised the question of Jesus' humanity, and ours, to the status of a crisis. Both Gospel and liturgy had affirmed that there was a deep Christian instinct that recognized in Jesus a special relevance for our own self-understanding. But how can such an intimation be followed up without one or another incredible distortion? As a matter of fact, there was a succession of such distortions successively rejected: Apollinarianism, Nestorianism, Eutychianism, etc. Then, finally at Chalcedon, they hammered out a formula that provided a frame within which the perennial controversies about Christology could find their crucial issues rightly oriented. Jesus, thus says the Chalcedonian Definition, is both *homoousion to patri kai homoousion hemin!* Just as he shares the divine mystery with God, so also he shares the human mystery with each one of us, and in so doing reveals to us the basic truth about ourselves: that every human *ousia* is an *inspiration* and project of God. Each of us is an inspired creature, in real analogy to Jesus, *kata te n anthropote tas* as far as his *humanum* is concerned!

Obviously, though, there's something question-begging in the formula, *homoousion hemin.* Do we identify Jesus' humanity from our self-understanding, or do we take him as our clue for a more valid self-understanding than we have found elsewhere? There are real difficulties either way, which is why Chalcedon has been such a perennial bother, from the Scholastics to Schleiermacher to Wolfhart Pannenberg and Peter Hodgson. On the one side, the prime image of our human horizon is affected by the deformations of sin and self-deception. Hence, the biblical notions of *sarx, soma,* and *anthropos* are not decisive; their interpretations were all too easily perverted into the radical antagonisms between Alexandria and Antioch—*Logos-sarx* vs. *Logos-anthropos;* monophysitism vs. Nestorianism. Over on the other side, though, the natural dominance of Jesus' divine office and ministry tends either to exalt him above the human level or else to conceive of man's divinization in contrast to his real humanization.

At any rate, it was Chalcedon's firm intention to reject both such assumptions. Christ's human *physis* was not a hypostasis, a thing; else you are back in the "two-things-equal-one-thing" bit. Instead, it is best understood as an intentional activity process, a complex energy system competent for the inspired tasks for which this particular *physis* had been brought into being (by the inspiration of the Holy Spirit through Mary the Virgin). The divine *physis* is also an energy system—"full of grace and truth"—with both *physis, hypostasis* and *prosopon* (personal appearance). These two energy systems were concurrent yet integrated in God's saving purpose and in Christ's specific mission on earth. This concurrence may be understood in any way that manages to avoid one or another of the *four* typical errors condemned by the fathers at Chalcedon: (1) Don't confuse them; (2) don't convert them; (3) don't separate them categorically and (4) don't deny their interaction. Otherwise, right on! And it is a lamentable sign of our blurred vision of the divine mystery and the human that we find it so hard to think of the two natures in other ways than those proscribed by Chalcedon. Unsurprisingly, therefore, the history of Christology and of Christian anthropology has been frustrating and baffling, the despair of all but the cockiest or blinded. But how much do we know about Jesus that can throw any light on our own *self*-identification? If, that is, we stress the uniqueness of each person, his and her own particular self, how can any *one* man identify his own unique self as norm or clue to any other?

Chalcedon suggested an answer here by nuance. Modern psychology (fifth-century style, that is) differentiated *hypostasis* (monadic essence) from *physis* (activity). The essence of a thing is *self*-possessed: a universal or a particular sample of some universal. The nature of a particular thing, however, is seen in its function: *physis* means *activity,* identifiable activity. Thus, the Chalcedonians denied that Jesus' *humanum* had a *hypostasis* or was a monad. Instead, said they, his human *physis* was actual and normal like ours, "sin only excepted." But this proceeded to spawn a whole brood of misconceptions because of the prevailing psychology pictures of the human self. If one assumes that a self is (or has) a hypostatic monad and then that Jesus lacked any such hypostasis, it would follow that his humanity was incomplete or so dominated by the divine hypostasis as to mark him off from all other humans, decisively. But if you take the other tack and insist upon a human hypostasis as nucleus of the human physis, you've started down the Nestorian slide—and still not faithful to the *homoousion hemin.*

This is why I'm inclined to recommend that we take our cue from Chalcedon and recognize that the *humanum* has no hypostasis or general essence and needs none; the self is neither monad nor lump. To be a self is not to be self-possessed; it is, rather, to be an intentional activity process identified by God's specific intention and differentiated by God's specific purpose, these together constituting each man's uniqueness. Such a *physis* is obviously still animal as well as human. No extra energy is added, no monad is inserted into hominid blubber. Mind, spirit, vision are all fueled by the same metabolic processes that energize our reflexes. But it is just this sublimation of energy, from libido and reflex to conditioned reflexes to concepts to self-consciousness (and all points between), that signifies the *humanum* and implies that it is indeed an inspiration, in the biblical metaphor of the human spirit as the sublimation of our respiratory processes. This notion of the divine "inspiration" of the *humanum* cannot be turned into a causal hypothesis and then confirmed or infirmed. But then neither can any other causal notion be made to apply to a genuine mystery. This is what John Macmurray had in mind with his aphorism that the self exists in act but not in essence.

Christians have believed that in Jesus Christ we find an actual human activity process replete with human self-consciousness; he was not a divine kewpie doll inserted into the body of a Galilean Jew. He is the restored, true *imago Dei*—image, not fraction. His coming to be the man he was, with a special *physis* and a special ministry from God, becomes an analog for understanding God's intentions in our becoming the humans we are, or were intended to be. All of which is to say that each human *ousia*—one to a customer!—is a gift (inspiration!) of God, a special organizing potency toward freedom, truth, and love. To be human is to be at once animal and spiritual; it is to be a bodily process equally inconstant and perduring, subject to the joys and miseries of the use and abuse of one's human capacities. To be human is to be self-conscious and conscious of others; it is to be aware, through one's own self-transcendence, of the encompassing mystery that brackets all human strivings and hopes.

Now, all of this, or something like it, can be read off the data of the Christian claim that Jesus was, and is, *homoousion hemin.* That claim begins with the testimony that he had an actual human history and a normal biological organism. This is what the row over his "rational soul and body" was all about; there was nothing superhuman about his humanity, not even in his *nous* (the Apollinarian heresy). What then was special about him was not his human constitution (*physis*) but his special mission, God's special inspiration and purpose for him, and the quality of his performance of that mission. But this implies that each of us is also a divine inspiration in some sense or other, a project and calling of God that makes us each himself and herself. To accept one's appointment as the person he or she was meant to be is to appreciate the Creator and to share in creation. To reject one's appointment, to rebel against its fulfillment or to attempt to frame a contrary existence, is to repudiate one's creation and divine endowment.

Now, what if God, of his own elect counsel and in the fullness of time, chose to create a human creature like ourselves but with a very special agency, a very special mission, and a very special destiny? There is, as far as I can see, no discontinuity between this sort of notion and any view that makes sense out of our existence as well. What if the hinge of God's enterprise of reconciliation with humanity turned on the exhibition in an actual human life of genuine mutuality between God and human beings, of God's patient love and unfaltering mercy, of the gift of freedom and the use of freedom that would, indeed, be a full, perfect, and sufficient revelation of God's grace as this grace is *for humanity,* for every single person? What then was there to hinder God from choosing when, where and how—in his own good time and according to his own good counsel—to create and inspire a specific human self to be "the right man on our side," to be the man for others, to be the man who is both *Ebed Jahveh* (servant of God) and *Ebed Adam,* servant of man—our brother, our high priest, our redeemer? This act of choosing would have been from all eternity because this was a purpose of God, an eternal purpose that his love should become fully manifest in human history for the fulfillment of the original purposes for the human creation. But its historical manifestation would have to be in a bracket of calendar time ["in the days of Caesar Augustus, when Quirinius was governor of Syria," etc.]. This was a bracket of human time in which a historical event became the manifestation of an eternal purpose.

In the very act of becoming a human being, Jesus of Nazareth became the *hypostasis* of God's redemptive love, wholly actual, wholly unique. He became God's self-chosen agent for God's self-presentation, God's self-chosen mediator, by which God could identify himself with us and enable us to identify ourselves with him. God was in Christ, not as a fraction of the human nature (or *hypostasis*), but as the divine axis of an actual finite self from top to bottom, from beginning to end. This was the *Ephapax,* "the once for all," because one such event was sufficient—all that was necessary or appropriate.

This divine investment in Jesus' human existence occurred at the very fringe of time and process and causality. There was no time span at the end of which Jesus became the Christ; there was no time when the Christ was not, when Jesus was and then *became* the Christ (adoptionism). From the beginning he was fully human, and he continued so—truly human, fully human, from start to finish. He was not called to be different from us in any decisive sense in which we are not different from each other, but rather that he might be the man in whom we could recognize ourselves—not humanness in the ideal Platonic sense (there's no such thing), but God's mirror to each human self—to each his and her own individual, unique, personal meaning. And this is why all of us read off *ourselves* for our knowledge of Jesus. This is why it is wrong to search for some sort of universal, timeless truth about *humanitas* in the biographical data. Jesus' revelation of God is God's revelation to you or to me, to each self his and her own self-understanding—since the individual is the *haecceity* of "humanity." From the beginning, Jesus Christ was by the elect counsel of God, a second Adam, not less but *more* fully than the first Adam. (You remember Irenaeus' notion of the Fall: that the first Adam was not actually a fully matured, fully complete human being and in trying to become fully complete and fully matured, he missed the way.)[1] Here, then, is the second Adam who, in trying to become fully human and fully mature, made it—continued fully human in every stage of life and so became maturely human.

Our savior is God; our savior is one of ourselves; and because this was a single event, we can speak of Jesus Christ only as "him," not as "them"; "he," not "they." And this, I think, is what the author of Hebrews had in mind, when he said, "So it is with Christ. He did not confer upon himself the glory of becoming our High Priest [i.e., he was not self-possessed]. This was *conferred upon him* [this was the inspiration of the Holy Spirit that made him who he was]. This [he goes on to say, and I take this very seriously as the clue to a genuine theological anthropology not merely for Jesus but for you and me] was *granted to him* [just as each priesthood is granted to each human being, by God] in the days of his earthly life; . . . and in those days he offered up prayers and petitions with loud cries and tears to God, who was able to deliver him from the penalty of death [not from death but from death's power to negate life's meaning]. Because of his humble submission, his prayer was heard. Son though he was by nature, he learned obedience through the school of suffering and once perfected [once "fully human"] he became the source of eternal salvation for all who obey him" [5:5–9].

Here, even within the New Testament itself, we have the *history* and the *kerygma* bridged in a fashion that foreshadows the Christological compound of Chalcedon. The humanity of Jesus was real, and this is where we must begin, and continue, and keep coming back to. His human self consisted of a special creation, a special office, a special ministry. But then you, too, have a special creation, a special office, and a special ministry. *No* one else can exercise *your* ministry, as no other person can exercise anyone else's special ministry. Yet each of us needs to accept, gratefully, the special ministries of others, just as we need to offer our own special ministries, to God and to others. Jesus' special ministry was to be that human agency and mediatorial reality by which God's love could, under the circumstances of our history, be manifest, efficacious, and powerful— in that time and in any time and in all time—for those who confessed him as Lord and Savior then, and for those who confess him as Lord and Savior now, or ever!

This, or something in this general vein, is how I believe we can talk in terms of contemporary anthropology, contemporary bio-chemistry, contemporary molecular biology, and still talk about a human being in whom God's special project was that of the reconciler, the revealer, the redeemer of everyone who responds to him in faith, of everyone who receives in and through him that love of God he came to manifest in word and deed—as his personal ministry and mission in the world. The baseline for every Christian confession to the lordship of Christ in "the modern world" now, or the modern world then, or any "modern world" that will ever be is the sincere acknowledgment that in and through Jesus Christ we have to do with the living God in his gracious concern for our fulfillment. This means that, however we stretch our minds, we are still dealing with the indefinable. What can be defined (given limits, that is) is, by definition, not God. Yet we also confess, on the warrant of the Gospels themselves, that in Jesus Christ we have to do with an actual historical man—not humanity in the abstract, but a human self like ourselves. He shared with us our *ousia,* just as he shared the Father's *ousia* with him. He has his own identity just as you have your own identity, but his identity was to reveal to others and to enable in others their recognition of what it means to be open to the mystery above us (God), the mysteries over against us (others), the mystery within us (ourselves). Jesus was not the ideal man. But he was a true man—in the only radical, fundamental sense of true humanity—open to God (faith), open to life and death (hope), open to mission (justification). Thus, he reveals to us what and who we really are, against the illusions we have of ourselves and that others have of us. He was unique in his divine mission and power but no less, thereby, an actual human being.

In a blurred and partial way, therefore, we are able to understand who he was from our own human experience, with its vague, deep stirrings of awareness of the divine companionship in which we also live, however obscurely, however uneasily. But at a profounder level, through him we come to understand ourselves—gaining new insights about ourselves from our ripening acquaintance with Christ. This is why it matters in Christian existence to live with Christ, to live in the Gospels, to live day-by-day in the presence of the same historical Christ who is also the risen and triumphant Christ. This is why the Sacrament of the Lord's Supper matters so much, not merely to call us back to a time that was, but to bring us into God's time that is and evermore shall be. This is why one's "daily walk with Jesus" is not mere pious nonsense. It is, indeed, the way in which we come fully to understand ourselves. As we live with the clues and the leads that the Gospels give us about the human *ousia* of Jesus Christ (and clues and leads are *all* they give us, for that is all we ever have about real mysteries), through those episodic flashes of insight that are the real reward of daily immersion in Scripture we come to know ourselves. And yet this is something that all too many Christians before us, and in our time, neglect, as if on purpose. We attend, some of us and somewhat, to his revelations of God, but we fail to appropriate or appreciate the revelations he offers to us of the truth about ourselves. If he is "our high priest and brother," he has thereby identified himself with the total range of our human upreach and downfall. "What he did not assume, that he did not heal," and this ancient formula from Gregory of Nyssa means that any reduction of the full, normal human selfhood of Jesus Christ is a diminution of his total significance to us as the God-man, the man for us and others.

In the modern world, we talk about persons as if we could identify them as persons from partial clues. And so we can also talk about Jesus in terms of those partial clues by which he was identified by his disciples, by the Pharisees, by the Romans; and all of this adds up to *his* "social self." We cannot say so much for his object-self, his so-called self-consciousness. We do not know a great deal about what he thought about himself. I remember being slightly "shook" when I first realized that the report of Jesus's agonizing prayer in Gethsemane was not heard by the sleeping disciples nor otherwise recorded. The answer, of course, is that what they tell us about him was not intended as a transcription but rather as *their* remembrance of the total impression he made upon them of his own self-understanding, as the special person he was. This is obviously uncertain, but neither is it false or useless. What do we know about Socrates, for example, since we have none of his directly recorded conversations, even though we have reams of the conversations of Socrates as re-presented by Plato? But the Platonic Socrates and the Aristotelian Socrates are different, and Xenophon's Socrates is very different. It has crossed my mind that if we turned a group of New Testament critics loose on the problem of Socrates, it would turn out that there was no Socrates after all. Honest-to-God atheists are more credulous in this matter, as in some others; there are not many people who have denied the existence of the historical Socrates outright! They only say that all we ever know about the inner self-consciousness of anyone is what we can infer on the basis of significant, partial acquaintance. I'm reasonably well-acquainted with my wife (we've been married 37 years) and we're both great gossips. This means that I come, occasionally, to think that I've accumulated enough clues to frame a total picture that represents her real self. And of course you know what happens. No amount of acquaintance concludes the task of identifying another self; yet, very little suffices for the beginnings of a reliable identification.

And we do know something about Jesus of Nazareth as he understood himself. For example, he did regard himself as a teacher of righteousness—or else all our texts are systematically perverted and we'd do well to drop the business forthwith. He did understand himself as an avatar of the "suffering servant" of Yahweh, and this helped to identify him in relation to the People of Yahweh. He understood himself as authorized to interpret Torah in terms of love, and this gave him his confidence in moving beyond the normal patterns of unofficial rabbinical teaching—and drove him to the cross.

There is, therefore, nothing absurd in the notion that God of his own free counsel and love elected to create and inspire a particular human being to be the revealer of his reconciling love, the herald of his humanizing kingdom. In the very act of his becoming a human being Jesus was the Word of God, and that Word was the infinite axis of his finite self. This was a unique event, yet it has been universally relevant to the whole human enterprise since then, and everywhere and for all time. This assumption of humanity occurred at the junction of time and eternity, finite and infinite. There was a time when his historical identity first became known and his human character as a prophet and moral exemplar made its impact upon the first disciples. He who is our Lord is also the efficacious mediator between God and man. For he is also our brother—*homoousion hemin!*

Yet as we come to Jesus and seek to learn from him, we discover that he has some strange effects upon us. He will not "stay put," even as we try, in church and in Christology courses (and lectures), to hold him at arm's length. We may, and often try to, keep him "out there" as a remote object for survey and speculation. But every now and then, suddenly and somehow, he changes this relationship and he becomes the inspector, judge, and assessor of our existences; from the one we appraise, he becomes our appraiser. We ask the text about his opinions and teachings, reserving the right to ourselves to decide if we agree or not. Then suddenly and somehow, *he* changes this relationship of inquiry and becomes himself the Way, the Truth, and the Life to us. He asks us what we are asking about the ultimate meaning of life and why we have missed the way. We look to Jesus as exemplar and then discover that he is pointing past himself to God, with the demand that we put first *God's* kingdom and *God's* righteousness above all else in life or death. We acknowledge his perfection and then discover that he is confronting us with God's demand for our perfection, and also offering us the means of grace whereby we may seek and strive for it. We find our hearts moved with compassion in the presence of his passion and death and then discover that he is converting our compassion, not toward his suffering and death, but toward the suffering and needs of our fellowmen, here and now. In Christ's companionship no one remains unaltered. He has a way of drawing us to the point of decision—for faith or against faith, for discipleship or rebellion. He confronts us with God's sovereign righteousness and reveals to us our own freedom to share in or to resist God's truth and power and love. And this way of acquaintance and communion, reflection and devotion goes ever and ever on.

Introduction

His Christology strengthened somewhat by deft appropriations of Transcendental Thomism, more especially along Rahnerian lines, Outler now moves to concretize his theological anthropology with reference especially to the notion of the *humanum,* precisely in its natural condition, as a divine intention. His distinctions here between the barely, the truly, and the fully human, for all their impressive rhetoric, have a more substantive function still, that of binding the argument of the essay systematically and integrally. Since Outler wrote this material, both psychotherapy and pastoral counseling came to place increasing emphasis on discovering more expeditious and effective ways than those charted by classical psychoanalytic theory of strengthening the ego in the interest of the care and cure of the soul: the ego's overcoming the downward pull of id and superego, so the dogma goes, is what will finally allow the sublimely human in all of us to assume its proper place over the whole of things. This lecture exposes the pretentiousness and precariousness of all such thinking, in the interest of what is genuinely liberating to our humanity, all the while exhibiting clearly the difference a well-formed Christian anthropology can make to the ways we view ourselves and others, certainly in the context of ministry but also and more importantly in the context of a deeper communion with all whom God continues graciously to love.

CHAPTER
5

On Becoming
Fully Human

My argument thus far has tried to make three points. First, whatever else it is, the *humanum* is also a radical mystery, finite and transcendent, rooted deep in nature and open to the infinite. Man is the animal who surpasses himself. Our knowledge about the problems of being human goes on accumulating, with real increments of self-understanding and power; our wisdom about the mystery of being continues to turn up fruitful insights but remains impervious to all reductionist analysis.

My second point was that, for all its complexity, the *humanum* is an integer, an organizing, goal-seeking process in which stimuli and afference in any part affect the whole through the various concurrent processes within the organism (electrical, chemical, psychic, etc.). Personal existence is a gift of God, a divine inspiration, a superordinate intention that coordinates a synergism of many different capacities and traits.

My third point was that Christians have a valid clue to the human mystery in the event of Jesus Christ, who shares both the mystery of the Father and ours as well, serving thus as the prime analog for our own relationships with God. In him we can recognize the interaction (*perichoresis*) of the divine and the human;

he is Love and Meaning incarnate, the Second Adam, the prototype for a new humanity. His own human nature was very special, not by constitution but in virtue of his perfect obedience in the faithful exercise of his human calling and powers, in his ministry of God's righteousness and love. Jesus is not the human ideal (or at least, this is a misleading way of talking about him). He is no model for simple imitation. But in his eagerness for living, his sensitivity and hardihood in suffering, his poise in the face of death, he discloses to us our own calling and possibilities. "Although he was a son," says our friend in Hebrews (5:8–9), "he learned obedience through what he suffered, and being made perfect [i.e., fully human], he became our source of eternal salvation" (i.e., our own experience of being fully human).

This may be enough to remind us of the utterly crucial distinction between being barely human and becoming fully human, and of the prime corollary of any such distinction, which is the tragic pall of human existence, the myriad toll of lives that miss their mark or never make it. To be barely human is to have been intended so by God; it is to be an inspired animal whose "living soul" is "the breath of God" (cf. Genesis 2:7). To be truly human is to have recognized this God-man relationship, even in alienation and tragedy. But to become fully human requires participation in God's creative process, acceptance of God's intention as both gift and task from God. It is to make an offertory of one's humanity to God and neighbor. The human animal has a triple syndrome of needs and goals that mark him off from all his animal cousins: (1) freedom normed by justice, (2) intelligence normed by truth, (3) love normed by community (neighbor) and communion (God). Anything short of this, or deviant from it, means personal existence in alienation from its ground and end.

But it goes with the human mystery (the *humanum* as God's sheer gratuity) that no one can manage the *transitus* from being human to becoming fully human by any virtue or achievement of his and her own. All our human choices are aimed at universal human goals—to grow and grow, always toward our uttermost possibilities. But apart from God's grace and the response of obedient faith, the *humanum* continues in its tragic muddle of hope and disenchantment, in all its baffling variety. This muddle is all too clear in the whelming tumults and agonies of our time.

Rebels and diehards share the same passion: to be and to have, more and more of their full humanity! The rebels hope to have what never was; the diehards hope to keep what they never really had. Both are more passionately moved by wishful thinking than reality.

The current crisis of religion (and the church) springs from the spreading conviction that the denial of human beings' full humanity has either been caused or reinforced by religious notions about their radical dependence upon God—as if faith and abjectness are identical, both intolerable. And now the world is full of unruly and rage-driven people who believe that they can snatch the new humanity from the toils of secular society; and if, in the process, God has to be hustled off the human scene, the gain for human autonomy is worth it. The common credo of the partisans of the new humanity is that humans now have their destiny in their own hands, alone. And with this has come a new urgency for instant full humanity. Now, given the moribund state of organized religion and its ambivalent dual role in conserving the heritage of society and affecting social change at one and the same time, it is all too easy to conclude that it is the secularist ideologies of the revolutionaries that deserve the credit for such partial victories as have been won in the warfare for the new humanity. This, in turn, spawns the graffiti of the new utopians: "The church has had it," "God is dead," "humanity is being born," "the revolution is a moral crusade" (in which human ends justify its infra-human means).

None of this can easily be denied or dismissed, but it does deserve a more critical unromantic assessment than it has had thus far in the rising tide of political hysteria. One can think of at least three lines of analysis that might reward real depth analysis—not here and not now—and one other "line of sight" that I'd like to develop, at least briefly, as a conclusion for this part of my argument. The first passing remark is the persistence of the Judaeo-Christian tradition and its values in modern man's agony for self-acceptance and self-expression. If I had even strong suspicions that the God of the Bible has been, and must be, some sort of antihumanitarian despot or even a cosmic Milquetoast, I'd have no human choice but atheism—honest-to-God atheism. But the fact is that the moral substance of the new secularism is derivative, from the Judaeo-Christian heritage, and the repudiation of that heritage is the prelude to the demoralization of the secular city. A second comment suggests another complex probe: If the bad conscience of the majority has been a powerful leverage for progress in social justice for minorities, what happens when that conscience turns self-defensive and counteraggressive? How many more will throw in with the fascist mind when stirred to violence by further violence? My third passing comment is a question: Is revolution our best hope or even a valid hope for the Parousia of the new humanity? If it is, then God bless all revolutionaries; even so, come quickly, O holy revolution! But what if the new utopianism is the old romanticism, with new mores of violence, self-interest, and cynicism? What if the secular visions of the new humanity are in conflict with the basic drives of the primate-predator that now serves as its most plausible model? What if the rebels are men from La Mancha—only now the dupes of rage rather than glory—with their dreams of man the self-possessed, man the self-righteous? What then, when comes their disenchantments?

These are loaded questions, I know, and yet their import is not that I'm an antirevolutionary, pro-establishment fossil—well, fossil, maybe, but not at all a neophobe. I, too, have a list of upheavals that I dream of being upheaved; there is my kennel of fat cats to be liquidated. My favorite verses in the Magnificat are those about the proud being scattered, the lowly being exalted, the hungry being filled and the rich sent empty away (Luke 1:51–53). Nor am I chicken, either. Sights and sounds of carnage make my temples throb, too; my fascination with disaster, especially when it happens to people I disapprove, reminds me of how far the work of grace has still to go in my heart. Actually, my rejection of revolution (in contrast to reform) springs from a slow-growing but firm conviction that revolutions, as a modality of change, are a counterproductive force in human evolution. Stalinism; Hitlerism; Maoism; the new class, race, and nationalist passions (white, black, or whatever) are all reactions against intolerable human indignities. Yet they must be judged invalid on their own premises and results. They have not served the *humanum* according to their promises; and it is a brazen hypocrisy that their victims go so little mourned. That metaphor about eggs and omelets applied to people and revolutions strikes me as a hopelessly inhumane view of the *humanum.*

We come back in the end, therefore, to the question that has plagued us all along: What is the *humanum* and what would it take to become fully human? Once more, then, *con brio,* let's try to push the case for Christian realism a little further forward—as far, that is, as we can see it through the darkling glass of a world in torment. Our first premise, you will recall, is that the *humanum* is not a *hypostasis,* not a thing apart. The self that emerges, grows and perdures, is a gift and a task. It identifies and organizes a complex cluster of organic processes and meshes them into an immense operational field—ordered and sustained, by what? We are selfed, but not *self*-possessed; we are normed by righteousness but we are not *self*-righteous; we are endowed with capacities for incalculable productivity but we are not *self*-sufficient, either as individuals or as a species. The ontological root of the *humanum* runs deeper than its animal base, though never apart. A whole person is a genuine integer of plural energy systems that are not simply convertible. His and her unique identities are an enduement; there are experiments in personality. The self is not a part of the organism; it is the organism in its dependence upon an activity of origination and maturation not itself dependent, which is to say, "God."

Self-consciousness is a transcendental experience in which a person recognizes his and her own bodily events and perduring identity in and through these specific bodily processes. It includes the awareness of these processes as organized and oriented within the bounded frames of space, time and causality and the unbounded upreach of aspirations that are infinite. Self-transcendence is, therefore, the prime potency for our humanization and our deformation as humans. The divine inbreathing that identifies any given self is a *concursus,* in which God's power, without ever becoming a component of our human *ousia,* confers its power to act humanly—which is to say, naturally and yet also uniquely. Any such process is open to maturation or else to tragic deviation. The human process reaches out beyond itself in freedom, reason, and love; yet it also wreaks havoc in the world. The difference in every case turns on our human responses to God's "inspirations" and here our options are two and only two: faith (free acceptance of one's self as God-possessed) or the delusion of self-possession and its moral corollaries.

The Christian tradition has turned up a variety of explications of this notion of the self as a process within the creative grace of God. The version that has interested me most of late is Karl Rahner's. The analysis is much too long and abstruse to try to "digest" here; besides, some must already know it. In any case, his twin conclusions, not original but profoundly probed, affirm God's creative relationship to the natural process in which the *humanum* emerges within the human and societal matrices that guide or mislead people in their forward and upward reach to humanization. This, obviously, is an updated version of the Thomist anthropological premise of body and soul as matter and form and its theological consequences: that human self-transcendence is to human self-fulfillment as grace is to nature. Thus, our dependence on God's grace is not at all unnatural. It is, indeed, our aboriginal resource from birth to death, from our animal origins to our transcendental destinies.

This *transitus* from barely human to fully human is by no means automatic, either way. It involves a precarious configuration of aspirations and activities—animal, human, divine, all organized around the imperious hungers of freedom, knowledge, and love. It is a tragic mix of good and evil, generated by the unlimited strivings that keep surging up from the depths of the human mystery. The process is both unique and universal; each person must have his and her own private program of self-realization. But the prerequisite and sustaining conditions of the process hold good for all. Three of these essential "conditions" of full humanity will suffice to make the case for our special marvel of selfhood in self-transcendence.

The first of these polarities in the human condition is freedom. To be human at all is to have escaped the complete domination of causality and happenstance; to become fully human means the attainment of responsible control of both the closed and the still-open options of existence: coming to be free toward one's past and toward one's future. The experienced need of freedom is boundless. No human being is ever fully sated; we beat our poor, splendid wings forever against the bars of finitude. The desire for freedom is an inner demand for options (i.e., activity). But it also has an objective, norming horizon, too, and that is justice. Justice, as norm for human freedom, is not so much an order of equity as it is a demand that freedom shall enhance freedom, freedom for others—all others, since all share our irrepressible need for freedom, too. This is why justice as a legal system tends to become impersonal, organized around the axes of power and property. Freedom in the service of justice is freedom exercised by the rule of the most freedom for the most people over the longest run. But just because it is an insatiable hunger, freedom is easily and regularly deformed and corrupted. Indeed, as Benedetto Croce contended, human history is the history of the struggle for freedom, but it is also the horror story of freedom achieved turning into tragic abuse. Freedom in the service of the self turns self-centered, and is thereby diminished for the self and for others. Freedom in the service of more freedom for others liberates the self from the tyrannies of self-will.

A second factor in the human drive to perfection is the desire for knowledge, the disposition to inquire and to form rational judgments. Our organisms are uniquely organized for attending to the world, for translating sentienda into signals, speech, science, art—and wisdom. The aim of this incessant curiosity is insight of every conceivable sort, from the most primitive *Gestalt* to the outer reaches of the sublime. To become fully human is to channel one's curiosity into a lifestyle of openness to truth and of critical analysis of what is proposed as truth. For this internal drive of the human intelligence has an objective norm, truth, and our inquiries are either normed by truth or else corrupted by our own powers of rationalization, our own cleverness in making the worse appear the better reasons. Here, again, truth is not a state of mental satisfaction (that "truth for me" bit is a narcissist slogan, generative of all manner of self-deception and false confidence). Instead, truth is that dynamic network of relationships and processes that bear the sign of order and benevolence. Our experiences of insight are deeply inward and spontaneous, but their referents are outward and orderly. Sincerity or earnest concern are conditions of valid knowledge, but not its norm.

The shadow side of this imperious orientation toward truth is seen in our fatal tendency to corrupt what knowledge we come by in the false service of self-interest. We know too well how readily the mind is deformed by disuse and misuse. Intelligence is easily perverted by prejudices and cultural mindsets that stifle or stultify the processes of critical inquiry and judgment. And worse: Our hunger for knowledge is corrupted by delusions of mental grandeur; the passion that built Babel still generates utopian dreams. The Genesis myth was a shrewd one: the easiest way to seduce the old Adam (then and now) was to bait him with false promises of knowledge that would dispense with wonder, that needs neither faith nor poetry. The hunger for knowledge is a yearning for omnipotence, the Faustian lust for glory that leads to the typical Faustian damnation. To be human is to thirst for knowledge; to become fully human is to have gained insight enough to order one's insights into intelligent service of the truth, not for me (or us) but for all.

The reason for this is that the final norm for truth is love, the third of our tripolar conditions for human fulfillment. Love is, obviously, the convergence of all our interests—animal, human, and divine—and the effort to wall off *eros* from *philia* from *epithymia* from *agape,* is poor lexicography and bad psychology. From reflex lust to lifelong friendships, to creative outbursts of all sorts, to the highest reach of mystic ecstasy, the impulses of love describe a continuum of appetence, all branded by the twin marks of self-transcendence: enjoyment and enhancement. The continuum is dynamic: In its orientation toward the animal pole, enjoyment tends to dominate; toward the divine, enhancement counts for more. Never the one without the other, however, in true love at any level so that even God is rightly said to have an appetite for creation and a personal stake in its enhancement.

There is another polarity in love. On the one hand, it requires an "other" for its own fruition. Self-love is either a misnomer or a perversion. Love, of every sort, is a giving and taking, an offertory and a Eucharist—an analog of grace. This is why promiscuous sex adds so little to the truly human, for either of the parties. In serving one value, it stultifies another and more uniquely human one: mutuality that abides—in faith, hope and joy. In any case, love needs an "other" (mate, friends, colleagues, society); self-centered love encloses a cipher. On the other hand, love is a longing never stifled: a constant appetence for joy. In other organisms, libidinal energy is controlled, within rough limits, by the interaction of other needs and drives, by the strange equilibrium in nature between aggression and constraint. In man, these limits are lifted. His appetence is manifold, and thus can be sublimated and redirected out to the boundaries of the imagination and beyond. But the truth remains that love is boundless, even though our experiences of it are often tragically limited or false. And we might remark in passing that even if you have discarded the cosmological "arguments" (they are sadly out of fashion at the moment), what *do* you make of the paradox of a bounded creature with an unbounded outreach and upreach? Transcendence toward or in what? Could it be that self-transcendence in general, and self-transcending love in particular, is the real *analogia entis,* after all?

To be human, then, means to be loved and loving; and love must be both free and knowledgeable. The gift of love must be free to be valid. It must be appropriate to be effective and intelligent to be appropriate. There is a priceless mixture here of self-and-other understanding, a clumsy phrase for "friendship," which is why the ancients regarded friendship as a better paradigm for love than sex or mystic ecstasy. But love is not immaculate. It, too, must be normed—by community. Love's outreach is for an "other" but never the other in sustained solitude. The sexual unit is a pair, the social unit is a family; but it is the community that is a requisite matrix for a human's becoming fully human. The horizons of community recede as we reach outward from self, and communion is the name for that experience of community surpassing local boundaries of place and contiguity. Communion is the experience of infinite outreach and of intimate presence. The humanization of a person is a function of his and her outreach in community; divinization is a function of upreach in communion with God.

But the self-same love that must needs be free and intelligent to be truly human is also capable of incontinent inhumanity as well. It is the same energy that is invested in a rape or a riot or a mother's love. Love and hate build institutions and tear them down. The hippy slogan, "Make love, not war," lights up the Jekyll-Hyde masks of our human *ousia*—transcendental and tragic. What is more, the tragedies of love abused are compounded by our powers of freedom and intelligence. Freedom gives love its lift; it also gives hate its opening toward the inhuman. Intelligence aims love toward productive expression; in the service of hate and fear, passion makes man's inhumanity to man hellishly inhuman. Thus it is that our goal of becoming fully human is firmly tied to the means by which our hungers for freedom, intelligence, and love can be satisfied in the causes of justice, truth, and community as these are defined and supported by their transcendent counterpart: God's freedom, intelligence, and love. It is God in whose service is our perfect freedom; God whom to know is life and peace, God whose *ousia* is love. The human never becomes fully human in alienation from God.

My axial thesis is and has been that to be human at all involves a divine inspiration of an animal process; becoming fully human is the acme of that work of love. There is no human *hypostasis.* Human "nature" is an activity, the prime proof of the thesis that grace does not destroy nature but perfects it. To be human is to be a bodily-event process in which God's grace and man's response are coapted and cooperative. All animals need freedom, but the human experience of freedom is unique in significance and outreach. To become fully human my freedom must become trustful and graceful, the atmosphere of God's healing grace. Otherwise, freedom becomes frenetic or throttled: unjust, unrighteous, unfree.

Again, to be human is to join in the ongoing processes of learning and inquiry, attentive to more than the signals of pleasure and pain. To be human is to thirst for insight, insights for coping with the world, insights that end in wonder, having probed at least a little into the encompassing mystery of being. But to become fully human, one's search for the truth must be pressed against and beyond its limit: the intellectual love of God. The life of the mind is not a luxury nor an alternative to feeling. It is, rather, the effort to rescue human energies from mindless excitations and discharge. But finite intelligence must be lighted from outside the parentheses of our knowledge and imagination, which is to say from the Infinite, from God's self-disclosures to human beings' self-understanding.

Finally, to be human is to be a bodily-event process in love, an organism striving for more than orgasm and herding. To love is to seek out the actual real good of others, to strive for that good with zest and courage, to enjoy and celebrate that good in festivals of community and communion. But human beings cannot love upon command or calculation, nor even with the strength of their good intentions. The power to love comes from the experience of being loved ("we love him because he first loved us") and the quality of our experiences of love sets the human limits of our prospects of becoming fully human. This is why our aspirations are so regularly defeated, why self-salvation is regularly self-defeating—except as we come to know ourselves beloved by the infinite "in person." This is why God's self-revelation in the Godmanhood of Christ is the lodestone of our true humanity.

The human adventure, therefore, is a divine project within the natural order: wholly natural in all its coordinate energy systems (biological, psychological, etc.), uniquely human in all its superordinate meanings. Any real success as animals has been closed to us; and our yearnings to play god are fatuous. It is only as each of us learns to accept his and her own specific *ousia* from God and seek its fulfillment in God's redeeming and sustaining grace that we come back to the hopeful rest and blessedness for which God made us.

But all such talk of hope and humanity is harshly negated by the grim paradox of life and death, by the prospect of the extinction that is the lot of all things, visible and invisible! Death is wholly natural, utterly inevitable, yet also a sort of metaphysical insult to the *humanum*. Our truly human aspirations are immortal as we are not. Death is, therefore, our most incongruous experience; literally, "the last enemy" of eternal meaning in our lives. And there is no hope in death for anything more than quiet oblivion unless what it was that intended me (and you) in the first place intends me (and you) still, or yet again, "in the last place" (*ta eschaton*). But what is it that intended me (and you) and whose sustained intention is the ground of our perdurance as persons? It was not nature. Nature intends the species and is sublimely prodigal in insuring its continuance; but it couldn't care less about *me* (or you) and our personal concerns. It wasn't "society." It intends vital statistics and, in some metaphorical fashion, it intends "us." But society is not personal and many illusions are fostered by the personification of social groups. I was not even intended by my parents. They did intend a "him" or a "her" but not me, although their loving ratification of me after I appeared was the forging of a bond of love that has survived their death.

What then? Would you believe—God maybe? Now, before you recoil from what may sound like a conjuring up the ghost of the dead god-of-the-gaps, you might do well to consider what a special gap there is in the emergence and progress of the *humanum* in the natural process. For unless nature is self-contained and unless the self really is self-possessed, there is an imperious need for us to account for both: nature and self-transcending self-consciousness. What other account is even partially intelligible save one that recognizes, not a god-of-the-gaps, but the encompassing Mystery of Being, Love, and Consummation? The denial of such an encompassment was humanity's first sin and could well be our last. Our only hope in life and death is God's intention that we be, and that we be from and to and for him. And if it is in this life only that we have such a hope, we are of all creatures the most miserable.

Being human and becoming fully human is a venture of faith, receiving our being from God's hands and being glad to have it so. But faith is a means, not an end in itself. Faith is in order to love as love is in order to goodness as goodness is in order to blessedness, which is what God's providence is and always has been all about. And so it was that the apostle of faith exhorted us to work out our own salvation, as if we could, accepting the agonies of freedom normed by justice, inquiry normed by truth, love normed by community. Then he added that we do this in fear and trembling, conscious of God's grace as the constant climate of our endeavor. "For it is God at work in us," not to displace or dominate but to inspire, intend, and bring us to our final end.

Being human, then, is a work of grace; life is meant to be graceful and grace-filled. Grace is love, and love is joy, and joy is the glory of our humanity. Something like this has always been the faith of the apostles and martyrs and the pilgrim People of God.

Introduction

At the time Outler was drafting parts of his Earl Lectures, he was busily engaged in working out a history of Christological thinking for a seminar he taught at Perkins School of Theology during the spring semester, 1968. Parts of the lecture material prepared for the seminar were subsequently reworked for the Earl series, especially for the second lecture. For reasons that are not clear, Outler chose not to include the material below, presented at the last meeting of the 1968 seminar. It is, of course, impossible to say whether this additional material would have enhanced the Earl presentations themselves. What it represents, however, is of interest in its own right, and especially in the light of the aims of this present volume. Here, Outler patiently reviews for his students a hermeneutical framework for thinking about Christological issues that had guided him for decades and by means of which he arrived at some of his most important conclusions about the doctrine of the person and work of Jesus Christ.

CHAPTER
6

The Man of God's Own Choosing

A s we conclude this semester's work, I would like to call to your attention some of the things we discovered in our historical review of Christological thought in the church. Christianity began with a *kerygma* (proclamation) about Jesus of Nazareth, about what God was doing in and through this man's historical career, and about how this Jesus had in fact been the fulfillment both of history and of humankind's eschatological hope. The Chalcedonian formula will later speak about "from before time he was begotten by the Father but in these last days (*ta eschata,* 'in modern times,' 'in the endtime,') he became man for us and for our salvation." The early apostolic preaching was a storytelling about Jesus as a special, unique, and final revelation and manifestation of God's intent and purpose in dealing with human beings through reconciling love. This was neither the only nor the last revelation of God, but it was the once-for-all revelation of God's love that illuminates and appropriates all other revelations of God before, besides, and hereafter. This story was not, in the earliest instances, accompanied by a metaphysical explanation. It did, however, presuppose a history. It was a *kerygma* about a history that had not yet developed into a dogma. In order, however, to explain the *kerygma* about the history, the church was forced in successive crises to develop an account at a theoretical level of what was at first both kerygmatic and liturgical.

The first Christian preachers told the story of Jesus and then gave that story its kerygmatic interpretation and demand. The early Christians developed a liturgy in which Jesus was the cult figure of worship, the sign of their dependence upon God for his saving mercy and grace. But in order to continue to tell and renew the story, the church had to develop theories that were then assessed according to their efficacy for preaching and worship. (The measure of a good Christology has always been whether it aids the preaching of Christ so that Christ is heard and confessed as Savior and Lord. A good Christology aids in the Christian community's worship insofar as it helps to confirm believers in their faith and good works. Christology that does not affect liturgy one way or the other is neutral, and Christology that interdicts worship is bad Christology.) Out of the effort to provide a theoretical accounting for the preaching and the worship of the church, based as that was on the history of the Gospels, arose Christological dogma.

Originally, dogma developed in reaction to heresy. In their effort to explain what Christians mean when they worship Christ in and through the sacraments, theories that did not offend the Christian mind—that did not undercut either preaching or worship—were simply taken for granted. Theories that did offend, that threatened either the efficacy of preaching or the validity of worship, were rejected as unacceptable and divisive. "Divisive" is the adjective that would in Greek be translated as "heretical." Heresy is that which divides Christians from the apostolic preaching, and from the gist and the essence of the apostolic liturgy or the apostolic worship. Dogma is the teaching of the church that is intended to stabilize the *kerygma* in its interpretation of the history.

So we have three components: (1) history, (2) *kerygma,* and (3) dogma. The history was deposited, insofar as it was deposited, in the Gospel stories and the oral traditions of the apostolic church. The *kerygma* arose out of the apostolic church and then was crystallized in the second century. It took until the fifth century for the dogma to become stabilized in the formula of

Chalcedon. There, the essential notion was that in Christ God was actively reconciling the world unto himself and doing it through one who was of the same *ousia* (being) as the Father yet who was also of the same *ousia* as our own, and that the two *physeis* (these two natures, this unity of two energy systems, divine and human) are neither to be separated nor confused.

For the subsequent history of Christological thinking, the difficulty was that the dogma began to dominate both the *kerygma* and the history. From Chalcedon to the nineteenth century, the true history of Jesus of Nazareth was predetermined by the dogma of the church. The orthodox doctrine of the person and work of Jesus Christ came to decide what parts of the New Testament and what other first-century references are, properly speaking, historical. But dogmatized history is bad history; no dogma can dominate history without corrupting it. As dogma dominated history, it also came to dominate *kerygma.* What is to be preached? Answer: What is to be preached is that which confirms the dogma. Instead of the dogma being an explanation of what was preached, preaching itself came to be a manifestation or a homiletical extension of the dogma.

The beginning of modern Christology can be identified as that point when the historical analysis of the data of early Christianity began to be applied to the New Testament and to the historical dimensions of the life and mission of Jesus of Nazareth. Initially, the application of this kind of critical, historical self-consciousness was in deliberate rivalry to dogma. As dogma had come to dominate *kerygma* and history, now history sought to dislodge dogma. The principal impetus of the long history of the "life-of-Jesus" research was to recover the historical Jesus from the Christ of dogma. None of the nineteenth-century "life-of-Jesus" historians take Chalcedon seriously. As the enemy of history, the argument went, Chalcedon must also be the enemy of truth. Through the nineteenth century, the application of historical methods to the study of Jesus—from Reimarus down to Wrede and Weiss, and on to Renan, Sheldon, Stalker, and Fosdick—included the attempt to derive the preaching of Christianity, the *kerygma,* from the newly reconstituted history alone.

This was the picture of Christ that nerved and fueled evangelical Christianity in the latter half of the nineteenth century and the first quarter of the twentieth: The example of Jesus (not the *imitatio Christi* because that is primarily the imitation of the suffering Christ) becomes the ideal of a new *imitatio Jesu,* and in specific, the imitation of the strong, courageous man of Nazareth, the son of the carpenter, the moral hero who was able to distill the quintessence of law and prophecy and to develop a moral teaching of ethical neighborly love that was superior to any other kind of religion, the man whose confidence in God was a confidence in God's support of the moral tissue and texture of the universe.

This was a Christology that went along with man's rising hopes for himself and for the human future, a Christology that matched the idea of progress and the vision of universal education that would bring universal harmony and peace with the kingdom of God on earth. With the shattering of these visions and dreams (especially by the first World War, the Great Depression, and the manifest failure of education to produce personalities that were harmonious and concordant), the disenchanted of the twentieth century were no longer impressed by the image of the prophetic Jesus, or of the liberal Jesus, or of Jesus the ethical teacher.

And so, the effort to make *kerygma* out of history tended to be discounted. What then happened was a new recovery of the apostolic *kerygma* by the neo-orthodox theologians from Martin Kähler, Karl Barth, Emil Brunner right on down to the present time—a *kerygma* about Jesus, or a kerygmatic message of the Christian gospel that could on the one hand dispense with dogma, with Chalcedon as Greek, and therefore as bad, and also with history. From Kähler on down to Bornkamm, Zahrndt, Bultmann, and Tillich, you can have a *kerygma* about Jesus without any serious reliance upon a historical reality. Even if there had been no historical Jesus (except in the barest sense), the *kerygma* still goes untouched, for it is not about the historical Jesus, but about God and humanity, and about the action of the kerygmatic Christ in transforming the relationship between God and human beings from alienation to reconciliation.

In the course of 150 years, then, you had the dissolution of dogma, first by history, in the interest of *kerygma.* Then, you had the dissolution of history by *kerygma,* but with no recovery of dogma. Now, in our time, the Christological task seems to be either to recover as much of the dogma as you can and put it into modern language or not to bother with the dogma at all. In the latter case, you then would have to choose between history and *kerygma*, even though the historical basis of the whole Christological picture is so tenuous and shaky that you really have no choice between the Jesus of history and the Christ of faith; the Christ of faith is what really matters. If we are to put history, *kerygma*, and dogma back together again in such a way that none of the three dominates the other two, then we have to ask new questions. The first question is not which one of the three is the controlling polarity, but how do all three interact with each other? How does history correct *kergyma*? How does *kergyma* correct dogma? How does dogma correct history and *kerygma*? How does *kerygma* correct history and dogma? etc.

The clue I take for starters is in the formula of Chalcedon, the nerve of which was the *homoousion hemin*. We had already got in Nicea the *homoousion to patri*—Jesus is of the same *ousia* as the Father. What Chalcedon contributed was the affirmation that Jesus Christ, Lord, Savior, the eschatological Son of Man, is of the same *ousia* as our own. But what is our own *ousia?* This is a question that involves both history, *kerygma*, and dogma, for if Jesus shared our *ousia*, then he shares our history and he is in this respect an historical figure. The Chalcedonian dogma prescribes not what the history must be but that there must have been some real history or the dogma itself is stultified. History is the literal prerequisite and precondition to any *kerygma* about Jesus Christ that has any significant resemblance to the New Testament witness. If there is no history, there is no *kerygma;* and if there is no *kerygma*, there is no need for dogma, whether there *is* dogma or not. The whole of the Christian enterprise turns around the proclamation that "God was in Christ reconciling the world unto himself" and that he was "in Christ" at a specific time, in a definite place, and in actual historical figure with a date and name and historical locus and matrix. In this respect, therefore, dogma requires history. If you take Chalcedon seriously, then you cannot dispense with history.

But history requires interpretation. There is no such thing as "bare" history, as "mere" happening. Once it is remembered or represented, history is remembered and represented within an interpretative matrix—in some sort of evaluation or assessment in which meanings are given and assigned to the historical event. The interpretation of the historical Jesus has to do principally with why he makes any difference to us. The answer to the question is that here, in and through the events surrounding Jesus, God has acted once and for all, and for all human beings, in such a way as to disclose and manifest himself as the God of judgment, mercy, grace—the God of our salvation and of human destiny. The history the New Testament contains is not a simple record of a transaction; it was the history that made possible our awareness of what God was doing, is doing, and will do. The *kerygma* is the kerygmatic transvaluation of this history, that itself has a history, the history of the interpretation of Jesus' meaning for each respective time. This means that the Christian *kerygma* is not one thing. It is open to transvaluation and transformation in different times, places, and ages. But if you kerygmatize the original history, then sooner or later you will have to dogmatize that *kerygma:* that is, you will have to have a theory that makes your doctrine of what God has done for humanity in Christ consonant with what we know about human beings in general, intelligible in the light of our current anthropological self-understandings. This has been the unsettling difficulty throughout all of Christian history. We, too, must ask, what can the *homoousion hemin* mean *today?* What would it mean to say that a Jewish rabbi in the first third of the first century shared our *ousia?*

In the fifth century, it would have meant that he shared a human *ousia* conceived in terms of a tripartite psychology, with a human *hypostasis* inside a human skin and three levels of psychic organization: (1) primitive neural irritability, (2) developed neural sensitivity, and (3) an *anima* or *nous* at the apex of it all. You can see how irresistible the Apollinarian heresy was: "Yeah, he's got the same stuff and things as our irritable organisms, but he has a different kind of *nous;* there was a different 'little man' inside him than there is inside you, and that different little man was really special!" The other possibility was to say that there wasn't just one little man inside Jesus; there were two: one divine, one human, and they got along very well, indeed. The divine would say, "Let's go," and the human would say, "Yeah, let's." The human would say, "I'm tired," and the divine would say, "Well, don't rest yet—a couple more charges and we will be to the top of Golgotha!" This is what Nestorianism comes to. It is incredible not because of some logical defect, but because it does not correspond to the *ousia* that we understand ourselves to be, and therefore because it cannot be the *homoousion hemin*.

Though we may have come a long way from the tripartite psychology of the fifth century (and before), modern psychologists still must talk about the human *ousia* in reductionistic terms: They talk only about the social self. With them, we can notice that the human organism in its fetal stage and early infancy has no apparent self-consciousness, self-awareness, or self-identity, and then we can go on to see the infant developing such out of an awareness of his own social matrix. The self he begins to be aware of is the registered sum of the reflected appraisals of his "self" by other selves. In my "social self" I am what I understand other people to suppose I am or have adjudged me to be. I am what *you* think I am. Now over against this social self there is a self that is the object of my own self-consciousness. For as I come to identify myself as others have identified me, I also come to identify myself from internal experience of self-consciousness and introspection. Thus, I become an object self to myself, and enter into a dialectic between my social self and my object self. Into the dialectic feeds not only the data of my social self but also the introspective insights that come whenever I experience myself as estimated and assessed by those other selves. I can modify the social self by reference to the object self, and I can modify the object self by reference to the social self.

But who is the self that is assessing these self-assessments? That self does not exist in space, time, and causality. It is, rather, the presupposition of all self-consciousness because the self that is conscious of the self is not itself the self that is conscious of itself. Here, we are quite literally poised against an infinite regress. There is a subject self, but "it" is not tangible and is never experienced as an object or as an entity. Modern psychiatrists, psychologists, and anthropologists can talk about human behavior and interpersonal patterns with increasing meaningfulness and precision, but they cannot identify as an entity the self that is involved therein. The only conceivable account that I can give for the fact that there are human selves and that these human selves are not simple summations or derivations or functions of their chemical and biological and psychological processes is that each self is itself a created project of and for and within these very processes. The human self is a very special thing because it was made on purpose to be special. It is a creation of God, a special and deliberate creation by which a mammalian embryo is invested (I do not know how and when) with the potentiality of developing both as a primate organism and as a human self. The self, however, is not a part of the organism but *is* the organism organized in and for this mode of identification. The self is the human organism in its specifically human order, reference, and capacity. It is the human organism open to the neighbor (which is more than just gregariousness; neighborliness is a different dimension of *koinonia*). It is the human organism open to God its Creator, the *imago* and *similtudo Dei*. And it is the human organism finally open to itself, to self-consciousness that never can be brought to adequate conceptual clarity. The human *ousia,* then, is a divine project that differentiates an irritable organism from its other biological congeners not in degree but in kind. It is an irritable organism that is identified not primarily as an irritable organism but as having a focus of meaning to God, the neighbor, and to itself. Here is the locus of freedom.

In psychology, the case for determinism is open and shut. As long as psychologists deal with human beings as irritable organisms standing within causal processes, they cannot make a case for freedom. Yet to deny the reality of freedom is also to deny the total testimony of human experience: personal, corporate, and religious. In the subject self there is the capacity to *love,* whose meaning comes from the special project of the human self and not from analogies in the animal kingdom. We are made to be the selves we are, and each self is lovingly made to be itself. The becoming of its being depends upon its acceptance of its having been made and its obedience in that state of having been made as a special project of God.

The essence of sin is either to deny that I have my selfhood from the hands of God or to acknowledge that this is so but to find it intolerable. Sinners hate the thought of being creatures of God. This is the worst indignity they can suffer and they will not have it! On the other hand, salvation is the acceptance of one's personal existence as bearing God's own design, potency, capacities, expectations—and of being glad that this is so, deeply moved to become what one is made to be by God. In these terms, salvation is not being snatched from the jaws of hell or being lifted up on clouds of glory. It is to become fully what one's self is and is capable of being, toward God, neighbor, and oneself. This is what is meant, also, by becoming "fully human." It is to become only myself, no more but no less either. It is to become fully and vitally participant in God's special creation of myself and of his other self-creations. This means that we become ourselves only as we become fully dependent upon the purposes, grace, and love of God and become fully humble to the divine support that makes possible our being human at all. To begin to be human is to have had a divine creation in and for us, our selves. To continue to be human and to become fully human is to participate as trustfully in this divine creative project as we began to be in its bare beginnings. There is real synergism here between what God is doing in and through and for me and what I am doing in and through and for myself, in and through God's own grace.

If the human *ousia* as such is a creation of God, if each human *ousia* is also a creation of God, and if the fulfillment of each *ousia* depends upon the human *physis* (energy system) that can participate in this created project of being a human self, then we can indeed talk, as we have all semester, about what it is for Jesus of Nazareth to have shared our human *ousia*. It means that he had a human history and that his biological organism, *qua* biological, was like anyone else's. It also means that, like everyone else, his human self was a special creation of God. What differentiates Jesus being special from my being special is not the degree of speciality, but what he was special for. Each of us is made not just for the fun of it but for a project, a mission, a destiny. For me to be discontented with what my destiny is is to repudiate my creation and my Creator together. Here we come back to the essence of sin. Though I may not quite or ever know completely what my destiny is, insofar as I can come to see it at all and affirm it and seek its fullness, I am "saved."

Whether through history, *kerygma,* or dogma, we believe that we continue to come to Jesus in order to learn more about *him*. In the process, however, we discover that he has some strange effects upon *us*. However we may try to hold him "out there" as someone to speculate about, suddenly and somehow he changes the relationship to become our inspector and our judge. From the one we appraise, he becomes the one who appraises us.

We ask him about his opinions and teachings, and reserve for ourselves the right to decide if we like them or not. Then suddenly and somehow he becomes himself the Way, the Truth, and the Life to us. He asks *us* why and what we are asking about the ultimate meaning of life. We look to him as exemplar and then discover that he is pointing past himself to God, with the demand that we put first God's kingdom and righteousness above all else in life or death. We acknowledge his perfection and then discover that he is facing us with God's demand for *our* perfection, even while offering us the means of grace whereby we may seek and strive for it. We find our hearts moved to compassion in the presence of his passion and suffering only to discover that he is redirecting our compassion away from his suffering and death toward the suffering and the needs of our fellow human beings here and now. In the presence of Christ, no one is to remain neutral. He draws us inevitably to a decision either for him or against him, for faith or against faith, for discipleship or for rebellion. This is the way in which he confronts us with God's sovereign righteousness and reveals to us our own freedom to share in or to resist God's wisdom, power, and love.

PART 3

Toward a Wesleyan Theology of Pastoral Care

Introduction

As is well known, the principal focus of Albert Outler's thinking during the last twenty years of his life was on the life and work of John Wesley. Often to the consternation of many of his most cherished colleagues and ardent admirers, he came to insist that Wesley's theology evidenced a breadth and depth sufficient to warrant the most extensive study and application to current issues in ministry. Outler believed especially strongly in the possibility of a theology of pastoral care explicitly oriented by Wesleyan insights, and in his unpublished papers there can be found a considerable variety of musings in this direction, from completed lectures to stray paragraphs all the way to not easily decipherable notes scattered here and there.

This section of the Outler papers on pastoral psychology attempts to give a bit of the flavor of this dimension of his concerns by presenting one especially well-received lecture. (Another presentation germane to the present concern has been included in the already published third volume of this series, entitled "Sin, Sins, and Social Dysfunction." It is a probing and provocative account of Wesley's reconsideration of the doctrine of sin, excerpted from the first of Outler's Everett W. Palmer lectures, on "Wesley's Gospel and Ours," which were delivered at the University of Puget Sound, Tacoma, Washington, in October 1975. In this particular lecture, Outler offers one of his most carefully thought-out arguments for the claim he made throughout his career that no theology of the *humanum* could be adequately a Christian theology unless it took with sufficient seriousness the reality and the awesomeness of human sinfulness. In this context, he goes on to offer John Wesley's doctrine of sin as the most creative and original within the Protestant tradition. The "Sin . . ." discussion is an excellent complement to the lecture presented as Chapter 7 in this volume.)

The following reflections on Wesleyan patterns of pastoral care represent the fifth in a series of lectures on "The Wesleyan Spirit," delivered at the Texas Pastors' School in July 1969. They include an engaging attempt to face uncompromisingly the "mental disorders" (to use current psychiatric jargon) of Methodism's founder while at the same time drawing out of Wesley's writings a perspective on pastoral care for the present day. Here also, though offered almost as a series of side comments, Outler makes plain what he believed to be most fundamentally lacking in pastoral theology at the end of the 1960s: its lack of attentiveness to a well-formed and adequately grounded theology of the *humanum.*

His observation is pertinent to pastoral theology in the 1990s as well. What is most intriguing about this presentation is the forcefulness with which Outler advances his strong conviction that in both Wesley's writings and in his pastoral practice can be found just such a theology. The possibility of working out a distinctively Wesleyan theology of pastoral care and counseling, especially for group settings, is here articulated especially captivatingly. And this particular possibility may prove increasingly important to the practice of pastoral care today once caregivers make the discovery for themselves that their soul-care can be as effective in groups as it has been believed to be with individuals.

CHAPTER
7

Wesleyan Patterns of Pastoral Care

John Wesley was a compulsive-obsessional neurotic, and although saved (and much mellowed!) by grace, he remained one all his life. He was a driven man and a driving man; his emotions were held with a tight rein; he would not, his father complained, even go to the bathroom without a pause for decision. He had a multitude of acquaintances who cherished their acquaintanceship, a sizable number of friends and colleagues devoted to him; yet no really close, "bosom friends" (not even his brother Charles who came closest). When, therefore, he reported that his heart was strangely warmed at Aldersgate, he was speaking consciously of a most remarkable experience.

The paradox of Wesley's relentless drive and rigid self-control marked his psychological character before *and* after the rise and spread of the revival. It had been formed, of course, in the Epworth parsonage. His father, Samuel, was preoccupied and uncoping. Jacky, as he was called, grew up under the regimen of women (six sisters at the time). The home was a model of strict order and decorum; it was part of Susanna's creed that children must learn to obey and share unquestioningly. "Break their wills before six if they are ever to be saved thereafter." What else she could have done is not altogether clear (what with nineteen children, chronic poverty, plus the uncouth atmosphere of Epworth itself). Jacky was surrounded by women but no romance, part of a family in heroic struggle for dignity despite poverty. And though his manners were charming, he was always thereafter ill-at-ease in high society.

This deficiency in sophistication is all too evident in his two hopeless love affairs and his disastrous marriage. Sophie Hopkey was an artless and uncultivated teenager when Wesley, Oxford don of thirty-four turned missionary, fell in love with her, or discovered, actually for the first time, a woman who wanted him to fall in love with her. It was a preposterous match, but when Wesley dallied and Sophie married another man, his wounded self-esteem was pathetic. Grace Murray, his second love, was almost equally unsuitable. The story of his rescue from that marriage is less credible than most old-fashioned novels, until one realizes how literally unsophisticated Wesley was. When, finally, he married Molly Vazeille, it was with a view toward having a home-keeper and occasional companion, not a wife and lover. Neither was ready for the other. John never understood Mrs. Wesley's loud complaints of his neglect of her or her jealousy of his popularity with the pious females in the Societies, and he was horrified when she turned to acts of petty revenge and finally left him. She never understood that she had married an institution and never appreciated the role thus thrust upon her.

All of which is to say that Wesley was uncommonly self-possessed, but without much self-understanding (he had too many misperceptions of his own motives and too much self-loathing). He was never wholly fulfilled in his own emotions and interpersonal relationships; he was not what we would call a model of mental health, as it is commonly defined nowadays. This diagnosis is confirmed when one observes Wesley's authoritarian tendencies, in his single-handed direction of the Societies and the Revival. He was never the tyrant; he would never *impose* his rule upon another. But to be "in connexion with Mr. Wesley" was to accept Mr. Wesley's governance, much in the same way he had been "in connexion" with Susanna.

What interest, therefore, could this man have for those of us concerned with what once was called "the cure of souls"? "Neurotic, heal thyself!" would seem the easiest way to dispose of such an uptight martinet. And yet it is simply a fact, bolstered by evidence, that a multitude of men and women were greatly aided by him in their own mental health and social adequacy, in their search for dignity and self-confidence. The annals of the Revival are full of the records of people who had found God and grace—and themselves!—in Wesley's preaching, in his societies, classes and bands, from his queer counseling mix of tenderness and harshness, of assurance and "rebuke," his incessant correspondence and episodic visitations. All this amounted to an actual increase in mental and emotional stability (real "courage to be") and in professions of joy and happiness that are hard to fault as phony or mere suggestibility. Such a fact requires accounting for in terms other than Wesley's personal charisma since this, obviously, will not wash as a plausible explanation. Indeed, Wesley understood this himself. He rarely presents himself as model or norm; his dealings with others exhibit what would now be called an exceptional "professional distance" or objectivity. I would not pretend to understand this paradox myself, but I have profited from pondering it and have come to a few partial conclusions in the course of living with this man over the past decade.

The first point worth mentioning is Wesley's powerful commitment to the principles of growth and nurture as utterly crucial in meaningful human experience. Growth is life's most obvious signal: Human beings are born to grow and develop; stunted or deviated growth is a human blight. Hence, Wesley is forever exhorting his people to grow, to go on growing, to seek and to expect the fullness of their potential development ("perfection") in this life. But human growth and maturation are not automatic or private. Growth requires nurture—food, education, social experience, faith, and grace. And nurture presupposes a social matrix. Wesley was clear in his understanding that humans are not solitary creatures. They must be nurtured and cared for; this nurture and care must be personal and loving, and the small group is the optimal setting for personal growth and nurture—first the family and then some sort of voluntary association.

Wesley was convinced that the Methodists had fared better than the other revival movements because of their superior provision for the nurture of the converts: in the societies, classes, and bands. This pattern of small-group discipline was Wesley's principal agency in the "cure" of those souls vouchsafed to him by the Revival. After 1739, at least, he was certain that genuine

Christianity begins with conversion, a decisive event, or series of them, in which repentance, trust, and assurance of sins forgiven ("acceptance by God") provide a person with a fresh, new frontier of faith and hope. Conversion may have gradualistic antecedents; the event itself is discontinuous and climactic. Wesley would have rejected out of hand Horace Bushnell's thesis about faith's imperceptible onset, or, rather, would have insisted that Bushnell's notion of nurture might better be understood as the life's agenda of the Christian convert. He would never have allowed the either/or disjunction, "Is religion caught or taught?" His obvious answer was "Both, but in the right order." Conversion, then, is the chief aim of Gospel preaching. But Wesley was emphatic: "Converts without nurture are like stillborn babies." "Follow the blow," he said, "never encourage the devil by snatching souls from him that you cannot nurture." And so the direct aftermath of conversion was membership in a "class" or "band."

The history of the religious societies in England, in the last quarter of the seventeenth century and the whole of the eighteenth, is a fascinating chapter in the longer history of the Christian cure of souls. The societies had appeared in the wake of the Stuarts' downfall, and their prime purpose was stimulus and support for those who sought more from faith than they found in church. They were not *ecclesiolae in ecclesia* (by contrast with their Lutheran pietist prototypes in Germany); they held the established church and her priesthood in moderately high esteem. They were not, therefore, rivals to the church or substitutes for her sacraments; they offered a complementary experience of intense exposure, encounter, and interaction transcending nominal Christianity, as they knew it. Their chief agenda was what we might call prayer and devotion—readings, testimonies, interrogations. But they also encouraged people to open their hearts to others in sensitive response to the opened hearts of others.

When young Charles Wesley and George Whitefield formed the Holy Club at Oxford, therefore, they had ample precedent, even in Oxford. And when John attempted to organize his Savannah parishioners into spiritual bands, he was combining the format of the religious societies in England with that of the Moravian classes, borrowed from the Moravians on the *Simmonds.* In England, he and Peter Böhler founded a society in Fetter Lane three weeks before Aldersgate; and in November 1738, we find

Wesley writing to James Hutton about some of the problems they were having with the Moravian bands with which Wesley was still associated. Incidentally, Wesley's main thesis in this letter is that the secret of group dynamics is for every member of the group to feel and be responsible for every other member. Hutton had been advocating special "monitors" in each band (Moravian style) to serve as official critics. Wesley argues against this relegation of a duty common to all to a single representative "reprover."

Experience in these early societies tended to be rather snug and cozy; they were not eager to expand or hive off. The success of the Revival, therefore, made the formula at Fetter Lane almost immediately obsolete. New patterns for the care of souls in quantity, increasing quantities, had to be devised, and here Wesley's psychological genius shows up impressively. Taking the old guidelines, Wesley adds three new features: (1) weekly collections for expenses and the poor, (2) systematic study and interpretation of Scripture and theological tracts, (3) systematic mutual interrogations. One gets the flavor of these exposures from "The Rules for the Bands," which were formulated in 1744:

> The design of our meeting is to obey that command of God, "Confess your faults one to another, and pray one for another, that ye may be healed" [James 5:16].
>
> To this end, we intend:
>
> 1. To meet once a week, at the least.
> 2. To come punctually at the hour appointed, without some extraordinary reason.
> 3. To begin (those of us who are present) exactly at the hour, with singing or prayer.
> 4. To speak, each of us in order, freely and plainly the true state of our souls, with the faults we have committed in thought, word, or deed, and the temptations we have felt since our last meeting.
> 5. To end every meeting with prayer, suited to the state of each person present.
> 6. To desire some person among us to speak his own state first, and then to ask the rest in order as

many and as searching questions as may be concerning their state, sins, and temptations.

Some or the questions proposed to every one before he is admitted amongst us may be to this effect:

1. Have you the forgiveness of your sins?
2. Have you peace with God, through our Lord Jesus Christ?
3. Have you the witness of God's Spirit with your spirit that you are a child of God?
4. Is the love of God shed abroad in your heart?
5. Has no sin, inward or outward, dominion over you?
6. Do you desire to be told of your faults?
7. Do you desire to be told of all your faults, and that plain and home?
8. Do you desire that every one of us should tell you from time to time whatsoever is in his heart concerning you?
9. Consider! Do you desire we should tell you whatsoever we think, whatsoever we fear, whatsoever we hear, concerning you?
10. Do you desire that in doing this we should come as close as possible, that we should cut to the quick, and search your heart to the bottom?
11. Is it your desire and design to be on this and all other occasions entirely open, so as to speak everything that is in your heart, without exception, without disguise, and without reserve?

Any of the preceding questions may be asked as often as occasion offers; the five following at every meeting:

1. What known sins have you committed since our last meeting?
2. What temptations have you met with?
3. How [were] you delivered?

4. What have you thought, said, or done, of which you doubt whether it be sin or not?

5. Have you nothing you desire to keep secret?[1]

In his annual rounds, Wesley would meet with the bands in each place, and often winnowed them of uncooperative or nonparticipating members. But the constructive genius of the process was its provision of things to do that ordinary people could do for themselves, and others—and in so doing, make a meaningful contribution, acknowledged as such by others. Band and class leaders were chosen in and by the group process. It was in the bands and classes that people who were faceless and worthless in the streets outside found respect, dignity, and a new vision of God and man and the human possibility.

And here we come to the heart and soul of the Wesleyan view of the cure of souls—his concept of the *humanum,* of every human being's basic relationship to God, neighbor, and self; of the nature of grace and, consequently, of "growth in grace"; of the growth process in which we recognize ourselves as truly human and in which we may hope to become fully human. It was less Wesley's special skill at counseling, or even at facilitating the group process, that marked off his crucial contribution. It was, rather, a special vision of the human possibility, of life's premises and promises that made the decisive difference; it was this vision that compensated for the hypertensions of Wesleyan zeal and indoctrination.

To grasp this vision, one must begin with the "hearing of faith"—the moment of actual conversion. The one who finally hears the good news of the Gospel is one who, beforehand, had been desperate, either from guilt or ennui or empty complacency. This one was, as Wesley says, "dead"—as also his or her religious beliefs, however orthodox and observant, were "dead." At best, he or she was an "almost Christian." The essence of the trouble, however experienced, was alienation from God, a spurious perception of God's wrath, mercy, or absence. This is the bitter fruit of sin, the source of its blighting power. Sinful human beings suppose themselves either as able to save themselves or else as already lost and abandoned (damned). The transit from the death of sin to the life of faith is the miraculous discovery (God's gift on *his* terms) of God's personal love and care, of his pardon and free grace—of his accepting and expecting love. Now the new person in Christ knows himself and herself as a child of God and realizes that *this* is what it is to be truly human: an *imago Dei,* a special creature of God, a divine project; an individual creation identified, sustained, and consummated by divine grace. The *humanum* is not a thing, a homunculus inside an animal skin. It is a unique mystery, inspired and sustained by God. We are created and held in creation by God, moment by moment, for life's full span—and this whether we live in rebellion or trust. Either way, we are in God's providence; there is no other ground or end of being. Wesley's version of Christian synergism begins and ends with God—with God's sovereignty, initiative, and untrammeled freedom. But it understands humanity's creation as a special and specific enterprise of God in which human beings' identity, freedom and transcendental orientation are all constitutive of the *humanum* itself—not canceled, or cancelable, by sin, even when corrupted and perverted, as it regularly is.

The human *in se*—what is in human beings to be and to do—is, therefore, still God's doing, still morally meaningful, still "good" in its residue and potential. And whoever lives and acts according to the highest leadings of his and her *in se* (created nature) is assured of the support and sanctions of grace. This is the true meaning of God's prevenience—not that God loves us no matter what (although he does), but that God's grace anticipates us at every turn, from conception and birth through all our crises to destiny's final climax, creating and holding open possibilities of health and growth and self-fulfillment but never imposing an arbitrary determination of character or moral action. Human beings are not just what they will and choose (the basic error of the extentialists), but they become what they will and choose within the atmosphere and options of God's grace (prevenient, cooperating, encompassing). We are not on our own and we cannot save ourselves. What we can make of our human possibility is regularly and inevitably tragic and subhuman. Secularism is the final betrayal of humanity's hopes of becoming fully human, and the manifold misery and meaninglessness of life, apart from faith and grace, are grim confirmations of this.

In this sense, we find our true humanity—we are justified—by faith alone, with no antecedent merit or claim. Wesley rules out all possibilities of self-understanding and self-acceptance prior to and apart from the perceptions of faith that we are ourselves because God made us so, keeps us so, makes our "perfection" possible—by creation and recreation, by his grace prevenient, justifying, and sanctifying. When we see ourselves in *this* light, it makes a decisive difference in our self-estimate and our attitude toward our fellow humans. Our self-loathing is reduced—can *we* despise what we know God loves?—but then also our loathing or envy or misperceptions of others: "brethren for whom Christ also died." Yet we are also prevented from swinging to the opposite pole of secular confidence and hope, based on the supposition that the human potential is somehow inherent, that the *humanum* is some sort of self-subsisting entity and therefore somehow eternal, *in se*.

Here, then, is a paradox: On the one hand our radical dependence upon God (not only "for life and breath and all things" but for personal identity as well!) and on the other, our meaningful independence (moral freedom and agency, the specifically human experiences of the transcendental outreach of human curiosity, the unrestricted desire to know), our freedom (the hunger for an open future) and our capacity for love (the need for harmony: within the self, with God, and with our human environment). People of faith realize that they exist from and for God, moment by moment (with no exceptions conceivable), and they accept this role of "absolute dependence" (this is faith). But they will also realize that they have been created to act responsively and responsibly within nature and the human order in terms of reason normed by truth, freedom normed by justice, love normed by community. This is the true liberty of the Christian, true joy and blessedness. This is what it means, or would mean, for a human being to become fully human (i.e., "perfect in love in this life").

By teaching men and women to understand themselves in this light—this special clutch of notions about sin, grace, and human perfection—Wesley gave them a perspective that also liberated them, more or less, from the strictures of the dependency patterns fostered by his own authoritarianism and rule ethic. What strikes one repeatedly about the reactions of Wesley's followers is a typical absence of any servility or parasitism. Somehow he managed to give them room to swing free, and rejoiced with them in their responsible use of their freedom, intelligence, and *self*-control. And this, one might think, is closer to "mental health" and "self-authentication" than most of what we see and hear about under those rubrics nowadays.

There is a partial explanation of how he did this in the curious fact that he never set much store by intense and symbiotic "I-Thou" relationships (a trait that sets him off sharply from most other pietists). For Wesley mistrusted bilateral relationships, save as they were sublated in some wider group setting or, better yet, in a triadic reference to God as the transcendent link between every human "I" and "Thou." His reason: the typical I-Thou bond makes for ascendency-dependency relationships. One of the partners dominates or is dominated, absorbs or is absorbed, leans too much or is leaned upon. And so Wesley took more care than most autocrats in discouraging satellite attachments and knee-jerk discipleship: always his stress is on the vertical reference to truth and love that transcends and judges both master and disciple. In this appeal to the lordship of Christ over all, he was able to encourage real parity in co-discipleship. One could argue with some plausibility that Wesley carried this stress on the transcendental too far, that human relations can and should be far more intimate and symbiotic than Wesley ever allowed. Maybe so, but we must not discount the prevalence of crippling ascendency-dependency patterns in human relations as we see and know them—in business, politics, the church, in friendship, love, and marriage.

In psychotherapy generally and in pastoral care especially, the trickiest of all problems (given relative competence to begin with) is the management of what is called transference and countertransference: the patterns of inordinate attachment and resistance of clients to counselors and vice versa. One of the most ambivalent of all questions in the cure of souls (old style and new) is whose soul is being "cured," the pastor's or the pastored, and the answer is often so ambiguous as to raise legitimate doubts about much of the enthusiasm with which some pastors invest disproportionate time in a few of their flock, leaving others to fend for themselves. By contrast, Wesley never wheedles, never blathers, is seldom intimate; he commands, directs, reproves, argues, appeals. Always he is pointing beyond himself to a higher authority to which his reader has equal access—to Scripture and its rational interpretation, to prayer and conscience, to God and his revelation in Christ. And always he is nudging his reader over toward his own freedom and responsibility as a basic stance, even toward Wesley himself. Wesley's consistent respect for the voluntary principle, even as it related to his own authority, underscores his concern that his disciples be free—under God. But *under God,* and *God's* righteous rule in human hearts and the human community. Wesley's most vivid abhorrence, apart from flagrant sin, was antinomianism—and this because of his conviction that when human beings become laws unto themselves, when the *in se est* is understood as autonomy or inherent goodness, they have corrupted the terms of their real existence as God's children and have begun to stultify their true humanity (which exists solely in our relationship to God).

But Wesley was also very much a man of this world because it is the human scene that we know and are involved in. He takes the sweet bye-and-bye for granted; he counts on it heavily for eventual redress of earth's inequities for the righteous. But he never dwells on it, and he is loud and clear that it must never be used as an excuse here below, here and now. And so he correlates the cure of souls with Christian manners, mental health with social aplomb and self-possession. This is the main motive in his otherwise intrusive advice about clothes and cleanliness, about diligence and thrift, about pride of craft and stewardship. He repeatedly makes the point that conspicuous and wasteful expenditure, or slackness, or improvidence all belie an unhealthful emotional insecurity, an absence of self-determination of one's own needs and their appropriate satisfaction. He decries fashion, partly because it is wasteful, but also because its slaves are not free. Clothes are for comfort and decency, not for decoration and display. Food is for nutrition, not for gluttony. This was Wesley's general doctrine of temperance, which never stretched to doctrinaire extremes. He was no advocate of self-punishment, no partisan of the shabby, sloppy, or shaggy (although he wore his hair long!). His point, consistently, was that a Christian's habits should support his and her Christian witness and service in the world.

There is not much of Wesley that will translate, word for word, into the language and practices of the modern world. For one thing, patterns of authority and leadership have altered out of all recognition since the eighteenth century; for another, all ancient notions of values and moral judgment have been rendered newly problematic, as if from scratch. The dominant views of psychology and personality have changed; the Rogerses and the Maslows and the Hiltners of this world have not read John Wesley much; and even if induced to try, they would find him unsympathetic. The theory and practice of group dynamics has taken new directions since Wesley's bands—some fruitful, some absurd. There would be no point, therefore, in my commending Wesley's way with people in quest of full humanity for us merely to imitate. On that score, however, I'd hesitate to recommend much of what passes currently as pastoral psychology and pastoral care—in view of the fact that the field as a whole is very far from having kept pace with the revolution in the human sciences (anthropology, biology, personality theory, etc.) that keeps on forging ahead with such bewildering complexity, to say nothing of the swift obsolescence of what may be called "modern" theology. Yet I am more convinced than ever that the basic substance of the Wesleyan view of humanity's incredible journey from the barely human to the truly human to the fully human is one of the richest of all available options. By comparison to the doctrines of human beings' radical evil and virtual passivity in relation to their ground of being, here is a concept that affirms and promotes humanity. By comparison with all reductionist estimates of humanity (the naked ape, "computaman" or whatever), here is a human agenda that recognizes our self-transcendence in utter seriousness and sees Christian faith and trust as the most "natural" terms of healthful, human living.

Wesley's ideas about the dynamics of small-group relationships and their role in the cure of souls also deserves reconsideration—all the more because of the current manic phase of what is hopefully called "sensitivity training," with its glowing advertisements of the benefits that will accrue as we gain release from our crippling inhibitions. But how is a healthful group formed, maintained, and made optimally fruitful to all its members? How are such groups reformed? How are people enabled by group interaction to transcend their dependence on this group or that? How can the transcendental reference of human existence be recognized and made evident in group relationships or in bilateral counseling relationships? Wesley doesn't have all the answers to all these questions. But he asks them, as few of us do today, and he would force us toward answers of our own, which is not always the way of our present-day medicine men and witch doctors.

Do you remember, from your own ordination, or from listening to others, the quaint words of the bishop's charge to us as elders in the Church of Christ?:

> You are [said he to us] to be "messengers," watchmen" and "stewards" of the Lord: to teach and to admonish, to feed and provide for the Lord's family; to seek for Christ's sheep that are dispersed abroad, and for his children who are in the midst of this evil world. . . . And if it shall happen that the Church, or any member thereof, do take hurt or hindrance by reason of your negligence, you know the greatness of the fault. Wherefore see that you never cease your labor, your care and your diligence until you have done all that lieth in you, according to your bounden duty, to bring all such as shall be committed to your charge unto perfectness in Christ. . . .[2]

Wesley heard these very same words from Bishop John Potter, who ordained him "priest" September 22, 1728. Now, obviously, this Elizabethan rhetoric can, and should be, demythologized and remythologized in terms to suit our own times and our own commitments to the care and cure of souls. But if these reformulated commitments of ours somehow fail to include an authentic vision of the human in God, a fruitful understanding of Christ as God's clue as to the full reality of our humanity, a welcome stress on God's presence not merely in personal or mass experience, but peculiarly in dynamic groups, then our patterns of pastoral care could be competent enough and still be barren. If, in our zeal for freedom, we fail to ground and limit our freedom within our existence as God's creatures, we shall find ourselves extolling what we cannot provide. If, in our hunger for dignity for all and peace for the world, we fail to call human beings to a recognition of their *dignitas* as God's gift and investment, we shall find ourselves asserting our own dignity and denying that of others, with all sorts of flimsy rationalizations as self-justification.

In the Christian cure of souls, the aid of all the human wisdom in the arts and skills of graceful human relations is indispensable. Pastoral counselors who are unfurnished with the best the human sciences can contribute are by so much a discredit to their calling. But the one thing needful, in all the changes and chances of psychological theory, has been a vision of humanity's plight and his promise as this is revealed in Christ and lived out in the community of the Word, the sacraments, and Christian comradeship. Given this vision in a context of freedom-loving self-respect and freedom-granting respect for others, deficiencies in temperament and technique may not be fatal—as we have noticed in Wesley's case. Without such a vision, the most equable temperament in the world and the best techniques will not suffice to lift personal existence beyond itself to a glimpse of the human mystery encompassed by the divine. And if you cannot do this for others, what are you doing posing as their pastor or counselor?

The word of grace is not a psychological gimmick or panacea. Religious cant is often a reinforcing agent in mental illness and emotional disturbance (not as much as it was, but only because of the fading of meaningful religious language in general). The Gospel is no more a specific for schizophrenia than for cancer. What matters, though, is that all human beings, well or ill, live by their notions of who they are, how they came to be, what they are up to, and where their real goals and satisfactions lie. Here, at least, the Christian pastor has something to offer that extends all his and her other services and transcends them. In such ministrations, the Wesleyan spirit is as relevant today and tomorrow as it was to men and women two hundred years ago.

PART 4

The History and Theology of Pastoral Care: A Course of Lectures

Introduction to Part 4

Albert Outler retired from full-time teaching at Perkins School of Theology at the end of the 1973–74 academic year. Previously, in his capacity as academic dean of the school, this editor had suggested to Outler that he might consider offering a course on pastoral theology that would afford an occasion for summing up his reflections on the discipline that had been of interest to him for over forty years. With enthusiasm, he agreed to teach a course entitled "The History and Theology of Pastoral Care," during the fall semester of 1973. Dr. Harville Hendrix, then a member of the Perkins faculty in pastoral care and now a well-known therapist, author, and lecturer in his own right, shared some of the teaching responsibilities with Outler in the course. Outler's lectures had a broader impact than they might have had otherwise, for they were delivered over closed-circuit television to which students in other institutions beyond Southern Methodist University had access. Restoration of the videotapes of his and Dr. Hendrix' lectures is currently under way at the Outler Archives of Perkins' Bridwell Library. Evaluation of the course itself was positive, and in some quarters bordered on what Outler termed the "embarrassingly glowing."

Outler's lectures for this course provide an unusually close look into the way he typically taught all his classes, mixing magisterial historical overviews with insightful comments on contemporary issues, garnished with good humor and conveyed with uncannily apt turns of phrase. Read in the context of his earlier discussions, these lectures offer more than a glimpse into how Outler's thinking matured over several decades. But in this editor's judgment, they have their importance not so much for what they reveal about their author, but for what they contribute to the discipline of pastoral psychology itself. For they bring impressively to fruition a perspective that insists that neither pastoral care nor psychotherapy can be well-served without theoretical reflection committed to seeing the *humanum* in its fullness, that is, in relation to its transcendent origin, environment, and destiny. The reflections Outler here offers set pastoral care on a firm historical foundation, make plain the continuing relevance of psychodynamic psychotherapies to pastoral care and counseling (and in the process show the silliness of a variety of still-popular technique-driven approaches to healing), outline an agenda for future discussion between healers from the pastoral and the clinical disciplines, and proffer a theology of the Christian life that contains within itself norms capable of guiding both ministers of pastoral care and counseling and psychotherapists alike.

CHAPTER
8

Introduction to a Course in Pastoral Theology

This is a course in *pastoral* theology, theology as resource for understanding the pastoral task and for one's own self-understanding in this particular profession. I'm interested in the pastor as a priest, i.e., one who loves others for God's sake and seeks to mediate God's love to them in fruitful ways. I'm interested in him and her as a diagnostician of the human situation, who understands the pathologies of human unhappiness, their symptoms and "causes," and who has a credible theory as to why people hurt and how they may be helped. We'll also be talking about the pastor as prophet and as moralist, as a keeper of conscience; for human unhappiness always has, amongst its components, moral and spiritual dimensions that are always personal and social. The pastor is, therefore, a moralist perforce (good, bad, or permissive). Beyond that, our concerns will focus more specifically on the pastor as psychologist and counselor, in view of the fact that, in our time, "pastoral care" has formed an alliance of sorts with psychotherapy. But we must not ignore the pastor as charismatic (i.e., as an inspired and inspiring person, whose spiritual gifts are both evident and infectious). Finally, we must not fail to stress the pastor's role as catalyst and change agent in the struggles of our society toward true and full humanity.

The ruling image that includes all these pluriform rôles and functions is the New Testament metaphor of "the good shepherd." This metaphor was either claimed by Jesus or attributed to him by the first disciples; it is an image of sturdy, unsentimental compassion, wisdom, courage, and resourcefulness. In the Bible, this pastoral imagery is rich and meaningful, and even in our time, when few of us have any firsthand acquaintance with sheep and shepherds, we still have no wholly adequate substitute for this composite figure. It suggests the interaction between the guide and the guided, the leader and the led, those in need of wise and loving help and those who can give it, the enablers and the enabled. The essence of shepherding, of course, is linkage: guiding a flock to where they can fend for themselves, guarding a flock from enemies and their own shortfallings, healing the ailing—and "carrying the young lambs in his bosom."

In the Christian tradition, the good pastor is a link between the "flock of Christ" and the God and Father of our Lord Jesus Christ. And this makes him and her a *theo*logian, i.e., a person with considered thoughts about God and about the divine-human relationship, which is the shortest and best definition that I know of "theologian." But *pastoral theology,* the good shepherd's considered thoughts about God and the human scene, is not a different kind of theology from all the other kinds. It is, rather, all the other kinds of theology focused on the pastor's total task, their convergence on one point: the pastor enabling people to think and feel and work as Christians, to rejoice and hope in God, to live abundantly, and to die triumphantly, as members of the body of Christ. It is, therefore, biblical theology (i.e., our basic data about God) adapted to the interests, capacities, and needs of people in contemporary society. But it is also historical theology (the residue of Christian reflection on the great issues of life and death and destiny through the course of twenty centuries), but aimed at providing a credible perspective upon the pastoral task in the light of the various ways it has been conceived and practiced. There are no models from this past that I know of that we can find and imitate, but there is genuine wisdom to be gained from our predecessors' experiences in trying to be good pastors.

Pastoral theology is also systematic and philosophical (speculative, if you like) in that it is concerned with the great central questions that have confronted the Christian mind and the range of varied answers that remain now as live options—e.g., "salvation," but with a crucial concern in how these questions are being asked now, and how they may be spoken to, now, in this new world that none of us really understands. Pastoral theology includes a serious interest in preaching, worship, and meaningful ceremonial, for no amount of personal and small-group experience satisfies our needs for communal and ritual linkages with the larger encompassing Mystery in which we live and move and have our being. Later on I'll be arguing for the urgent need for the hallowing and re-sacralizing of life that has been "secularized" in the wrong ways or for the wrong reasons; now, I want only to assert in passing that no pastoral theology that fails to understand the force and effect of myth and ritual in human life is adequate or authentic.

But, finally and most of all, pastoral theology is moral theology. The good shepherd must know what is good and bad for the human condition, what is right and wrong, and why—how to analyze and assess what were once called "cases of conscience." For despite the immense and still largely unrecognized revolution in the modern conscience, the absolute crux of the pastor's task is moral guidance, with all that that entails. At the bottom of every behavioral disorder is a false perception of the good and the right, of the grounds and motivations for authentic and truly human action. And this is the business of ethics, of morality: the question as to what constitutes responsible behavior, the source and outreach of human responsibility. Here again we are talking about something more than abstract notions—rather, about ethics in action, of freedom normed by justice, of self-fulfillment normed by community, of life bracketed by birth and death but encompassed everywhere by God's grace. Pastoral theology, then, is all you know about God in Christ, all you know about the *humanum* and its disorders, all you know about the human possibility and its terms—all of this brought to bear on the complex enterprise of being a *good* shepherd, living for others and for their best good.

And there is more: For the good shepherd is a competent psychologist and counselor; he/she is open and sensitive to all the social and moral issues that stir the community's conscience, or ought to; he/she is prepared not to be ministered unto but to minister and to give all for the help of others. Good shepherds must themselves be a living letter, known and read by all, which is to say, they must have experienced what they are trying to communicate: they must have recognized their own lives as a gift from God and have accepted that on God's terms; they must have lost their need to dominate and must have found courage to lead; they must be alive and open, truly loving, and therefore compassionate: grace-filled and grace-ful! This means what used to be called "converted" and what is now called "transformed" or "liberated" or "self-fulfilled." It further means a basic security with God and with one's fellow humans, *all* of them, in principle at least. You can translate this back into Latin and it comes out *curatores animarium.* For longer intervals than I can account for the church has survived without great theologians or great exegetes or moralists, but it is never more than one generation of good pastors away from real disaster. And current demoralization in the Christian pastorate is the most sensitive and precise of all the measures of the magnitude of the current crises within the churches!

This course will be a first attempt on my own part to apply all the theological disciplines to the daily and yearly round of pastoral care, my first attempt in twenty years to combine, in a formal course, a lifelong vocation as a historical theologian with a long-standing avocation in psychotherapy. You'll notice that I've started with Freud, assuming that we would agree that *there,* in some significant sense, is where the new era of modern psychotherapy really begins. I was strongly tempted to include some much older landmarks (Gregory's *Liber Regulae Pastorales* or Butzer's *Care of Souls* or Baxter's *Reformed Pastor* or St. Alfonso Liguori's *Moral Theology* or Washington Gladden's *The Christian Pastor and the Working Church*). And then there are significant omissions of contemporary sources and discussions in the list I've finally come down to (Hobart Mowrer, the wide-ranging debates on pastoral and medical ethics in abortion, organ transplants, euthanasia, etc., the drug scene and alcohol, and the determinists' bid to assume responsibility for the human future). My fundamental conviction is that to see both classical and contemporary sources in anything like an intelligible perspective we need to see the pastoral office and enterprise as it has been understood and practiced across the centuries, in other crises and transformations of the Christian community. There are not many synoptic views of this tradition (these traditions) and the ones I know strike me as woefully inadequate. But then, in trying to do better, in territory that is at least partially familiar to me, I began to see why. We need a good history of the experience of effective working pastors and how they put their theology (and psychology, etc.) to work for the people of their times and places. But this would be exceedingly difficult, and I feel thoroughly frustrated in having to crowd what I hope will be a useful perspective for you into three lectures. My hope, of course, is that some of my larger (and occasionally outrageous) generalizations will spark off some interest for some of you—to follow up on your own.

CHAPTER
9

The Pastor as a Professional Person

An older friend of mine, who is as dismayed as I am with what the world has come to, turned on me the other day with a complaint that the clergy have been derelict in their duties as keepers of the public conscience. "The clergy," said he, "have a responsibility for leadership in the moral field that they have let slip from their hands.... The clergyman is a very special someone. He stands in a special place; he has special authority. Not because he has had education in theology and perhaps in psychology, but because he is 'a man of God.' He is dedicated. He is unselfish. He has no wish to hurt but only to help people— and this is rare. The clergyman cannot minimize *sin* and maintain his proper role in our culture. Failure to do this is *his* sin. The clergyman inevitably evokes transference effects from his parishioners and hearers, and these reinforce his rational and moral authority with them."

I confess that I was as astonished as some of you must be by this reference to the clergy as authority figures, *ex officio.* For although my friend is eighty, he is as fully liberated from the old stereotypes as any man I know (and has been for longer than I have known him). He is, as a matter of fact, one of the more eminent shrinks in this country. But what blew my mind was his reversion to an image of the clergy that was common in his youth but that few of us can recognize anymore, and that fewer and fewer of our layfolk (the younger ones especially) do, either. It put me in mind of the great days of the parson (in all his glory)—the person of the town: the man of learning, wisdom, courage, and grace, with a certain spiritual aura that somehow outshone his human failings, a person deserving reverence, of some sort, for what he represented ("a man of God"). George Herbert wrote one of his better poems about him, that we'll mention later, and spoke of the parson's "pulpit as his stronghold and castle."

I can remember when something like this was still so, and there are residues of this ancient reverence for pastors still left in the nooks and crannies of our racial memories. But for the most part it all sounds a mite quaint and unreal. For my lifetime has coincided with what we might call "the passing of the parson." Today's pastor, on the average, is better educated, more sophisticated in sociological and psychological understanding, with more institutional support for progressive social action and less inhibited by dogmatic sectarian biases than any generation since the apostles—but with less prestige and less *ex officio* authority than any of his and her predecessors since the feudal chaplains and chantry priests of the Middle Ages. That *is* an unnerving paradox, isn't it? What status or influence we have nowadays does not come from our office, as such, nor any of its emoluments; and this has cut deeply into our sense of professional dignity, identity, and self-confidence. For if we are better educated, so are our people; and they, as we, are immersed in the hurricane tides of information and opinion that swirl through the communications media, and our voices are all too often echoes of that uproar. If we are sophisticated in psychology, so also are our people (or at least enough of them so that even our paramedical status at its best, which is none too good, doesn't snow them as it might otherwise). And if we are liberated and broad-minded, so are they (at least the young). If we are nondogmatic and ecumenically minded (in our own eyes), their most natural reaction is, "So what? Who isn't?" And if you speak of the pastor as "a man of God," they, and we, must quickly speak of the priesthood of *all* believers, which has come to mean that everyone can, on principle, and does pray on his and her own. Thank you very much indeed for next to nothing!

The result is a profession without much left of its original reasons for being defined as a profession. We are, many of us, men and women with ambiguous feelings about our professional identities, and we have warranted doubts about any indispensable rôles and function we may have, if any, in modern society. Whatever you can do, somebody else can do as well or better, except to speak of God and the Gospel in tones that often sound uncertain and embarrassed. Save for fundamentalists, with whom we would not wish to be seen dead, not many of us are prepared to speak up, resoundingly and credibly, about sin and God's judgment against it; of repentance and pardon; of life, death, and resurrection in the grace of God, "who in Christ was reconciling the world unto himself." In many ways, therefore, the modern pastor is in mortal peril of redundancy—in the eyes of the world and in his own eyes. Who really needs him/her, and for what— save as auxiliaries in other helping services, bit players in other scenarios, or else specialists who have declined any general responsibility for the whole flock of Christ? None of us could object, on principle, to a notion of pastor as an auxiliary to anybody: a humble, modest helper to other real professionals, extenders of services that are initiated and supervised by others. The notion of servanthood is still embedded in the literal meaning of the word "minister."

But who really *needs* a pastor for his and her opinions about public affairs or community problems, unless those opinions are clearly derived from a distinctive perspective on such affairs (viz., a theological understanding of life, death, and destiny)? Who really needs a pastor for the ritualizing of life's crucial transitions: birth, puberty, marriage, death, unless she and he can anchor those events to their transcendental moorings and do so convincingly, which is to say with intelligent convictions of one's own? Who needs pastors for their bonhomie and friendliness, unless this is a graceful expression of their habitual generosity of spirit, springing from their love of God and neighbor? Who needs Christian pastors as social service workers or teachers, or psychotherapists or TA trainers if their anthropological frame of reference is indistinguishable from the prevailing humanisms and naturalisms of our time? Who needs pastors for their vision and courage, their political savvy, unless their revolutionary ends and means are different from the utopian or nihilist goals of the secular radical? Who needs pastors for their leadership in worship, if worship is nothing more than some overrated form of collective magic (or, alternatively, a weekly dose of reassurance)? Who even needs pastors for their alleged and traditional "power of the keys"? Here *my* answer would be "Everybody," but then your next question—reflexively, I should think, if you really are "modern"—would be, "What keys?" "What power?"

And this brings us to the heart of our identity crisis as professional persons. We are all too often people without a message, except of the same general sort available elsewhere in society (admonitory, hortatory, moralistic, etc.), maybe with more piety and less prestige. We are all too often people without a medium, except the same deeply ambivalent and demoralized society in which the whole world lives, where true community is all too often small scale and episodic. We are people without authority, save our own personal stature and charismata, whatever that may mean. You may, indeed, have solved your own identity crisis (and God be praised for that), but who is interested in your identity, and why should anyone be? You may be able to help individuals and small groups to new levels of liberation and joy, while an overburdened, fragile planet shudders under the agonies of injustice, indignity, inhumanity. You may be afire with prophetic indignation—with few troops to muster and no precincts to deliver—a moralist with no ultimate sanctions for your values, a romantic who continues to tatter the rhetoric of love in scenes where self-interest has already been canonized.

Now, obviously, nobody that I know of ever consciously intended anything like this outcome from their valiant and high-minded struggles against the repressive societies in Western culture since Plato (at least), or the false supernaturalisms and superstitions that have dogged Christianity since the apocryphal Gospels, with their inclusion of God as an episodic cause among natural causes, a *deus ex machina*. There was clear gain in the triumphs of liberalism and in our human self-awareness of our own responsibility for the quality of human life, in our deliverance from the old tyrannies of priestcraft and proof-texting. Any nostalgia for those good old days is just that—nostalgia, which normally is no more than self-indulgence. But these triumphs are hollow and disenchanting to many of us because of a very much larger and more radical discontinuity in the Western tradition that has become evident in the past two decades, a break with the past that few historians have recognized clearly and none has explained to my satisfaction. My concern with it here is its impact on the pastoral office and with its radical import for any updated notion of "the power of the keys," which, as I have suggested, is the chief distinctive claim that the pastoral office has ever had.

One way of identifying this quantum leap toward social disorder (at least temporary social disorder) is to look at the collapse of conventional moral demand systems that once controlled the collective behavior of a working majority in the populations of Western societies, the collapse of the traditions of *ex officio* authority and of accepted authority figures at every level of social organization: from the family to the schools, civil governments, courts, business and labor; the erosion of taboos of every sort and the fading of divine sanctions for or against what human beings do, or fail to do, to themselves and others. Given this perspective, the easiest way to see what's happening is to ponder the steady rise of what used to be called psychopathic and sociopathic behavior—i.e., reckless, ruthless, remorseless—along with the rising, whelming flood of passionate self-assertion and self-righteousness amongst all the various self-identified groups and movements that I know. Notice, too, how this self-righteousness has come to be bolstered by a universal sense of victimization. The Siamese twins of anxiety and guilt have been disjoined and guilt succumbed in the operation. Psychiatrists of quite different persuasions are beginning to report this basic shift in the character disorders of their patients, especially the younger ones. Now, as I take my daily dosage of heavy pieces explaining mass murders, prison riots, promiscuity, hijacking, terrorism, and ripping off as a lifestyle (this litany is random and also endless), I feel like the postoperative appendectomy case: it hurts only when I laugh.

Christian pastors are caught in the churning middle of this huge upheaval; they have joined the ranks of the victims and victimized. If they try to reassert their authoritarian rôle of yesteryear, they'll find themselves with their limp Bible or gaudy chasuble with nobody paying much attention (except a geriatric remnant of varying ages). Not even the Jesus freaks or the pentecostalists will stand hitched, nowadays, to *ex officio* authority. And if you abandon your claim to the power of binding and loosing, in some credible sense, your alternative is to become a sort of religious cheerleader or drum major in the parade of the cults of reassurance as they march from Coué to Carnegie to Peale to Tom Harris. If you try to rehabilitate or update the notion of *sin* (some notion of a radical human flaw), you are confronted with the valid challenge of moral relativism and the still vividly remembered spectres of religious obsessions. If you cry, "Woe," your voice is lost in a dismal chorus; if you cry, "Peace," you're conning somebody. What then, conceivably, is the pastor's professional rôle, vocational identity, personal dignity, final justification?

The only answer I can see (a partial one, of course) would begin with our recognition that the deepest hungers of the human heart have not yet been stilled or sated by any of the ministries of secular societies (not even the best-intentioned ones). Humanity is under abuse around the world. Business and labor continue to conspire to do in the consumer worse than ever. And still the human spirit reaches up and out and beyond itself; it will not finally settle for the husks of technology, racism, greed—not even for creature comfort. It will not write "Ichabod" over the portals of its future. This spirit flares up like tinder in response to a visible, credible truly pastoral figure like John XXIII and is not wholly extinguished when his vision is deferred. What is crucial here and now is this grudging admission that human beings need moral guidance as much as any thirteenth-century peasant (or prince) or any seventeenth-century antinomian. An appeal for something like the pastoral office keeps re-forming in our hearts. The power of the keys may go unexercised, but something like it also goes a-begging.

Paul Pruyser has lately raised a lonely voice in support of defining the distinctiveness of pastoral work among the helping professions[1] (and I keep quoting psychotherapists because of their residual prestige as having been our liberators from religiosity and moralism). He points to the fact that pastors still have readier access to larger segments of the population on terms that allow for serious interpersonal encounter than any other professional group in our society; and then he chides us for our appalling neglect of such an opportunity and challenge. He speaks of such pastoral activities as "pastoral conversations, pastoral convening, pastoral care in situations of crisis and *kairos*, pastoral counseling, pastoral use of sacraments and the means of grace (including preaching and teaching), and pastoral enabling." His main thesis is that if pastors who have gained their own freedom to let others be free were also willing and able to provide guidance to others in their being free and responsible, they would be rendering a truly distinctive and professional service, needed by all, and actually acceptable to more people than we may have supposed.

But the efficacy of any such service depends upon a crucial proviso that Pruyser prescribes but flatly refuses even to try to fill out. The pastor, says he, must have a *theo*logical diagnosis of the human malaise; he/she must be able to lead people to a deeper and more authentic awareness of their human flaws and their involvement in them, to a more realistic acceptance of their responsibilities and a more honest recognition of the terms of personal and social rehabilitation. He applauds James Lapsley's rhetoric and program in *Salvation and Health* (viz., a working theology that combines psychiatric wisdom and skill with frank talk about God and man and "salvation").[2] He challenges the clergy "to put your shoulder under a task that not only badly needs doing but will be an exciting venture." Pruyser's final word is almost brusque, but a valid warning to those of us still working through our own transference-dependence complexes vis-à-vis psychotherapists we have known and worked with: "I will interpret any attempt at asking me or any other psychologist to develop a pastoral-theological system for you as an act of abandoning *your* [pastoral task] altogether."

I, for one, regard this as a prophetic sentence against us, and a reasonable challenge to us. We may, or may not, agree on what a thorough and valid diagnosis of the human malaise would amount to, or its indicated therapy, or its long-range prognosis. I know what a can of theological worms this opens up, and I have by now an ingrained aversion to glib God-talk. But that this inquiry about divine-human interactions (and their implicates) defines the hermeneutics of the pastoral task and thus also the pastor's identity as a professional person seems to me painfully clear and its imperatives painfully urgent. A good pastor is a good diagnostician of the human condition! But diagnosis, as we know, is a tricky business—in medicine, in education, in the ultimate issues of faith, hope, and love. There is, on the one side, diagnostic overkill. But then there is diagnostic complacence. Theological diagnosis over the centuries has swung between the extremes of Pelagianism and hyper-Calvinism, and now we are apparently in for a season of a new hypostatic schematism: too much parent, too much child, too little adult, etc. For now, my question is whether our various attempts at diagnosis will take the theological and moral dimensions of human destiny, here and hereafter, as real and decisive, even if also as vague and subject to the rhetorics of metaphor and mystery. Either we seek and find transcendental grounds for self-denial and self-fulfillment, or all the secular reasons for *self*-denial will quickly lose their grip upon the human will. Or, if this is incredible, all the other grounds for any one of us interfering with any of the rest of us will have to be functions of utility, power, or passion. That way lies the dark—the death of God and of Man—unmourned in an idiot universe.

But pastors have to be more than diagnosticians, if they are to be professional in any complete sense. They must see themselves as a guide and comfort to troubled consciences and as a goad to untroubled consciences. They must understand themselves as priest, twixt man and God, between earth and heaven, between the linear and ecstatic. Moreover, it goes with our job to try, as best we can, to hallow life once again, to re-sacralize it, to recognize its suffusions of mystery, tragedy, and glory—the interdependence of a theology of the Cross and of glory beyond the Cross. You cannot do this by fiat, of course, but if there were enough of us who understood life in these distinctly religious terms, those of us whose experience of life included real intimations of its holiness and of its interface with the infinite, the taste and feel of our existence—and that of others—might be altered by the fallible means of infallible grace that we can administer all too fallibly.

But there is a fatal hypocrisy in praying "Hallowed be thy name" and then failing to proceed with equal emphasis to "Thy kingdom come [here and now], thy will be done on earth." To punctuate this sentence properly is to have discovered the true

Christian secularism: No one will ever know the harm that has been wrought by that conventionally misplaced comma that allows for the familiar abstraction: "Thy will be done [comma] on earth as it is [as a matter of course] in heaven." For the nuance in this reading is that earth and heaven are mere correlatives (and they are in a way). But the real priority in Jesus' original petition is a moral and secular one (not eschatological, yet; that will come later, in due course). "Thy will (of love, justice, and salvation) be done on earth"; this is the Christian charter for a permanent revolution in human history. The good pastor is, therefore, a harbinger of the kingdom, a catalyst of change (i.e., he/she triggers interactions in others; and even this metaphor is misleading, since, technically, catalysts don't get used up and good pastors do). But the changes they are after are significant personal and social responses to divine imperatives, to divine promises, to divine power—in the humanizing of life and its divinization as well.

Professions are identified by their collective intentions and their specific functions. Within very rough limits, lawyers know what they are *for*, in society (besides being for themselves), and all their shortcomings fail to negate their professional ideal image. So, too, with doctors—from GPs to ophthalmologists who restrict their practice to left eyes. Pastors are as much professional persons as they, *if* their intentions and functions are understood and acted out in terms of basic human needs to which they can minister, however inadequately, as servants of the servants of God. Nothing less than this, and nothing much to the contrary, will tell them, or the rest of the world, whether they are truly professional persons or one more of those human anomalies that so confuse our view of the human potential at its best.

CHAPTER
10

The Good Shepherd: Changing Perspectives (1)

It was the act of God in Christ, reconciling the world unto himself, that brought the Christian church into being; and both the ministry and mission of that church are defined, ab-originally, by *Christ's* ministry and mission. It was he who came not to be ministered unto but to minister, and to give his life in redemptive love. It was he who was recognized as "The Good Shepherd," who cared for God's "little flock" at the cost of his own life. He is our High Priest—our only one, according to the New Testament—and all human ministry in his name is a per-petuation, an extension, an expression of that primordial mystery of Love Incarnate. The "pastors and teachers" (in Ephesians 4:11)—notice the pairing there; it is significant—are a part of that ministry: the shepherding, guiding, nurturing, safeguarding part. As a rule, the shepherd doesn't feed the sheep; his job is to enable them to feed themselves, to lead them into green pastures, to find ways for them to fend for themselves. Yet, in the early church, there was urgent need for guidance, nurture, discipline— and inspiration! We know precious little about the very first Christian groups in that period when the nascent movement was still evolving in its original Jewish matrix. Our information here is largely about the Pauline churches, which have been taken as more typical than they probably were—mainly because of the shape of the New Testament canon and its Pauline core. By the time Christianity actually became visible in the Roman Empire (Pliny's "Letter to Trajan"[1] serves as a convenient landmark for this), the Christians had already been excommunicated by the Jewish rabbis at Javneh and were trying to find their groping way into an uncertain future that they had never expected to have to negotiate, certainly not the future they were, in fact, confronted with. Moreover, Christianity was illegal and "underground," since the Christians rejected the civil religion of the empire and were no longer exempted from it, as the Jews had been.

In those late New Testament letters commonly called "The Pastorals" (1 and 2 Timothy, Titus, James, 1 and 2 Peter, Jude), many of these problems are reflected, and we can readily imagine what kind of pastoral care these people needed. Their original rootage in Judaism had been lost, and this posed a problem about the Old Testament in the church and its continuing authority for Christians. Their earlier eschatological hopes had been shattered and now had to be transvalued. New Christians greatly needed valid teaching, since in the Hellenistic world the New Testament Gospel was all too easily misconstrued. New Christians (and old ones, too) needed moral guidance, for the Christian lifestyles and ethical standards were cross-grained to all prevailing customary morality anywhere in the ancient Near East. This meant firm discipline because their new-found liberty in Christ (liberation from superstitions and bondage) was, by itself, a powerful temptation to antinomianism.

Think what it was like to be a Christian in the second century: with no fixed liturgy, no official doctrine or creed, no single pattern of polity or ecclesiastical discipline, with sophisticated "gnostics" always about, eager to reduce the offense of the Gospel (its scandalous story about Jesus as the Christ or its self-evidently foolish claims that the Savior of mankind was actually one of us ordinary mortals). The Gnostic proposal was that the Gospel needed to be retuned more closely to the then "modern mind." The second century was "a world come of age," with a surpassing confidence in some kind of secret wisdom (gnosis = self-understanding = self-realization = union with the divine), and this is very much like our world, "come of age" even if with different definitions of wisdom (liberation = peak experiences = self-fulfillment). The intelligentsia were contemptuous or patronizing. Always there was the threat of persecution and often its bloody reality. Under such pressures, pastoral care evolved on four levels—with a variety of combinations:

1. *Sacramental fellowship.* ("Breaking of the bread and prayers," "the showing forth of Christ's death till he comes again," "discerning the body of Christ") in which the Christians were drawn together—frequently, regularly—to remember, to repent, to be renewed, and to grow up into Christ Jesus, to maturity.

2. *Moral guidance.* The forming of a Christian conscience and the shaping of habits that would translate "the fruit of the Spirit" into a communal lifestyle in which they could function as public virtues and inner compulsions. Quite literally the law has nothing to say about "love, joy, peace, patience, kindness, goodness, fidelity, gentleness, and self-control" (Galatians 5:22–23) because you can't legislate for or against dispositions.

3. *Christian discipline.* The Christian groups managed to pick up more than their share of weaklings, hustlers, neurotics, antinomians, et al.; it almost asked for them. The moral atmosphere out of which they came ranged from one extreme of asceticism (the loathing of the body and this world) to the other extreme of brazen amoralism. These converts had to be sought, welcomed, and winnowed; they had to be taught; they had to be kept on probation (for two years, as a rule) and then they had to be disciplined—by pressures ranging from partial suspensions to expulsion. There were stations for the different gradations of penitents: (1) "hearers" or "catechumens"; (2) "kneelers"; (3) "co-standers"; (4) "weepers." Moreover, the business of "confession" (exomologesis!), "penitence," and "absolution" were public (i.e., in the full congregation or group).

4. *Spiritual consolation.* Life in those days was burdened, difficult, dangerous. Yet the Gospel of faith, courage, and joy was, indeed, gospel. What impressed pagans the most about Christians was their joy and courage. And this Gospel of

130

high spirits was preached, exemplified, and made real in the valley of the shadow of death by good shepherds (sometimes by the bishops-presbyters-pastors [the terms were almost interchangeable until late in the second century at least], and also by the spiritually mature layfolks, by the widows and deaconesses, etc.). I'd just as soon not get swamped in the tricky questions of ministerial orders or apostolic succession at this stage. Obviously, a stable scheme of order and ordination evolved later, and there may have been more continuity in it than can be proved from the very confusing medley of terms and references in the literature that we actually have to go by. The only two points to make here for our purposes are (1) that there was no clear-cut uniformity in the polity and order of the first two or three centuries and (2) that the pastoral tasks (priestly, prophetic, diaconal, judicial, and charismatic) were, more often than not, performed by those who happened to have the requisite gifts, graces, and fruits for them. This is the primitive actuality of the priesthood of all believers: not every man his own priest, but all Christians as priests and pastors for others, as the need arose and as they could respond. This mutuality of caring and helping is seen in *The Shepherd of Hermas,* in the counseling role of Justin Martyr, in the pastoral concerns of Irenaeus, Tertullian, and the great Alexandrines: Clement and Origen.

But one of the most crucial of all the pastoral concerns in this ante-Nicene church was unity: unity in the local group(s) and unity throughout the round of all the local churches in the *oikoumene.* This is the literal meaning of "catholic": one part related to the whole; the whole as more than the sum of its parts. And this was the prime concern and function of the chief pastors, in their localities, in their regions and in the *oikoumene.* They were both symbols and agents of *koinonia*, for the Christians—from Mesopotamia to Britain, from North Africa to the dark forests of Germany. I'd prefer to waive the question of the Petrine supremacy with no more than a passing comment that there were good and sufficient reasons why the chief pastor of the empire's capital, the bishop of Rome, did become the chief symbol and agent of the unity and community of catholic Christianity, *primus inter pares.* The so-called primacy of honor is a plain historical fact; the primacy of Petrine jurisdiction is, of course, still in dispute.

The survival of Christianity, from the fall of Jerusalem (70 A.D.) to its "emancipation" by Constantine (313 A.D.) is something of a marvel, a succession of crises for which the church was chronically ill-prepared and from each one of which she emerged reflecting a strange paradox of amazing continuity and decisive change. Just as a twenty-year-old is both identical with the two-year-old he was and yet unrecognizably different, so the Christian church in its last great general persecution (under Diocletian—303–310) was still "apostolic" and yet now unrecognizably different from its earliest origins in Jerusalem and Antioch. Its transplantation from Jewish to Christian soil had forced on it an identity crisis; it wasn't a Jewish sect, it wasn't a Greek *thiasos*. But what was it? The persistence of history, when they had counted on an early apocalyptic climax, had forced on them a crisis of continuity. The civil persecutions forced a crisis of survival. The disruptions of the third-century empire forced a crisis in their concern for culture and for the hostile world around them.

If you can understand how they managed all this, you've already begun to understand both the ways of Providence and the essential functions of the good shepherd in the vicissitudes of communal Christian living. For in these centuries, the good shepherd emerges as a person (1) who understands the Christian Gospel and the Christian life well enough to interpret it to others and to help them unravel their misunderstandings of it; (2) who could hold a group together, could link them with God's means of grace, could preside over their celebrations and rites of passage (including death!), who shared their concerns and their fate (even to martyrdom); (3) who could teach the uninstructed with simplicity and could hold his own against the intellectuals and in a police state; (4) who kept the Christian conscience alive and the Christian commitment to the Christian ethic and so wielded the power of the keys "to loose and to bind" (sins on earth and in heaven); (5) who was inspired and inspiring, who could lead people to the outer limits of spiritual insight, ecstasy, and joy, yet also with courage and love and deathless hope.

Those who know this period I have been trying to characterize will recognize, as I do, that these generalizations are inferences from a meager and diverse literature—as diverse as Ignatius (the pastor of Antioch who was deeply concerned about the sacramental, doctrinal unity of the little scattered Christian groups, centered in their pastor), to Justin (who was a sort of pastoral counselor; his "thing" was the intellectual riddles of Christian versus pagan and Jewish "philosophy"), to Irenaeus, pastor of Greek colonists in Gaul (whose "thing" was "continuity" along with a wonderful new explanation of Christian salvation), to Tertullian (a layman, moralist, and *enthusiast,* literally), to Clement and Origen (schoolteachers, sort of), to Hippolytus (whose "thing" was liturgy), to the Pseudo-Clement, whose image of the church is a ship, with God as owner, Christ as captain and pilot, and the pastor-bishop as *proreus*—a sort of lookout and helmsman.

From all this, one gets the overall impression of a representative leader, relating his people to God through his teaching of the Christian story through the sacraments that recapitulate the Christian story. He is the representative of the catholic (whole, universal) community who could relate a local group to the whole People of God; he was the keeper of their consciences, not just by his conscience but "by the mind that was in Christ." As far as any human agency can be invoked as a historical force, it was this sort of pastoral care that explains the church's survival, in the ferments and turmoils of those crucial centuries—and in essence, ever since. Its central focus was diagnosis (sin), therapy (the new creature in Christ), and the dedication of the new creature to a life for others in Christ's spirit (the Christian life). This was a doctrine of radical human equality, the only kind there is really: the equal need of all humans of God's unmerited love and pardon. And the final assurance of this was the Christian confidence that both life and death are equally encompassed by God's grace. "Therefore," said the Christian pastor—even before, or apart from, any funeral!—". . . stand firm [hang in there!] . . . and work for the Lord always, work without limit, since you know that in the Lord your labor cannot be lost" (1 Corinthians 15:58, NEB). That's the work ethic in a form that Max Weber never understood!

Then came Constantine. And the church that had barely survived its worst persecution under Diocletian suddenly found itself, first emancipated, then favored—a half century later established as the state religion of a police state. It was the most drastic change the church has ever experienced—until now, maybe—and her responses to it were deeply ambivalent. From having been "out," church membership began to be "in," and this produced the largest bulge in church membership in the shortest time in the whole of church history.

In most of us there is this reflex aversion toward mass religion: It *can't* be for real. This is the residue in us of what was the prime impulse of monasticism, and then later pietism and now, in our time, the new encounter culture. The first monks began with a sense of alienation from the straight, self-serving religiosity of the popular churches; they amounted to a real "counterculture" (which is one reason why they annoyed Theodosius so much). Their choice was to flee the elegant decadence of Constantinople and the grubby affluence of Alexandria out into the deserts of Cappadocia or Egypt. Here they sought to escape the world, the flesh, and the devil and to find their own ladders of ascent to God—true happiness in "mystic sweet communion." Monasticism was at first eremitic but not for long and never typically. At bottom it was the intensive small-group experience that is the driving and pulling force of monasticism. Its essence is not asceticism nor virginity nor any specific formula for salvation, but in the settled conviction that human existence for the general mass of humankind is hopeless unless they become like us (who have finally found the best life has to offer, here and hereafter). This monastic premise is very nearly self-evident. But the conclusion—that we happy few have found the way out (a formulary way out)—is what constitutes the half-truth of monasticism. The differences between Mt. Athos and Esalen are more in matters of style and taste than in psychological dynamics, even in the apparent contrast between the burden of sin that the monks carry and the burdens of freedom loaded onto the new ecstatics.

Meanwhile, back at the overrun ranch of the "Great Church"—in Constantinople, Rome, Alexandria, Antioch—the pressures of change had gotten out of hand, literally. Before Constantine, pastors had had scant responsibility for the *oikoumene* ("civilization") and even less direct political leverage (save as an underground within the civil service) . Now they were involved in social and political responsibility up to their ears; after Theodosius, they would become civil servants! The emperor had gambled a good part of civilization's future (as he knew it) on Christianity as a unifying, stabilizing force. So what should the Christians do but fall to quarreling amongst themselves as to how this rightly should be done? Immense, confused debates boiled up, enlisting great theologians and dock workers—along with thousands of "average pastors-bishops" who could not fathom even the key terms in the debates! In the seventeenth and eighteenth centuries, there were those who saw the church's civil establishment as the New Jerusalem coming down from heaven to earth; and then there were others (John Wesley among them) who saw it as the church's "Fall," from whose dire consequences we are not yet extricated. And there are those, nowadays, who speak of post-Constantinian Christianity (they mean post-Theodosian, i.e., post-establishment Christianity) as if they really supposed that a return to the catacombs (or even communes) made any sense whatever; as if there were no radical differences between a Christianity perceived as a real challenge by secular society (as then), and a Christianity (as now) that can be (has been) dismissed by secular society as no big deal at all.

What I've been asking you to do is to imagine the pastoral office in all this turmoil and the transforming pressures upon it. In summary, they produced a shift from the earlier lateral dispersal of gifts and roles throughout the churches (and the unity springing from that *concursus*) to a pyramidal model of ministry, in which unity and authority come from the top down through a system of spiritual hydraulics run by spiritual plumbers. The functional ministry of sacraments, service, and shepherding turns into an official ministry in which the bishop is the pastor, with the other clergy deriving their pastoral authority from him (in their communion with, and obedience to, him). Functional ordination becomes sacerdotal—a "second baptism," as it was called. It created a higher order than the generality of baptized/confirmed Christians. Out of this change, the clergy emerged as a new social class in imperial society, with distinctive garb and insignia of rank—the symbols of *ex officio* authority. Before you sniff at this—or covet it!—try to understand how, in a secular culture, where power and the signs of power were crucial, if the Christian pastor is to have any power of the keys (i.e., spiritual authority), he and she have to have an "awesome" status (literally), in order to be privileged and immune. Chrysostom describes the ideal pastor thus:

> He must be dignified yet modest, awe-inspiring yet kindly, masterful yet accessible, impartial yet courteous, humble yet not servile, vehement yet gentle, in order that he may be able easily to resist all these dangers and to promote the suitable man with great firmness, even though all men gainsay him, and reject the unsuitable with the same firmness, even though all favor him; he must consider one end only, the edification of the Church. . . .
> A priest must be sober and clear-sighted and possess a thousand eyes in every direction.[2]

In the West, where the twin concept of law and peace had created the empire (*lex et pax Romana*), a whole set of juridical images evolved to help define the pastoral office in the new situation—where *lex et pax* depended now more and more on moral influence and less and less on legislative fiat. One sees this in Ambrose's little treatise *On the Duties of Ministers*,[3] where the pastoral virtue most earnestly stressed is "philanthropy," which then still had its root meaning, "active love of *hoi anthropoi*," of humankind. This was the same Ambrose who had brought Emperor Theodosius to abject, public penitence—not once but twice.

One of the best summaries I know, of the good shepherd's image in this dangerous new world can be found in one of Augustine's late sermons (just before the darkness fell, as the Vandals were closing in on Hippo, as Rome had fallen two decades earlier). Augustine for most of us means the theologian; his own self-image was as pastor, and he was so identified and accepted by the whole of Christian "Africa." In sermon 209 he defines "pastoral" in terms I'd be willing to start from today:

> Disturbers of public peace are to be rebuked, the low-spirited are to be encouraged, the infirm are to be supported, objectors confuted, hypocrites guarded against, the uninstructed taught, the lazy aroused, the contentious restrained, the haughty repressed, litigants pacified, the poor relieved, the oppressed liberated, the evil borne with if need be—and all are to be loved.[4]

Rhetoric? To be sure, but rhetoric with disaster looming before him and a twenty-five-year track record of actual practice behind him. We could do with some of that rhetoric today!

Already, the two geographic regions of the church, Eastern (Greek) and Western (Latin), were drifting apart, and since, from now on, we'll be dealing chiefly with the West, I'd like to offer you a scandalously brief comment on what I take to be the essential difference in Orthodoxy's understanding of the pastoral office from the dominant perspectives in the West. In essence, it is pneumatological: In Orthodoxy the good shepherd is, first and last, a charismatic person, a person gifted by the Spirit and generous in the sharing of his gifts and graces. The sacramental life of the *koinonia* was maintained by the priests (who might also be charismatic); the governance of the church was maintained by the hierarchy (who also might be charismatic). But the care of the soul in its spiritual journey (the overriding concern of Eastern Christianity, then and now) is the function of those already on that journey (priests or not). This is why the greatest Orthodox theologian (and saint) that I've ever known, Georges Florovsky, has always been more interested in the Quakers and the Pentecostals than in any of the other Protestant groups. In Russia even now the role of the *startsy* continues. A *starets* is an "elder" (man or woman) whose spiritual wisdom and fidelity and grace-filledness and courage give him or her influence and authority in guiding the spirits and, above all, the consciences of the faithful.

If the fourth century was Christianity's most expansive epoch, then it should also be added that the three centuries from 500 to 800 may have been its most audacious. For as Roman civilization fell apart under the pressures of the Gothonic migrations (and its own senescence), the Christian church undertook to fill the vacuum and to try to civilize and Christianize the nascent European civilization at one and the same time—with the unlikeliest candidates for either job one could well imagine. For those first Europeans were not savages (in any standard anthropological sense); they were simply wild. Their turbulent energies were bridled, insofar as they ever were, by tribal customs, by clan loyalties, by blood ties. The notions of *lex et pax* were simply incomprehensible to men for whom violence was routine and fame and glory (inside the clan or "family") were supreme values. These first "Europeans" were religious enough; it was only that, for them, religion was a service function of tribal and feudal life. Thus, the pastoral office, in their case, had to mean: (1) civilizing; (2) evangelizing; (3) civil administration or, alternatively, defense of the church's rights, wealth, and freedom; (4) technological progress, which meant that pastors, as well as the monks, were leaders in agriculture and handicrafts of all sorts (short of weaponry!).

The overwhelming challenge to any such enterprise was lay patronage and lay control. That old wheeze about the rancher who, when asked if he belonged to a certain church, replied that he had a church that belonged to him, takes us straight back to the feudal concept of the chaplain or the chantry priest or the manorial vicar. And the fact that pastors were usually literate compounded the problem. For the typical feudal noble (with descendants in modern skyscrapers and on many a campus) regarded learning as a commodity to be hired and exploited (what the word "clerk" has come to mean). This was the beginning of that anti-intellectualism that has stifled the Christian mind; it is the mindless counterpart to the clericalism that, from the other side, seduces it.

At any rate, the pastoral office in the early Middle Ages evolved under these pressures, with all sorts of defense mechanisms aimed at exercising or defending the power of the keys within a constituency that was willing to use Christianity but not eager to be transformed by it. The chief pastor becomes "the Lord Bishop," a sacral and secular potentate. The church created its own system of courts and canon law and defended the immunity of the clergy from secular jurisdiction. This, incidentally, is the origin of "penitentiary," a place where an offending cleric can be sent to repent! This was the pragmatic sanction for clerical celibacy, pastors without hostages to the vicissitudes of lay support! This was the issue at stake in the investiture controversies that raged from before Charlemagne's time to the Vatican-Fascist struggles of the 1920s.

With Charlemagne and the Carolingians there was a brief flowering—of civilization and Christianity (with Alcuin and Scotus Erigena). Then the dark came down again, as far as anything close to an equipoise between secular control and the church's struggle for autonomy. The doctrine of the "Two

Swords" (Gelasius) was honored more in the breach than observance, with the church yielding more and more to the irresistible temptation to use its spiritual sword as a tool of deception and superstition. There was the age of the "Donation of Constantine," forged (as it was discovered later) in order to bolster papal and clerical claims to *ex officio* authority. This was the period of the Isidorian Decretals and the legends of saints and the miracles of the various shrines, etc. Protestants have had a field day with these corruptions, with scarcely a murmur against the obvious corruption of their acceptance of the tyranny of lay power *cuius regio, eius religio* (secular divine right monarchy).

But the really effective instruments for pastoral control of these violent but superstitious peoples were the penitential offices, on the one hand, and the sacraments on the other—with both hands working to the same end: viz., to tame the fierce, unbridled passions of their people, to reinforce the Christian ethic, and to open the kingdom of heaven to all believers—along with threats of the terrors of hell. Professor McNeill has told the story of the development of the sacrament of penance and of the Celtic penitential practices and their influence throughout medieval Europe.[5] Its gist is that this tradition helped form a Christian conscience amongst peoples in circumstances where it's hard to imagine how anything else might have done so—at least not by itself. Outbursts, remorse, and punishment were all commonplaces in that society; what the Christian pastor had to do was to interiorize moral restraints against tantrums and outbursts ("berserk" was a Norse word for them that has stayed on in our own vocabulary). He also had to turn remorse (sorry enough to say you're sorry) to contrition and repentance (sorry enough to quit and to give being good a real try).

The pastor had to change the notion of punishment from the status of civil penalty to that of eternal damnation, that is, to change the sense of guilt from a social matrix to a divine one. And the most effective weapon available for this transformation was not preaching nor counseling, not even temporal punishments, but the sacraments and their power to let people into the church (baptism and confirmation), or to ease their way out (extreme unction, which originally had been for spiritual healing), or to ordain (to the ministry *or* to marriage), and most of all to admit to the solemn and dreadful Eucharist, and to excommunicate. Thus, penance and the Eucharist were yoked: Confession was made auricular and private, penance formalized and qualified, and absolution made prerequisite to Communion. It was a logical development and it's hard to see what alternatives there were, given all the circumstances. But it was also a high price to pay for pastoral authority. The image of the pastor-priest as shaman became so firmly fixed in the Western mind that it is still one of the first free associations in every anticlerical mind since Frederick Barbarossa!

CHAPTER
11

Changing Images of the Good Shepherd (2)

We left Frederick Barbarossa fulminating against popes and priests, a prototype to European anticlericals ever since who see in Christian pastors a shaman and a tyrant—pious enforcers in an inequitable society, enemies of freedom and progress, charlatans battening off gullibility. This was Voltaire's target and Tom Paine's; theirs is the prevailing image in the psychiatric literature from Freud to Fromm, to Allen Wheelis as well as in much revisionist history. The drumfire has slacked off lately; our threat to secular control is too weak to warrant further denunciations, except in the sociology and psychology textbooks that define religion as either superstitious or moralistic.

But there was another side to medieval religion, and in it the good pastor plays a crucial role. For European Christendom, all things considered, was an immense achievement and the rôle of Christian shepherds in its career (clerical and lay, male and female) is one of the most impressive I know of, before or since—though I've no defense for all its tragic shortfalls. Between them, the monks, the friars, the pastors, and the schoolmen of the Latin church transformed a brawling motley of hotheaded, violent tribes into the makings of a dynamic civilization that might also have been something like a humane one, for this was its basic intent.

"Christendom" (as they came to call it) had a common language for its thinking, lawmaking, worship, and commerce: Latin was more nearly universal than Greek had ever been. It had a common framework for civil and canon law so that the notions of equity and justice were no longer tribal. It had a common intellectual perspective, now scornfully called scholasticism. But it meant Thomas could be read and argued with—in his own tongue—by more people then than now. And Bishop Grosseteste could travel from Lincoln to Rome and never ask for a translator or an interpreter en route. This civilization had a common religion, with myths and symbols that had common meanings for peasants, emperors, and popes; and something like a common conscience that could be enforced by ordinary pastors with some sense of reinforcement and consensus from the universal church. It built cathedrals and parish churches and abbey chapels that still bear witness to a special sense of sacred space. Its view of life was organized around a series of twin foci: nature *and* grace, secular *and* sacred, law *and* Gospel, earth *and* heaven, time *and* eternity, etc. And for all the tainted monks and nuns, all those greedy friars and venal priests, the medieval pastor, by and large, was more closely involved with the common people (wielding more authority and influence) than we today. Grosseteste justly complained to Innocent III that the low level of clerical morality was a blight in the church—and Innocent agreed. Jacob of Voragine spoke of the pastor, not as shepherd but as a fisherman, and this metaphor (*halientia*, the art of fishing) becomes a technical term for what we call evangelism.

The administration of penance was one of the main concerns in medieval Christianity, and here we must mention the rise of the most misunderstood and easily abused of all its developments: indulgences. Here, of course, all Protestant free associations leap to Luther's Ninety-five Theses. But what we keep forgetting is the good essence of the notion of the communion of saints and of our own participation in the sum total of all the good that saintly souls have ever done. To trade on this superabundance is both crass and superstitious; to ignore or reject it is to forget part of what it means to belong to the extended Christian family—on earth and in heaven. For example, my Ph.D. diploma is sort of an indulgence. It says that I once met certain requirements (and leaves unsaid that I paid tuition), and that I am entitled to all the entitlements of membership in the Academy. But it means that I had shared in the superabundance of learning and culture and academic merit amassed in a great university and that I was welcome to all of it. I remember the debate about indulgences in Vatican II, and it got pretty silly when they began to quantify the business. But then a bishop, who wasn't the sort to buy and sell the gifts of the Spirit, asked me, almost plaintively, I thought: "How do you live without the merits of the saints?" I dutifully explained the Protestant answer (about the sole merits of Christ, etc.)—and then he said, "But these are Christ's merits, too, in other lives like ours. Are they to be despised?" And I realized almost for the first time that the old either/or was inadequate on both sides.

A great resource for the medieval pastor and friar was the immense fund of illustrations for preaching and pastoral conversation that had accumulated in the collections of *exempla* that the people seemed not to tire of hearing. Chaucer's *Pardoner* tells how "lewd folk loven tales olde" ("lewd" here meaning "uneducated," which *is* something of a switch, isn't it?). Everybody knew the Bible stories and the pastor could always draw a moral thence to good effect, a resource long since denied us today when one can sport a B.A. and be mole-ignorant of the biblical heritage! My point in all this is that pastors and people lived in the same world; they had a common universe of discourse and values, a common diagnosis of the human flaw, a common concept of *humanum* and a common hope of glory. The abuses were dreadful, and became intolerable. But what goes unrecognized are the unsung heroes and heroines, the saints and victors.

One of the medieval church's greatest contributions was her serious attempt to help people face death and die well. She knew, as we don't, that part of the art of living is learning how to die—and to "die" in advance of physical death so that we can go on living out our lives in faith, hope, and love, without a crippling fear of death. So the *ars moriendi* grew up in an age when death was a familiar companion to great and small. *Everyman* was an endlessly popular morality play, with much slapstick and gallows humor. But it and the block books (fifteenth-century comic books), plus the constant reiterations of the liturgy taught Christians to face death, in life, with courage and dignity. And if you are at all moved by the Vaughan Williams' setting of "For All the Saints Who From Their Labors Rest," you've still an inner, emotional clue to this whole great tradition. If not, you've got problems.

Where it all went wrong, of course, was that, as Roland Bainton says, the price of Christianizing the pagans was the paganizing of the church. Church and culture were too nearly collapsed into a fatal embrace. A more precise way of putting it was that Europe was never Christianized. Christendom was never more than a partial vision. The church sought secular power for the good of the *saeculum*, but in this process, even when it won, it lost (as at Canossa and in *Unam Sanctam*). The Crusades were a well-meant crime, and their benefits were far more in the secular than the sacral order. The truth is that the secular princes never really acknowledged the church's claims to judge them (of which more later). Thus it was that, when the plagues and famines of the fourteenth and fifteenth centuries revealed that the church could not fend off the little people from the wrath of God, an unconfessed disenchantment with Mother Church and Christendom set in. And what did it take to push that disenchantment to revolt? Five things, convergent: (1) nationalism (which is to say, tribalism renascent); (2) humanism (antiquity reborn); (3) mysticism (the church as auxiliary to individual, or small-group, spirituality); (4) a substitute for ecclesiastical authority (*sola Scriptura*); and (5) a new doctrine of justification. Two, one, and three, taken together, are now called the Renaissance (with the church abiding and abetting it)—even in the cause of nationalism, for the Renaissance papacy was itself a sort of Petrine nationalism. Three, four, and five were, of course, the detonators of the Reformation.

Renaissance men and the Reformers were united in their rejection of papal supremacy and priestcraft, but all their other ruling concerns were divergent; they were, in fact, rivals. The Renaissance was a many-splendored thing, but its central focus was on humanness. The Reformation was even more variegated, but its defining concern was always and everywhere on the sovereignty of God. The Renaissance was catholic and cosmopolitan and could not only coexist with regal and priestly powers (with an inner detachment from their claims); it depended on their patronage for support—in literature and the fine arts. The

Reformation had to depend outright on the secular authorities even to exist, but its kingdom was not, primarily, of this world. The Renaissance took synergism for granted; the Reformation saw in human pride not only the first of the deadly sins (all the medieval moralists had done this), but the one sin that generated all the others. If you want a litmus-paper test of any truly Protestant opinion, ask about its attitude toward pride and human self-sufficiency: This is the psychological essence of the so-called Protestant Principle.

But all extremes create their own ironies so that in Protestantism the fervent stress on theocentrism had its human focus: viz., *salvation,* God's ways with man, *Christus pro nobis, Christus pro me.* In Protestantism, the alternatives to faith (theonomy) are either despair or autonomy, with autonomy the preferred choice by a wide margin. This is why rationalism, science, technology, and elective politics have flourished in the Protestant societies despite all theocratic claims to the contrary. The alternatives to saving faith, in a catholic ambiance, are atheism or syncretisms of various sorts; which is one reason why Italy, Spain, and South America have followed such separate cultural paths into the modern world from those of Northern Europe and North America.

All of these changes in the sixteenth century, not to speak of other concurrent revolutions, affected the pastoral office and the pastor's self-image. The most radical shift was from the pastor as priest and confessor to the pastor as preacher and teacher. In the Roman Catholic Church the power of the keys resided in the sacraments; in Protestantism, it was Scripture, the power "rightly to divide the Word of Truth." *Sola fide = sola Scriptura,* etc. Pure doctrine replaces correct liturgy as top priority. Luther spoke of the church building as a preaching place—literally, *eine Mundhaus.* And the business of preaching was not rhetoric but doctrine, and the burden of doctrine was not speculation but an evangelical judgment against sin and an evangelical consolation for the penitent. The Protestant preacher had a generic diagnosis of the human condition and a sovereign remedy for it. The pastoral task was, first and foremost, to prepare and to enable the people so that they could hear "the Word rightly preached" and faithfully receive "the Sacraments duly administered."

But the shepherding tasks remain, despite doctrinal changes, so that Protestant pastors, of all sorts, took the Scriptures as their shepherd's crook and dutifully ventured into the fields of re-proof, moral guidance, and spiritual consolation. One of the earliest treatises in this field is called *Der Hirt* (Zwingli, 1524).[1] Its theme is repentance, based on scriptural insights about sin and of God's remedy for sin in the atoning death of Christ. But pardoned sinners are still in need of shepherding and pastors must do everything, in love, to upbuild and increase their flocks. They must be faithful and brave, they must be diligent and wise; they must fend off the wolves and the false shepherds (the papists).

Luther and the Lutheran pastors were diligent pastors; Luther's *Table Talk* is a jumble of pastoral conversations, with real dialogue, real passion for souls, with shrewd insights and earthy humor. The Lutheran pastor is directed (in the Large and Small *Catechisms* and in the *Postils*) to smell out pride and self-deceit, to tell the Gospel story in so many different ways that young and old alike—Bauern and burgermeister—might somehow hear it for themselves and see how it applied to them. The Christian life is strenuous; the Devil sees to that! But it has no business being gloomy. "When the Devil tempts you to doubt God's mercy—since you already know you don't deserve it—say, 'Away with you, devil. I will now sing and play in praise of my Lord Jesus Christ' " (Luther). The Lutheran chorale is a group experience; they are not meant to be heard but sung, in chorus! And the Lutheran pastor can either sing well or else at least delight in it with the others. And he will be sensitive and swift with his consolations—to the sad, the sick, the dying and the bereaved. He will recognize all families as the model of the true church and his own first of all; pastoral care, even more than charity, begins at home.

Given this concentration on salvation, the function of the confession of sins and true repentance becomes primary, and all Lutheran liturgies (and those derived from them, like the *Book of Common Prayer*), begin with confession. Thus, absolved, the congregation can get on to the other elements of worship (normally with the Service of the Word as the centerpiece) . But this presupposes pastoral preparation of consciences beforehand, and pastoral follow-up. The Lutheran pastor and his parishioners, ideally, have a common frame of demand and expectation, focused on human beings' chief business of salvation. How can I find a merciful God?

But their schism from the Catholic past, which had never been fully assimilated in the northern fringes of Christendom, made for serious disruptions in the continuity of Christian teaching in the newly liberated territories. Moreover, since church governance was now, in most Lutheran territories, a branch of civil government, supervision was uneven and inadequate. The so-called *Saxon Visitations* are reports of examinations of pastors and congregations by officials of the Saxon court, and they reveal this unevenness quite frankly. The enterprises of Christian nurture and of theological education had fallen into arrears. There is the story of the pastor who, when asked about his study of the *Decalogue,* replied that it was on his list of planned readings but he had not, as yet, been able to obtain a copy of it!

The only exceptions in the sixteenth century to this continuation of the interdependence of church and state were the Anabaptists who (as congregationalists, charismatics, and low church) were the first post-medieval men and women with convictions about religious liberty, the separation of church and state, the church as a voluntary association, etc. But their time was not yet come; they would have to wait first for an interlude of anarchy in seventeenth-century England (and the triumph of "toleration" after that), and then for the American experiment in the radical separation of church and state. Meanwhile, Lutheran pastors constituted a new social and vocational class—men of great authority and influence, based on a mutual agreement with their people, that the power of the keys was rooted in Scripture and its authorized interpretation. If that ever were to go, the pastor's fulcrum would be lost. And now, for many, it has gone.

The other basic shift from Catholic to Protestant models of pastoral care has already been implied—from compulsory celibacy to something like compulsory matrimony (and family). Here, the old choice between ordination or matrimony (as one's basic vocation) was elided, and the married pastor and his family become more dependent on lay support than ever, and the wife and children were closely identified with the father's vocation. The positive side of this, of course, was its transplantation of a sort of Christian asceticism out of the monastery and convent into the world. And the example of the faithful, wise, gentle, firm *Hausvater,* with a loving, supportive wife and relatively well-behaved children, was one of the most effective influences in his pastoral ministry. The overall contribution—social, cultural, religious—of "preachers' kids" in the last four centuries (with horrendous and well-publicized exceptions) is out of all proportion to correlative factors, and its import for one's theory of pastoral care needs to be newly examined. We cannot, I know, revive it, *simplex,* but must its values be lost?

John Calvin and the Calvinist traditions (for they are pluriform) are stereotyped for most of us by their stress on God's sovereignty and a theocratic vision of society. Say "Calvinism" and most people's free association will be "Predestination," "Puritanism," "Genevan theocracy," or "Servetus burning." For Calvin himself, and for Reformed pastors in general, theology was an auxiliary function of shepherding. The aim is the shepherding of souls, guided in their theological and moral insights by biblical truth "to the greater glory of God." Both pastors and laypersons understood the right answer to the first question: "What is the chief end of man?" Answer: "To glorify God and to enjoy him forever." God's glory is, or may be, served by all that happens; and this is why no proper Calvinist is ever as troubled by the notion that a large fraction of mankind is destined to damnation as non-Calvinists think they should be—and this might even include him. "Are you willing to be damned for the glory of God?" was a serious question, seriously posed, to Calvinist ordinands. And its contradictory poses a real dilemma: "No" is a clear sign of self-interest; "Yes" a sign of self-abandonment.

The twin focus of pastoral care in the Reformed tradition was evangelical repentance, on the one hand, and moral conscience on the other. The most typical notions of repentance teeter on the precipice of self-detestation and self-reproach, for the essence of conscience is always self-denial. But the Reformed pastor was able to work, often with fruitful effect, in turning these negatives into positive values and hearty and abundant Christian living. Of all the Christian traditions, Calvinism has been the most vigorous ("dynamic," if that's your word as it is for Hiltner and Pruyser [both Calvinists by heritage, at least]). Non-Calvinists have always been at a loss to understand why anyone as abject before God as a good Calvinist ought to be, is so vertebrate before others. He will plunge into politics, he will overthrow the government, he will lop off kings' heads, and he will die before he'll kneel before the pope—or anybody else. He and his kind will overleap national and cultural boundaries more readily than Lutheranism or Anglicanism (though usually not racial ones), and he makes an industrious, thrifty, and sober workman, merchant, or tycoon. All this after singing in church, "Would he devote that sacred head for such a worm as I?"

But the fact is, of course, that good Calvinists are not abject before God, really, and yet neither proud nor wheedling either. They have a contract in their pockets, the Scripture. They are great ones for covenant making and covenant keeping. And since salvation is from the Godward side of the Covenant of Grace, and since it depends on Christ's merit and not their own, they are freed up from a great many existential anxieties that gnaw away at Lutheran and Catholic consciences. Yet the care of consciences was the main business of the Reformed pastor: How to interpret the covenant and its imperatives, how to be faithful to one's Christian duties, and, above all, how to deal with doubtful or troubled consciences, since every Calvinist knows in his and her bones the ambiguities of moral choice. (Yet they have lost religion if ever they let that serve as an excuse for any lapse from being conscientious.)

Anglican Christianity is different from anything on the continent, and the pastoral office in the Anglican tradition reflects this difference. Simply stated, it is that the Church of England rejected the papacy (that is the one point on which more Englishmen have agreed, for four hundred years, than any other), but did not abandon its catholic heritage in other ways. Anglicans were Protestant; most of them take church-state interdependence for granted; most of them were intolerant and monopolistic. But they were never Catholic enough to impress the Romans and never Protestant enough to convince the European Protestants, nor their own home-grown Calvinists. One must, therefore, always speak of Anglican versus Puritan, of the Church of England versus Dissent; and must always bear in mind the protracted struggle over the Crown (i.e., the seat of civil power and its constitutional form). The Tudors rescued England from the bloodletting Wars of the Roses, only to expose it to the dangers of Spanish-papal domination. This, more than Henry VIII's lust and lechery, accounts for the Act of Royal Supremacy; the confiscation of church wealth and property; the creation thereby of a new nobility beholden directly to the Tudors, of the Edwardian

Prayer Books and Homilies and of Queen Elizabeth I's equal rejection of the papists and the Puritans. It explains why the English would take James Stuart for king and then William of Orange and, finally, George I of Hanover (a weird collection) all because they were alternatives to continuing threats from the pope and Spain and France. It explains the Civil War and Commonwealth, and the fact that, ever since, all true Anglicans (including the Whigs) have been allergic to the bare thought of bloody revolution—why, for example, they resisted both American and French revolutions.

In this tradition, pastor and priest have been seen as two modes of the same office, with preaching a distant third responsibility. The Puritans tried to put preaching first, and their efforts mark the shift of the center of gravity from sacrament to sermon. As the Puritans were forever talking about conscience (in the atmosphere of devotion and prayer), the Anglicans talked about devotion and prayer and their fruitage in moral rectitude. In George Herbert's *Country Parson,*[2] Jeremy Taylor's *Rules,*[3] and Gilbert Burnet's *Discourse of Pastoral Care,*[4] one can see the faithful and diligent Anglican parson busy with his flock—instructing, guiding, consoling, and, above all, gathering them into "the communion of saints."

The Puritans were deeply troubled about the compromises in the Church of England: vestments, prelacy, auricular confession, priestcraft, and regal power. The Thirty-Nine Articles had been their chief concession, but you can look at any *Book of Common Prayer* and see that the Articles are not its internal canon. Thus, the Puritan cause progressed from scruple to controversy—and to a near win when, in 1595 William Whitaker's nine "Articles" on double predestination, election, imputation, and perseverance were approved at Lambeth Palace by Canterbury and York, only to be ditched by Queen Elizabeth I, Peter Baro, and Bishop Bancroft.

For the Puritan pastor, the great business was sound and fruitful learning—chiefly in Scripture, but also about Scripture's bearing on earthly affairs, not least of all politics. Scripture is the font of revelation and wisdom; it is the prime reference for preaching and for the determination of cases of conscience. Indeed, preaching and moral counsel are not to be divided. The best preaching is "painful" preaching (as Thomas Fuller called it;

"plain and home" is Wesley's phrase), which means that you start with a human situation, find the right Scripture for it, crumble your text, and then apply it for all it's worth. The normal place for this is, of course, the pulpit, but it is equally appropriate for counseling and for pastoral conversations of all sorts. And since the basic biblical images and stories were part of the common culture, the Puritan preacher could afford to be indirect, allusive, and (in that limited sense) "nondirective." For example, John Wilson has an interesting book about the fast-day and thanksgiving-day sermons preached in the Puritan parliaments; and there were literally hundreds of them, none short. Though they were all biblical, and all very much aware of the violent issues in controversy on any given date, there were very few explicit political proposals offered to the perplexed legislators. The aim was to call the lawmakers to their account before God and to admonish them to consider the grounds on which their accountability might be expressed.

"Painful preaching" was also diagnostic. It varies from the "disjointing of a broken soul" (hence consolatory) to "the clarifying of doubtful consciences" (hence critical and monitory). These phrases are Thomas Fuller's, describing William Perkins as "an excellent surgeon" and spiritual physician. Thus, pastoral care was a follow-up to preaching and a preparation for a more profitable hearing of the Word. The popularity of case-manuals—by Perkins, Ames, Hall, Taylor, Sanderson, Baxter—bears witness to their relevance. We can take Baxter as spokesman for this whole tradition, for he is curiously representative of the best on both sides. He was a chaplain in Cromwell's army (and anathema to the Cavaliers). Yet he was denounced as Arminian by John Bunyan—and warmly approved by Wesley! In *Gildas Salvianus, or, The Reformed Pastor,* he describes the pastor as shepherd. "As a lawyer is a counselor for men's estates, and the physician for their bodies, so the pastor is counselor *for* their souls—and must thus be ready with advice to those that come to him with their cases of conscience."[5] Baxter, incidentally, anticipated Wesley's class meetings by almost a century, by inviting interested parishioners to his home in Kidderminster on Thursday evenings for "spiritual conversation."

CHAPTER

12

Changing Images of the Good Shepherd (3)

In our last look backward, before we come to our own times and their problems, I propose a brief view of some of the ways in which the pastoral office evolved in the Roman Catholic Church from Trent to Vatican I. Then I will turn to a longer survey of the American experience. This omits the rise of pietism in Europe and the Evangelical Revival in Britain, and the rise of Enlightenment Protestantism in Europe—except in their decisive impingements on American Christianity. This is the only way I could see how to make sure that we get the American scene in our sights, especially since it heavily dominates all our present options and prospects.

Rome reacted to the Protestant Revolt slowly and uncomprehendingly. Nobody there, including the really great ones like Cajetan and Contarini, could quite imagine that the church that had survived the Great Western schism, the conciliar movement, and the Renaissance papacy could be balked for long by the scattered and disunited dissidents of Germans, Switzers, English nationalists, Dutch traders, and Scottish fanatics. In an ironic way, of course, it wasn't Rome's corruption nor Protestant heroism that saved the Reformation. It was the *Turks,* who were banging on the gates of Vienna, no less, and so distracted

Charles V that by the time he was ready to tackle the German and Swiss schismatics, the cost of their suppression would have been prohibitive. Later, there would be holy wars, first in France where the slaughter of the Huguenots strangled all other hopes of reconciliation, which then made the Thirty Years War so desperate and destructive, which in turn hardened Cromwell's anti-Catholic line in England and Ireland.

But Rome was adamant. Second guessing history is often silly, but it is worth wondering how much of a concession would have weakened Luther's support, what might have happened if serious internal reforms—like those set in motion by Ximénez in Spain and Contarini's group—had not been squelched. At any rate, Rome underestimated the force of the alienation that had been unleashed, and so moved to set her own house in order too little and too late (to put two clichés back to back!) The focus of this effort was the Council of Trent, and we are still in urgent need of a really careful, thorough ecumenical study of Trent; for more was accomplished there than the Protestants were ever willing to recognize, and with enough errors so that Trent is the acid test of how history, once canonized, can ever thereafter be transcended.

Rome's twin concerns at Trent were (1) to dispose of the heretics and (2) to revitalize her own pastoral ministry. We'll skip the first and move to one of the council's most positive consequences: reaffirming the primacy of the priestly role of the Christian shepherd, giving the priest-pastor a far more arduous task in pastoral care than anything since Gregory's *Pastoral Rules.*[1] Reforms in the dispensations of indulgences were instituted and widely enforced; an immense reform in theological education was launched, which is only just now being dismantled. If the prime target of Protestant pastoral care was the Christian conscience, the Tridentine reform was aimed at the reform of the confessional and the sacrament of penance. This, after all, was what the Ninety-five Theses were all about. Leadership in this level of reform was given by St. Charles Borromeo, St. Philip Neri, and Blessed Robert Bellarmine.

But the problems of casuistry remained, and here a literally tremendous controversy blew up within the Roman Catholic Church. Protestants could have learned more than they did from the controversy, if they had not dismissed both sides as papists, since it was the Catholic analog to the quarrels between the Calvinists and the Arminians. This was the debate about divine sovereignty and human freedom, about nature and grace, and about the ethical grounds of judging "probable" sin. It finally focused on the agonizing question of synergism between Baius, Bañes, the Dominicans, and the Jansenists (along with Pascal and Port-Royal) on the rigorist side, and Bellarmine, Lessius, Molina and the Jesuits on the other. It was a real cliff-hanger, too, full of blood and thunder, and the rigorists came within a hair of winning. The final (?) result was a papal suspension of the question, with both sides forbidden to tax the other with heresy or heterodoxy.

The heart of it was pastoral: How severely are sinners to be dealt with? How wide is the gate of Christian hope? The rigorists believed, with the honor of God at stake, that grace is dearly bought: This is the *theologia crucis*. From which it follows that Christian discipline must be strict and scrupulous. Out of this doctrine of grace flows a whole theory of ethics and moral guidance that informs all the pastor's dealings with his parishioners and the nature of his spiritual and moral authority in these dealings. The Jesuits believed, with human freedom as their prize, that grace is sufficient as offered by God in Christ and efficacious when accepted in faith's freedom. The details of their probabilist theory, and their distinctions between prevenient and exciting and sufficient and efficacious grace we can leave, though the problems they point to are up for grabs all over again today. What matters is that the synergists had a theology, a Christology and an ethics that informed their pastoral diagnoses and care; and it is this constant correlation between one's theology and one's understanding of pastoral care that I'm trying to illustrate in all the different ways I can think of. On this score, Pascal turns out to have been more clever than just in his lampoonings of the Jesuits, in his *Provincial Letters*. I remember in Rome, at Vatican II, running into attitudes or judgments that I would have called "Puritan" (I was hesitant about that phrase for Romans). Then I heard them label such things as "Jansenist," and suddenly realized how deep and abiding this rigorist-synergist rift in the Christian mind runs, even yet.

After Bellarmine, Busenbaum, and Escobar came the greatest (or at least the most influential) of all modern Roman Catholic pastors and casuists, San Alfonso de' Liguori. Liguori, roughly a contemporary of John Wesley's though neither knew of the other, took the Jesuit heritage (though not himself a Jesuit; indeed, the founder of the *Redemptorists*) and stiffened it in the interest of more effective and rigorous pastoral discipline. Whereas Jesuit "probabilism" had tended to take the less rigorous of any two moral alternatives (as binding, that is), Liguori shifted the burden of proof over onto the conscience of the believer: Only when there is a reasonable doubt as to moral obligation or sin can the conscience be absolved ("equiprobabilism"). Liguori made heavy demands upon pastors and confessors that ought still to be heeded: Ignorant, incompetent, casual handling of penitents is itself sinful and unconscionable. The good shepherd is responsible for knowing his job, with all the wisdom he can muster from Christian moral theology and with all the grace he can claim as he himself grows in grace. Liguori is perhaps the most widely representative of all "modern" Roman Catholic pastoral theologians up until our own time.

We can mention only in passing the tradition of mystical piety in St. Francis de Sâles and his varied experiences with godly but also neurotic ladies like Madame Guyon and Madame de Chantal. His older contemporary, Pierre de Berulle, is remembered less for his own piety (rich, warm, and sophisticated) than for a crop of effective disciples, the greatest of whom was St. Vincent de Paul, who combined mysticism and philanthropy (social action) in a most impressive fashion. Note that all of these great pastors were founders of religious societies within the church catholic—the Redemptorists, Salesians, Vincentians— and so perpetuated pastoral and missionary styles that still persist today. There's a lesson in this for Protestants who, when they have something special going, tend to split up into sects, schools, or denominations. Yet one of the crucial tasks in all fruitful pastoral care is to help the person or group into a larger incorporation in the *koinonia* of Christ.

In America, from the beginning (always excepting the Roman Catholics and the Lutherans, partially), the pastoral office was affected by the ecclesial theory of voluntary lay support and the practical circumstances of religious pluralism in the new country. Even in colonial New England and Virginia, where there were establishments of sorts, the role of lay elders and trustees (or vestries) was greater than it had ever been in England; and after the Revolution the twin principles of separation of church and state and religious voluntarism altered the pastor-pastored relationship out of all recognition. This was reinforced by the pervasive influence, in American Christianity generally, of low church, non-liturgical, individualist, and small-group traditions that, in Europe, had been called "Anabaptist." In Europe the Anabaptists had been successfully put down or driven to the margin. In America many of their cherished emphases finally triumphed, affecting all American Christianity. This was associated with the radical informality and constant adaptations on the frontier, as the new country moved westward from its seaboard linkage to Europe. In the new country, the ninety-nine to one ratio between "folded sheep" and "lost sheep" was drastically altered and has remained so (with fluctuations) ever since.

By the same token, and for the same reasons, pietism came to be a powerful force in the American experience—in Methodism and the frontier sects (yet it left its mark on all the churches). And here the charismatic character and role of the pastor-evangelist (and all other spiritually minded, morally wise men and women) came to be crucial, and almost always outside a sacramental framework (or, at any rate, any doctrine of the sacraments that gave the priest the power of the keys). The pastor's role as counselor in an itinerant ministry in a mobile society became, typically, *ad hoc* and episodic. The pastor as prophet wielded significant influence in a disorderly society, but largely in terms of restraint of the popular vices of drunkenness, lechery, violence, and greed. Temperance and abolition became the two most massive causes to which Christian pastors lent their voices and influence. But it was the pastor as inspired and inspiring leader—revivalist, small-group leader, etc.—that contributed most (especially in the days of the *Second Great Awakening*). On this score, of course, the ordained pastor (or the learnèd parson) had scarcely any advantage over spiritually gifted men and women who had never been inside a seminary. Mrs. Phoebe Palmer had more influence on the spread of the idea of "holiness" in the Methodist churches than any professional theologian of any sort.

The key to interpreting American Christianity is the fact that it became even more narrowly focused on "salvation" than any other major development in Christian history, for soteriology was the centerpiece of pietism and pietism was the main moving force in American Christianity. "Are you saved?" was an intelligible question to all and sundry, and all three possible answers ("Yes," "No," and "Maybe") had a high level of specificity for all the concerned parties. With this went a corresponding de-emphasis on speculative theology and an overwhelming stress on "experimental," "practical," personal religion. These factors, in turn, bred the anti-intellectualism, biblicism, pragmatism, and individualism that is so familiar in the American tradition.

Thus it was that in America the theology of pastoral care came to be organized around "conversion," "regeneration," "Christian experience"—i.e., soteriology—with characteristic presuppositions about diagnosis (original sin and total depravity), about therapy (imputation of Christ's righteousness, linked to a Christology that took substitutionary atonement for granted as "orthodox"), and about prognosis (heavenly bliss for all injustices here below). In this context, the pastor was evangelist and witness, above all else, and proclamation was not absolution but the promise and hope of salvation. Soteriology and eschatology became the two poles of the Christian life, to an unprecedented degree.

But the Civil War and its sequel—the Gothic Age of American expansion, industrialization, and the consolidation of the middle class as flywheel and gyroscope in American society—altered American Christianity more drastically than has often been realized. Our history books dwell lovingly on all the details of colonial America, of frontier America, and the Civil War. But the America that is our own living memory emerged after the Civil War, and most of us know less about that epoch (from Grant to Taft) than any single segment of our three and one-half centuries. This was the America that spread and grew rich off the newly subjugated South, the newly emancipated blacks, the newly opened Western lands and the new, unassimilated ethnics; the America of the tycoon, the WASP, the newly confident middle class and the churches that had made suitable accommodations to the new situation. The phrase for this is "Culture Protestantism," coined, I think, by Troeltsch to apply to a very roughly analogous phenomenon in nineteenth-century Germany but much more applicable to American Protestantism. My point is that it was this Christianity that has given most of us our operating images of "institutional Christianity." This is what most of us have in mind when we speak of the faults and failures of "the church"; this is the paradigm to which we are attached or from which we are alienated, and this is the frame within which the conventional definition of pastoral care was so firmly fixed that it still controls our more recent deviations from it. I mention this because it is, relatively speaking, so small and so recent a slice of Christian history that we ought not to let it dominate our perspectives as it has—and still does for many.

It is also the context for the rise of the Social Gospel (America's unique version of it) in response to urbanization, industrialization, and the human casualties of "the system." Pietism, in all its forms, has held to the premise that changed lives can change society; regalism to the premise that the ruler's wisdom (i.e., civil power) can change society; sacerdotalism to the premise that a Christianized community will be ideally humane; classical Protestantism to the satanocratic premise that secular societies can't be changed by much (the Christian's citizenship is in heaven). The Social Gospel proposed a real switch: A changed (i.e., reformed) society will change its members from inhumane to humane, from selfish to sharing, from oppressive to liberating; and until society is changed in these respects, it will damn its members faster than evangelism can snatch them from the pit.

Our concern here is with what all this did to rôles, tasks, and images of the good shepherd. And the short answer is that it split up its components and made rival types of them. Here, more than before, we see the "prophetic," "priestly," and "pastoral" rôles of the Christian minister being differentiated and specialized. The prophetic rôle got divided into "preaching" and "social reform." And this was the age of the gr-r-eat preachers (Phillips Brooks, Ernest Fremont Tittle, Harry Emerson Fosdick) and of the great social radicals (Rauschenbusch, and Harry Ward and the young Reinhold Niebuhr). In this process, the priestly office came under increasing denigration—conformist if not reactionary. The pastoral office suffered, too; visiting the sick (i.e., the physically ill), burying the dead, comforting the mournful, offering moral guidance was less and less valued, compared to the excitements of the pulpit or the picket line.

As the rise and spread of general education began to narrow the gap between the culture in the pulpit and the pew and as other social forces began to dim the luster of the older image of "the parson," a very interesting series of new movements began to evolve in Liberal Protestantism as basic alternatives to the conventional patterns of church life that had come to seem too conventional and outmoded. The first of these was "religious education," the first proposal for a major transformation of the church into a school. It came with all necessary provisions for nurture, worship, pastoral care, and social reform, all informed by a new Dewey-ite theory of learning and character formation. It never succeeded in displacing the church. But from 1900 to 1940, or thereabouts, Christian education was the pastoral theology frontier in most mainline Protestant churches, and its influence may be seen in the powerful bureaucracies it developed in most of the denominations.

Less of a displacement than an extension was the "foreign missionary movement." It, too, had a theology and a program that challenged the local congregation's concern with itself. And, at the time, its colonialist and imperialistic aspects were invisible to WASP eyes. Now it is in profound disarray yet remains as the most massive bureaucratic empire in the United Methodist Church and in many other Protestant churches.

The Christian pastor today is more nearly cast adrift and on his own than any generation for centuries—with no credible paradigms to go by, with insights from the past to help but no models to resuscitate and reinstate. He and she are confronted with radical questions about professional identity and distinctive tasks. But Christian pastors have a heritage, more than most of us have ever really reckoned up or sought to claim for ourselves. Pastors today are free (actually forced) to seek new ways of doing their pastoral things, including the theology that will sustain both these things and those who do them. It is to this cause that this course is dedicated.

CHAPTER
13

The Rise of Modern Psychotherapy and Alliances with Pastoral Care

We are all familiar enough with the fact that, for a full generation now, pastoral care and pastoral counseling has constituted a movement of its own. It is related casually to the churches but differentiated more and more clearly from the inclusive vision of the pastoral office as we have seen that vision, in its variations and mutations, over the centuries. As a movement, it has always been concerned with the psychotherapeutic orientation of the clergy. Its concern is twofold: On the one side, to help ministers to enough emotional health and self-understanding for themselves so that they become less menacing to other emotionally unstable people than they might otherwise be; it is a fact that the clergy as a class have more than their share of neurotic demons and worse temptations to Yahweh or martyr complexes than the population on the whole. The other face of the same concern is a practical program of clinical training ("clinical" here used in a very loose and mildly pretentious connotation) so that parish pastors would have a modicum of applicable skills in recognizing and responding to symptoms of emotional distresses and a modicum of therapeutic resources—for first-aid and supportive therapies, for intelligent referrals, and for competent paramedical cooperation with doctors and the healing team. Now, with all the various new developments in group therapies in "the encounter culture," the movement is multiplying its outreach to a larger fraction of the population (church and community), with results that we shall have to examine and assess still further as we go along.

I would be the last person in the world to depreciate any part of this development or to sing small any of its literally epoch-making contributions to the life and work of the church or to the new levels of comprehending and responding to the human malaise that we have come to in our time. The societies in our Western past were, for the most part, repressive; their taboos and moral demand systems were keyed more closely to social order than to human freedom. The astounding victories of freedom's course in our time are due, in no small part, to the multifaceted influences of modern psychotherapy; and the rôle of the clinically trained parish pastor in all this (along with the pastoral care specialists) is truly impressive.

My own first glimpses of this new frontier run back into the mists of prehistory (i.e., before there was a movement and not many pioneers). It was in my seminary days when B.D. theses were required. My own academic major was theology (historical theology at that), but my vocational interests were pastoral (they still are, in a curious, frustrated way); and so I asked myself what I could do for a thesis that would focus on the pastoral office and also garner the smatterings of my widely scattered interest. So I proposed to the faculty committee a topic with a 180° angle: "The Use of Psychotherapy in Pastoral Work." What was even more preposterous was that they solemnly accepted the project, partly because it had not been preempted (to their knowledge or mine) in 1932, partly because they didn't know enough about it to know just how preposterous it was, and also partly because we were very fond of each other and they believed that it might be a useful lesson in the delicate balance between curiosity and foolhardiness!

I mention this as evidence for my own partial identification with the pastoral care movement, before there was one, and as the beginning of my marginal involvement in it ever since. My

Yale Ph.D. was in patristics, but, on the side, I also managed a sizable chunk of the residence requirements for a graduate degree in psychology (in the Institute of Human Relations). Later, when I'd returned to Yale on the faculty, I absorbed a series of seminars at the William Allenson White Institute of Psychiatry in New York. Twice I came within a hair of going whole-hog into medicine (or, alternatively, a Ph.D. in clinical psychology)— on a premise that I would still defend: viz., that scientific psychiatry is the paradigm for any fully respectable specialization. My decision, in each case, therefore, was a vote for the generalist conception of the pastoral office and, for myself at least, a judgment that pastoral care as a paramedical specialization would always be something of a professional anomaly. How I got to be neither a doctor nor a pastor nor any other one "thing" is another story that we can ignore for our purposes here.

For one of those purposes is to examine how and why (especially why) the pastoral care movement came to be so narrowly focused on, and joined with, modern psychotherapy and its developments; so specialized that the phrase "pastoral care" has, for many, the specific meaning of care for a special fraction of a congregation or community; and, thus, how the larger scope of the pastoral office in the whole church (and in society at large) has been dissociated from it. Another of my purposes is to lay out the background for a less obvious (or more debatable) conviction, viz., that the pastoral care movement has been operating now for a full generation on the ideological capital of Freudian and post-Freudian psychology, on the one hand, and of liberal Protestant moralism, on the other. If it is true (as I believe it is) that the presuppositions of these wedded traditions are losing their ideological dominance, and if (as I also believe) the pastoral care movement, as a movement, is running out of steam, in terms of its need for new conceptual breakouts from the naturalistic and humanistic traditions in which it has grown up, then it would seem to me to follow that we are on the vague uncharted boundaries of a new frontier for pastoral care and, maybe, the pastoral ministry as a whole—just as we were in 1928 when what is now so commonplace seemed so visionary.

This is why I keep harping on the theoretical and theological aspects of what seems so obviously to so many as preeminently practical and clinical and pragmatic. For I am convinced that the notable successes of the pastoral care movement stem from its not fully comprehended involvement in the great central concern of modernity (viz., psychology) and that its failures (insofar as it deserves any such judgment) stem from an inadequate theological response to the problems and challenges posed by modern man's psychological preoccupations. This thesis may be readily understood and then assessed, if we will recall the fact that the Christian gospel is, and always has been, a message about God in Christ reconciling the world to himself but with no single or specific philosophy, political theory, natural science, sociology, or psychology all its own. No age of the church has been able to make good its single claim to any one such philosophy as having a monopoly. Bultmann was not the first genius to discover that Scripture contains all the problems and primal insights of Christian wisdom, but does not have its own philosophy, science, or psychology. Nor was he the first to claim that he knew which specific "philosophical pre-understanding" was most aptly fitted to the really valid understanding of biblical truth. There were good reasons for him to choose Heidegger and existentialism but not to claim that now, finally, we had reached any sort of terminus.

The business of exploring all available secular wisdoms as interpretive matrices for Christian truth and self-understanding is an old story, a perennial quest. It began with Christians having to choose between the available options for a metaphysics that helped make the most sense out of the intellectual problems generated by the Christian mystery: materialism, Epicureanism, Stoicism, Aristotelianism, Platonism, and their permutations. The central issue in the choice was a vision of metaphysical reality that either confirmed, or at least did not infirm, what Christians believe about their lives from God, in Christ, through the Holy Spirit. *Fides quaerens intellectum.* Their choice of Platonism (in general) was the most crucial event in the development of Christianity for at least ten centuries, and has left its vital residues in every one of our theological traditions. Its first premise was (is) that the human analogue of, and access to, divine reality is the idea. Hegel made this point in modern times by arguing for an identity between the rational and the real. The point that concerns us about this first great alliance between the Christian message and a great secular wisdom is that it generated a whole succession of theologians—great and small—who responded to the challenge to think through the problems of Christian teaching within the great general ideas of Platonic idealism, without reducing the Christian message to a subspecies of Platonic philosophy, ethics, and lifestyle.

This is one main hermeneutical key in the interpretation of every Christian theologian from Irenaeus to Clement, Origen, Athanasius, Augustine, Erigena—to Hegel and Hartshorne (with necessary qualifications, of course). The response to Platonism also spawned a rich crop of heretics and heresies—Gnosticism as a generic name for the impulse to seek salvation in a secret wisdom for a special few and to leave the generality of humankind to its sodden fate of inauthenticity! The response did something more, however: it saddled Christianity with its own cognate dualistic psychology—body-soul, matter-thought dualisms—with their implicit denigration of body and matter and their further implication of mechanism as the truth about body and freedom as a function of spirit. This is the taproot of the special kinds of deterministic and necessitarian theories in Western civilization, from Augustine to B. F. Skinner (strange bedfellows as they may seem).

A thousand years into the development of Christianity another major transformation in the intellectual climate in which it lived took place, and another basic choice had to be made as to what sort of philosophical pre-understanding suited the Gospel best, *now*. (This, of course, is what we mean by "modernity," isn't it?) If the simplest word for the Platonic outlook is vision, then the word for the Aristotelian perspective might be observation. In both, the crucial question is the meaning and correlation of perception and conception, i.e., both of them are distinctive epistemologies yielding distinctive metaphysics, ethics, and politics.

Again, let us not stay to debate the merits of Platonism versus Aristotelianism, and Christianity. I note only that the twelfth- and thirteenth-century recovery of Aristotle as a font of secular wisdom generated another succession of *theological* responses that run from Albertus Magnus and Thomas Aquinas to Bernard Lonergan, et al. This was a tremendous achievement—but with its price of false disjunctions between naturalism-supernaturalism, reason-revelation, and a deep, pervasive secularism in those who opted for the *mundane* level of all these vertical orientations of existence. The best Christian Aristotelians really do understand how grace fills out and completes the deficiencies of nature; the average is liable to settle for any sort of culture Christianity that seems handy (with suitable supernaturalistic adornments and escape hatches). What matters is that Christian thought in the thirteenth century was able to react positively and constructively to a new view of the world and of human beings' place in it, without surrendering its essential mystery, credibility, or the pastoral power of the keys.

Then came the Renaissance and the rise of modern science, and with it all a radically new view of the world and the inherent coherence of nature and the natural order. Nature was recognized as a domain of laws, laws that describe regularities that are quantifiable and verifiable; and man's prospective mastery of nature was predicated on his capacity for natural knowledge and his capacity to apply it in his own self-interest. The chief casualty of this new worldview was miracle, and with it any easy and glib doctrine of providence. Thus, Christianity faced a new challenge of immense import, and the ways began to part between theology and philosophy. First came the rise of astronomy and physics and the ruling general idea of mechanism and mass in motion. "The laws of motion are the laws of all things," said Galilei; and the laws of motion are quantifiable, subject to experimental verification, and they do not require God as more than creator: artist, architect, and divine mechanic.

It took Western Christianity two centuries to accommodate its by now integrally "classical theism" to this new naturalism, mechanism, and scientism. Of course, the process is still going on. Indeed, this is what "neoclassical theism"—in the endeavors of Hartshorne, Ogden, Cobb, et al.—is still all about, at bottom: Christianity in a naturalistic perspective. Here again, my point is that Christian worldviews (and life views) change with the changing premises of secular wisdom; and theology that fails to respond, positively and constructively (without surrendering its essential claims, its vital message), is doomed to obsolescence, and with that, its power to inform and sustain the pastoral office, i.e., to produce a "modern," credible, relevant pastoral theology. Deism was one such theology, in the seventeenth and eighteenth centuries; fundamentalism is its opposite number in the nineteenth and twentieth centuries.

The physical sciences came first—from Bacon to Brahe, Copernicus, Galilei—with their great basic charter in Newton's *Principia Mathematica.* Luther and Calvin denounced the development, and Descartes and Spinoza provided philosophic alternatives to scholasticism that intended to conserve a religious view of life in this new world. Most theologians, too, tried their hands at surveying "the wisdom of God in creation" and the consonance of revealed religion with natural. This is, indeed, almost the title of Butler's famous *Analogy of Religion, Natural and Revealed.* Practical, pastorally minded men (like Hervey and Wesley) provided a theology of pastoral care for people with a naturalistic world order (if they would allow for a supernaturalistic context for that order).

The progress of the biological sciences was slow, but their challenge to the Christian worldview was even more unsettling, finally, because of the startling implications of "modern" biology for human beings as natural creatures, an item in "the domain of animate nature." Here again, the Christian mind had to identify the challenge and to recognize that what really threatened was not the essential biblical revelation of humanity as God's creature and bearer of the *imago Dei,* but of the Aristotelian and Cartesian biologies that Christian theologians had borrowed and had come to think of as integral to their system. Yet the battle between Darwin and Moses goes on. We have learned enough about evolution to know that it has no credible account of the origins of human life, personality, and self-transcendence, yet it contains enough to have come to take for granted humankind's integrated place in nature. This affects our self-understanding and the way we interpret life and human values to each other.

The chief by-product of the increasing triumph of science and the scientific worldview was called "Enlightenment," the awareness that humans can and must think for themselves, plan for their own affairs, take history into their own hands. The Christianity that accepted this Enlightenment premise was called "liberal," "modern," "progressive." Its great architects (Schleiermacher, Ritschl, Bushnell, et al.) accepted Kant's thesis that speculative theology is a futile exercise and that Christian truth must now be grounded in "experience," in "moral concern," in "human values," all under and within the scope of God's primal and final sovereignty, all focused on the incomparable "Event" of Jesus Christ but all validated in the personal and social consequences of human life and death. Liberal Christianity, at its best, *was* evangelical, Christocentric, and deeply spiritual. But it was grounded on assumptions derived from the intellectual, moral, and human perspectives of nineteenth- and twentieth-century science. And the crux of its power of the keys (i.e., that science and reason do not reach to the inner courts of human decision, human fulfillment, and hence our need of God in Christ through the Spirit) depended on science's tacit admission that its boundaries ran up to but not beyond the mysteries of human freedom and of human self-transcendence. Interestingly enough, men and women in the exact or rigorous sciences even now have a tendency to make some such an admission ungrudgingly; they know that the reach of rigorous hypothecation and verification stops at the borders of the finite.

So far, then, so good—sort of. Christian theology, by the hardiest, has managed to respond to the successive crises of having to choose its philosophical and scientific pre-understandings, always by holding fast to its basic insistence on human beings' radical dependence on God's sovereign providence and redemptive grace. Always the task of the thoughtful Christian, concerned to support the Christian pastor with a credible account of the ways of God to humanity, has been to find the right way to understand and interpret the essence of the biblical Gospel: "It is he who has made us and not we ourselves"; "without me you can do nothing"; "thou hast made us for thyself and our hearts are restless until they find their rest in thee." Given this confession, the rudiments of Christian faith, hope, and love are still in place.

But with the emergence of the social sciences out of their biological and physical ancestors, yet another—and now essentially different—challenge to the Christian life view began to be even more and more evident and aggressive. Put as simply as possible, it is the challenge of human autonomy—of the irrelevance to the human scene and to the human potential of any divine reality on which human existence depends, or any genuine personal and moral interactions between the human self and its divine Creator, Savior, and Consummator. The conscious foe of Enlightenment humanism was *heteronomy*—the human will controlled arbitrarily by another's will, human or divine, without its own moral and rational assent. Its avowed goal was *autonomy:* each making his and her own *nomos* and binding themselves intentionally to their own inherent values. The premise of this program was a basic conviction about human perfectibility: the human entelechy within the individual and any truly free society. Given freedom, equality, justice, and education, the *humanum* will grow up toward its own self-realization, by a psychic and moral tropism; where it fails or deviates, the causes are mundane and accidental. And there is no help beyond.

This is Bonhoeffer's *mundige Welt;* this is Freud's gospel of ego overcoming the id and the superego. This is the premise of Rogers' *On Becoming a Person*[1] and the assumption of transactional analysis. This is the contemporary *Fragestellung* or problematic of all serious Christian theology—and of much that is neither serious nor really competent. This is why I regard our epoch as the time when Christian theology, ethics, and spirituality have either to deal with psychotherapy in a positive and constructive way (without surrendering the mystery of salvation from God in Christ through the Spirit) or else fail, for the first time, in its power to transvaluate its message and lifestyle in reaction to a major transmutation of the secular wisdoms of the modern world. Second- and third-century Christianity created a Christian Platonism; in the thirteenth century, it developed a Christian Aristotelianism; in the seventeenth century a Christian naturalism; in the nineteenth century (and the first half of the twentieth century) a Christian liberalism. And now, the challenge is comparable—albeit far more difficult and confused—to create a pastoral theology that takes the secular wisdoms of depth psychology, group psychology, and sociology with utter seriousness, without surrendering the Gospel or accepting autonomy as its true meaning. Feuerbach's proposal has at last come to be widely accepted—theology can and ought to be reduced to anthropology. The "Death of God" episode was shockingly bad theology but an uncommonly candid revelation of how far human autonomy had come to be the ground tone in our society and in the churches.

What matters most to us in this course—or at least in my argument here—is that the pastoral care movement recognized the reality and pertinence of this challenge of secular psychological wisdom from the very beginning. And the movement rather quickly formed a practical working alliance with the psychotherapeutic movement, even at the cost of a specialization that disengaged it from the total enterprise of the pastoral ministry. It is important to see how and why this happened. Three reasons, at least, help to explain it. First, psychotherapy (in its varieties) offered a powerful and valid antidote to *heteronomous religion;* there's no denying that there was a horrendous pileup of heteronomous religion in the churches (the bitter fruit of culture-Protestantism or of obscurantism) with its dreadful entail of neurosis, hysterics, and hypocrisy. Pastors could see for themselves what the psychiatrists had been saying since Freud: that heteronomous religion was unhealthful; that people who lived in dreadful guilt and fear of God's wrath were bad news to themselves and others; that a heteronomous religion was unfree and subhuman. This is the "religion" that human beings needed to be cured of, what Bonhoeffer had in mind with his old pietistic phrase "religionless Christianity."

Second, psychotherapy offered pastors a new and fruitful access to self-understanding of their own hang-ups, neuroses, and tendencies to use other people rather than serve them in their own best interests. The fraction of neurotic reactions in seminarians and the clergy has always been higher than their proportion in the population at large, and the clinical training of clergy in the various programs has been of immense value in aid of an emotionally healthier clergy (comparatively speaking, of course). And now, with the new psychotherapies, one can see batches of liberated clergy turned out in fortnightly revivals. Like all pietists, those who have had the special experiences of psychotherapy not only tend to herd, but also to view the unliberated with that special sort of sympathy that alienates more often than it reconciles; this, too, has tended to reinforce the specializing, monasticizing tendency of the pastoral care movement. Third, psychotherapy has provided clinically trained pastors with a whole panoply of tools and procedures for dealing with disturbed and distressed people that their predecessors did not have. Sometimes, some of these were intuited, but without a decent theoretical framework—etiological, diagnostic, and therapeutic.

I have already listed the basic benefits of this alliance between psychotherapy and pastoral care (in *Psychotherapy and the Christian Message*): (1) respect for persons; (2) the rejection of the older mind-body dualisms that have befuddled Christian anthropology since St. Paul's time; (3) the inner meaningfulness of apparently absurd and rational behavior and rhetoric; (4) the fine art of listening; (5) the human organism's capacity for growth; (6) the dangers of traditional moralism and the futility of judgmental attitudes; (7) the unhealthful qualities in much of what passes for religious experience and behavior; (8) the conception of endo-psychic conflict; (9) the sovereign virtue of outgoing love, compassion, and practical helpfulness as therapy and redemption. David Roberts before me, and James Lapsley currently, have tried to show how fruitful a working alliance between psychotherapeutic wisdom and skill would be, together with fresh opportunities for their help, in the psychopathology of ordinary, everyday living. This, of course, was Tillich's concern and that of Reinhold Niebuhr. None of us thought of himself as a substitute psychotherapist, and we were even more cautious then than most pastoral counselors are now about attempting extended counseling programs with those we could diagnose as at all seriously disturbed. Although we were (and are) deeply concerned for a serious dialogue within the psychiatric theorists, and thus were rather closely related to people in the medical schools and psychiatric clinics, we never thought of ourselves as paramedics nor were we ever so regarded by the doctors and scientists.

For the first stage in every one of these historic coaptations between secular wisdoms and Christian theology is the Christian eagerness to learn from the world and to assimilate the world's wisdoms wherever they apply or however they may be put to real use in the cause of Christian reflection or of practice. This has happened in sizable measure. The authoritarian pastor; the insensitive, heavy-handed moralizing pastor, the pastor who is deceived by transference phenomena, the pastor who aggravates hysterics and guilt neuroses are less numerous and less of a public-health menace than two generations back.

But the vital second stage has not happened: the development of a pastoral theology able to cope with the theoretical assumptions and implications of modern psychotherapy, in any and all of its sectarian schools and programs. We are now thirty years into the alliance and most of the serious and fruitful struggles with the existential and ultimate concerns implied by the psychotherapeutic problematic have come from the other side: Freud's *Civilization and Its Discontents,*[2] Jung's *Modern Man in Search of a Soul,*[3] Fromm's *Escape From Freedom* to *The Sane Society,*[4] Pruyser's *Dynamic Psychology of Religion,*[5] etc., and now Philip Reiff, Andrew Weil, and Allen Wheelis. All of these contributors are humanist in their basic outlook and all their contributions are conceived within the perspective of human autonomy. Religion is an observable phenomenon, but its own claims to I-Thou relationships with God, and Christianity with its confession of Jesus Christ as our Savior to the glory of God the Father are put down to illusion or to the human recognition of the Void from which we are thrown up and into which we sink back. Most of these men are moralists—as Reiff has shown in Freud's case—but for most of them the virtues to be acknowledged and served by persons in society are immanent in the *humanum* and need only an optimum environment to develop and find self-fulfillment.

On the side of Christian thought and the theoretical structures of a pastoral theology to fit these new wisdoms about human beings, the results (over a generation) have ranged from tentative to promising to inadequate to bankrupt—this in an astonishingly thin bibliography, considering the number of people at work in the field and the magnitude and urgency of the problem and its probable import for the Christian future. This verdict, that pastoral theology is the least-developed segment in an overall situation of theological underdevelopment, is not bitter nor recriminatory. It is, however, a confession and a monition. David Roberts and I once agreed that pastoral theologies would best be expected from the people in pastoral care, since amateurs like ourselves were bound to be suspect and were already specialized in other disciplines. This, I happen to know, was also Tillich's feeling and expectation—and Reinhold Niebuhr's. But what we had expected and hoped for has not yet come to pass. For what is needed is not just the monographic literature on slices of the endeavors of pastoral care, not just manuals, or case histories (many of them fictionalized, in part or whole), not just analyses of the applications by Christian pastors of the applicable techniques of the newer therapies; but Christian theology that is fully cognizant of the current challenges of autonomy, that is psychotherapeutically and pastorally oriented, and that is still rooted and grounded in the essential Christian convictions, experiences, and lifestyles. Here one can think of Williams, Hiltner, Oden, Clinebell, Oates, Vaux—and Tournier in a way; but then you begin to run out of names and you have to confess that even the names recited represent forays into the field rather than any encompassment of it.

Thus far, the alliance between psychotherapy and pastoral care has been one-sided and not yet close to that fruitful synthesis of secular wisdom and the Christian revelation that marked all previous crises when the Gospel was under stern challenge of obsolescence. Yet the whole future of the pastoral office and its role and function in what will be left of the church depends on a pastoral theology that matches the autonomous principles of modern psychotherapy with the Christian claim that theonomy is the truth about human life and death and destiny!

CHAPTER
14

From Couch to Carpet: Vienna to Esalen

Of all the secular wisdoms in the Hellenistic world into which the Christians had to venture in the second century, they chose Platonism, even though it entailed a switch from their biblical tradition of thinking of the high God as personal to one or another concept of God as impersonal being: immutability, impassibility, etc. And it was one of the functions of the merging doctrine of the Trinity to explain how God was both transcendent and immanent, and still personal in both aspects.

1. "God the Father Almighty, Creator of heaven *and* earth" (transcendent, sovereign being—the immutable, impassible One—the God beyond Yahweh);
2. "Jesus Christ his only-begotten Son" (personal, mutable, "was crucified, dead and buried—and descended [even] into Hades");
3. "The Holy Spirit, the Lord and giver of life" (immanent, subjective, existential).

Thus, Christian Platonism was an enrichment of the Christian vision of the human, the divine, and their interpersonal relationships. The price for this was a congeries of dualisms: body-mind, matter-spirit, earth-heaven, time-eternity, human-divine.

The implications of this dualistic tradition are still with us—in our attitudes toward the body, the *saeculum,* of life and death and immortality. It persists, with variations, in science: Most of the neurologists I know (Charles Sherrington, Wilder Penfield, James Skinner, et al.) are dualists, and so are many mathematicians and physicists.

In the thirteenth century, thinking Christians had to choose between the *via antiqua* and the *via moderna.* The "modern way" meant the naturalism and secularism of Aristotle and the Arabian rationalists (plus Maimonides, the greatest of the Jewish Aristotelians). St. Albert and St. Thomas met this challenge by bold changes in the traditional views of reason and revelation and of nature and grace: a Christian naturalism and a Christian humanism. They thought they could show that the basic premises of human experience (motion), of thought (causality), of choice (value), of conceptualizing (design), and of finitude (contingency), all lead finally to the radical either/or of infinite regression or else "God." They thought that if nature is impersonal, grace is personal and that grace does not rival nature but redeems it. This allowed for a full acceptance of the best of Aristotle minus his atheism! The price of this was a Christian rationalism: The confidence that all the fundamental truths of Christian *theology* (short of the Incarnation, Redemption, the Resurrection, etc.) are rationally demonstrated by the true philosophy—in short, by a Thomist monopoly in philosophy.

With the Renaissance and Reformation, the ways parted, philosophy dispensing with theology as obscurantist and theology trying to fight free of the humanistic presuppositions of modern philosophy. Even so, the Christian reaction was again positive and enriching: natural theology (i.e., modern science seen through theistic eyes), natural morality (i.e., human virtue reckoned as inherent, or "natural"). The philosopher-scientist could survey "The Wisdom of God in Creation"; and the Christian theologian could welcome the exciting discoveries of the vastness, the coherence, and the beauty of the cosmos as these were unfolded in an endless succession of exciting scientific discoveries. Sir Isaac Newton wrote a commentary on the Apocalypse and nobody thought him daft; John Locke was a devout Christian (by profession and intent, at the very least). All of which is to say that the Christian revelation and the best wisdoms of the world were still in vital balance. The price of this accommodation was an ominous overconfidence in the symmetry between reason and revelation, plus a bland kind of moralism and optimism that would flower in Leibniz and be denounced by Voltaire (in *Candide*). It also meant a new version of dualism, this one between nature as mechanism and the human spirit as spontaneous and free. "The man-machine" would become a commonplace, from d'Holbach and LaMettrie to Watson and B. F. Skinner.

With Hume, Voltaire, Kant, Rousseau, et al., a new challenge was posed to thoughtful Christians—under a self-chosen label "Enlightenment." The positive essence of "enlightenment," as Kant defined it in 1786, was human freedom to think for oneself: to dare to trust human wisdom, without theological tutelage. The self-conscious intent of the great Enlightenment frontiersmen was anticlerical, anti-Christian. Hume certainly thought Christianity expendable; Kant conceived of a valid "religion within the limits of unaided reason" (*blossen Vernunft*); Voltaire hated priests and kings and Christianity with equal vehemence.

Yet Christianity neither rejected the Enlightenment outright nor surrendered supinely to it. Instead, it created what has been called "Liberal Protestantism," "Enlightenment Protestantism"—with great pioneering, synthesizing thinkers like Schleiermacher, Ritschl, Bushnell, Rauschenbusch and many more. Its methodological formula was brilliant: Accept the liberals' thesis of freedom; then show that freedom itself is rooted in human feelings of radical dependence and self-transcendence, in divine moral imperatives that are not mere human preferences. And if this is so, then the human is still related to the divine; God is still ground and end of all our truly human being. The cost of this accommodation, of course, was the abandonment, with varying degrees of reluctance or enthusiasm, of Scripture as literal or infallible, and of the Christian tradition as normative. Here is where the critical analysis of the Bible as literature and history began; here is where the historical traditions of the Christian community began a series of devaluations. If you could relegate something to a "prescientific" status, its contemporary irrelevance is virtually demonstrated.

The challenge of biology (i.e., of evolution and the notion of the human as animal) was actually a variation on the Enlightenment theme and a further reduction of human pretensions to self-transcendence. Most of us have some living memory of the violent combat between Darwin and Moses, between "modernism" and "fundamentalism": It still rages, now that both Darwin and Moses are outmoded and the Scopes case ("Tennessee monkey trial") is long since forgotten. Here again the basic formula was: Accept evolution (what other alternatives?) and then show that even the evolutionary process is dependent on God and that the *humanum* emerging in and from that process is a unique and self-transcending creation whose fully human fulfillment depends upon moral and spiritual outreaches and upreaches that are transcendental, numinous, religious—unlike all other animals that we know. Here again, secular wisdom is neither rejected nor the Gospel surrendered, even if the mix is altered out of all recognition to historic, traditional Christianity.

This syndrome of challenge and response never ceases, however, and in the twentieth century the prime secular wisdom with which Christianity is involved is the psychosociological vision of man as a free, autonomous animal whose values and virtues are immanent and inherent, and whose religion, if any, is an exalted vision of the human community in the natural world: our capacity and our obligation for *self*-realization in ourselves of the human potential. This is a numinous vision; it is exalted; it is transcendental—or at least metapersonal, metahistorical (and, in that sense, mystical). But it has eliminated God, on principle, or divinized the human; it has reduced theology to anthropology. And it is this worldview, this life view and this political climate in which the modern Christian pastor has to breathe and think and exercise ministry. We were promised that the gates of hell would not be able to do the church in, but what was said about a rival gospel of human autonomy?

It may very well seem that I have been summarizing a two-millennia series of retreats, of holding actions, of salvage operations; and in a way, that is exactly what has been happening to Christianity. One might even wonder how Christianity has survived at all. Moreover, as some in every generation before us have supposed, our time just may be the end of the line; for, clearly, this current challenge is the most formidable of them all, thus far. For if autonomy *is* the human condition, then *theonomy* is a term and a notion that will have to go into the historical lexicons of what people once thought. Our choices will be between better and worse versions of humanism, moralism, utilitarianism—all within an increasingly vivid purview of the predictable exhaustion of the earth's resources for human survival.

But this challenge of autonomy—stark, bold, and confident—does serve to identify our own equivalent to all the prior gauntlets that Christians have had to run. It defines our theological task in its unique and distinctive elements, and it points out the precise focus of our intellectual and spiritual conflict. This time the odds have gone up, as part of the general inflationary spiral. To reject the secular wisdoms of psychology, sociology, and their harvest in the human-potential movement would be a form of decerebration, a *sacrificium mentis* that God has never asked of us (and will not honor). To surrender, to accept the verdict of autonomy as final, would be the living end, since Christianity has no *raison d'etre,* no reason for survival, without its stubborn witness to God in Christ in the Spirit and to a lifestyle that is derived from that witness, with all its implications for human existence. Time was when Western culture was so deeply sacralized that it was, in fact, unworldly and otherworldly. Pietism blurred the vision of Christian secularity and came close to denying that it was this world that God so loved, this world in which Christ died to save us all, this world in which God's will is to be done. But that time has gone—and with it the appropriateness and applicability of the gospels of secular*ism.*

Time was when criticism was our first priority—criticism of our cultural heritage, criticism of all the received wisdoms of the past, of all the customary moralities that have hobbled the human spirit. There is still no warrant for abandoning our rights and obligations for clear-eyed, high-minded critical independence. But we had best also be aware of how fragile and emaciated our Christian heritage has become, how literally precarious the Christian future, how fatuous *any* Christian hope will be in a world finally committed to autonomy as the human ideal. Ethical monotheism was never closer to defeat since the struggles between the Hebrew prophets and the worshipers of Baal. We need to see this challenge as it has developed over the past century and as it is mirrored specifically in the evolution of modern psychotherapy from Freud to Maslow—from that famous couch in Freud's home office on the Berggasse in Strauss's Vienna, to the shag carpets of Esalen and Sacramento and Los Angeles, wherever "trust circles" are being tested and games of "Lift" and "Life Cycle Fantasy" are being played out.

With regard, first, to Freud: I should like to emphasize the parallel developments of modern medicine in general and of psychiatry in particular, its revolutionary consequences in all of our basic concepts of the human condition, the human flaw, the human potential, and the terms of our final salvation, if any. We keep forgetting that Freud began his medical career in the very dawn of the epoch of bacteriology and of physiological process as the twin foci of modern medicine. Pasteur, Koch, Brücke, Meynert, et al., had just opened a new chapter in modern medicine—in which, incidentally, the progress of diagnosis so far outran any of their resources for therapy that the histories of medicine from 1875 to 1930–1940 read like horror stories for real. You could diagnose diseases that you couldn't cure, and explain their causes. Victories in our own lifetime over bacterial infection and physiological malfunctions have, indeed, been miraculous. With them have come a rising curve of longevity, and a new dilemma. As old killers are vanquished, new ones come and, *pari passu,* emotional and mental disorders gain new visibility and create new tensions in human society. But one of the consequences of all this is that, just as many "somatic" diseases become manageable (with the ironic limits of omnipresent death), psychic (and psychosomatic) illnesses still remain easier to detect than to diagnose, easier to diagnose than to cure, easier to cure by reducing symptoms than by full restoration. Even so, we are still falling steadily behind the proliferation of psychopathic and sociopathic disorders that overload the weakening fabric of public morality, not to mention our jails and so-called correctional facilities. "Crime in the streets," however, is matched by amoralism and antinomianism in those sectors of society seldom charged with outright crime. Psycho*pathy* and psychotherapy are still out of balance—if psychopathy is understood, literally, as suffering of the *psyche,* and psychotherapy, also literally, as the *therapeia* of that suffering.

Freud did not invent psychiatry, of course: the word means literally the *iatreia* of the psyche and runs back to Klaus Harms of Kiel (and before). Incidentally, the difference between *therapeia* and *iatreia* originally pointed to differences in their resources: *therapeia* is a healing by "scientific" or rational means; *iatreia* had the general connotations of "sacral" and priestly cures (as in the cult of Aesclepius). Moreover, before Freud's time, Emil Kraepelin (of Heidelberg) had charted the field of "modern psychiatry" in his famous and now outmoded *Textbook of Psychiatry*,[1] where psychopathology was described by types and labels that still remain in some popular literature: "dementia praecox," "paranoia," "asphasia," "psychoneurosis," "hysteria," etc. And Richard Krafft-Ebing (in Graz) had finished his famous *Psychopathia Sexualis*.[2] What Freud did, being a physiologist, was to reduce the most obviously *mental* disorders to functions (malfunctions) of psychic energy and to ground *that* energy in the primordial energies of organic process. This is why *The Interpretation of Dreams*[3] is the landmark in the Freudian revolution: in its linkage of the most evanescent of all our experiences with the physiological processes of appetence; the correlation between all mental constructs generated by these insatiable appetites, and monitored by their physiological controls, pleasure and pain (*Lust, Unlust*). This, of course, is why "sexual" and "sexuality" for Freud, became virtually coextensive with human appetence. He never denied the mental and he could abide, with some impatience, animistic terms like "soul" and "conscience." What he insisted on, however, was the exclusive rootage of psychic phenomena in physiological process; and with this one stroke he cut the bonds of the psyche with all real transcendence. This, as I read it, is the essence of the Freudian revolution and all its mutations ever since. He was himself a moralist, his own life the soul of decorum. His sense of the tragic untowardness of life was early, constant, and profound. But he laid an interdict on every serious notion of the transcendent as anything more than mental constructs. Even at best, they are unscientific, illusory and inimical to the human sense of reality.

Given this radical naturalism, Freud's inquiring genius led him to discover the uses of abreaction (Brener had already discovered this procedure, or was it Socrates?) in getting at the Unconscious. From that he could move on to a topography of the Unconscious and its dynamisms: id, ego, and superego and finally to a therapeutic procedure called psychoanalysis, in which the therapist served as midwife to the patient's self-regeneration. This was "depth psychology," all right, but also radically immanentalist. It was maieutic, obstetric, which is the reason for that couch and the doctor in the background (i.e., the ultimate in indirect communication). It was "scientific," too, although I still remember Professor Woodbridge (of Columbia) grumbling in a seminar (back in 1936) that there were more hypotheses on any given page of Freud than a scrupulous investigator could verify or infirm in a life of honest experimentation! Most of all, however, it was the charter for radical human autonomy.

Orthodox psychoanalysis has had three crucial drawbacks: First, it was dogmatic and polemical; second, its inventory of prospective cures was limited (most of the psychoses, alcoholism, and homosexuality had dim prognoses); and third, its range of prospective patients was extremely limited because of the time and expense involved. Both of the major Freudian heresies, Adlerian and Jungian, were more open to the notion of transcendence (especially Jung) but neither in terms that found their lodestone in the historic Christian tradition of *theo*-nomy. Then, with the rise of the so-called cultural analysts in America (Alexander, Horney, Fromm, and H. S. Sullivan) there were further radical modifications of psychotherapeutic doctrine, with more and more emphasis on the ego ideal, on the psychic components of psychosomatic illness and with an increasing frankness as to their humanistic, moralistic social concerns. Indeed, we tend to forget that Erich Fromm and Herbert Marcuse share strikingly similar backgrounds and at least one common concern, the early Marx's vision of the fully human society (which also means a wholly autonomous society). One common aim in all these post-Freudians was to shorten the time span of effective therapy and to lay more and more weight on the patient (and society) for self-understanding (i.e., self-therapy). This opened the way to the "client-centered therapy" of Carl Rogers and the Gestalt therapy of Fritz Perls—and for the entry of a new breed of pastoral counselors onto the scene. Before, pastoral counselors had no credentials at all for scientific psychiatry, and none for orthodox psychoanalysis except in very rare cases.

But in Rogers, Perls, et al., the presupposition is that neurosis, especially, is essentially a form of alienation from the neurotic's social environment—a maladjustment of interpersonal relations. They have been overly-dominated, insufficiently understanding or supportive, interfering, moralistic, immature. A further presupposition—the crucial one—is that the neurotic still retains the latent power of reintegration and maturation within himself and herself and that therapy, in essence, is a provision of an interpersonal environment in which this human potential can grope and practice its way to freedom, self-affirmation, self-expression, trust, love, and happiness. In Rogerian therapy, the essential transaction is intelligent acceptance; Gestalt therapy called for a somewhat more complex analysis of a typology that is obviously a variant on the Freudian topography—this one the so-called parent/child/adult vectors in every psychological transaction.

Here, we are a long, long way from Brücke's *Physiological Institute* and from Freud's physiological reductionism. We are also at an almost equal distance from rigorous, scientific experimentation—or even verifiable hypotheses that take more than a rough-hewn pragmatism and human shrewdness to see if they "work" and how well. Moreover, we have a therapy that may be "indicated" for unhappy, unfree, unfulfilled neurotics that becomes absurd and even dangerous when extended to truly autistic characters or to psychotic and psychopathic behavior. God knows that there are enough neurotics in the world to justify any and all serious efforts to reduce their suffering and enhance their human joy. But that "client-centered" therapy, Gestalt therapy, or transactional analysis should be called "medical" and "scientific" is nonsense—on any ground except the pseudopriestly authority our society confers on M.D.s (and some of them on themselves). This, of course, is why almost any reasonably well-educated, reasonably free and self-possessed, reasonably entrepreneurial person in our society (like pastors and industrial or management psychologists) can share in these new modes of therapy (as deacons if not priests)—since the priests themselves are no longer scientists, by any canon of science that I understand, but rather *shamans* and "medicine men" (and I do not speak here pejoratively).

Three things give me serious pause about this so-called human potential movement, in all the forms I have seen it (from Rogers to Perls to Maslow to Assagioli to Whomever): (1) its pietism; (2) its superficial links with experimental science (blood and drug chemistries and neurology, most of all); (3) its ideological gaps that seem so cheerfully ignored. Thomas Oden has pointed to their pietism and I think I understand what he means.

But I myself profess a slight acquaintance with pietism and for all my enthusiasm for its intensity, vitality, and nurturing power, I also know of its radically sectarian spirit and its powerful tendencies toward self-righteousness and hypocrisy. As for the human potential movement's shortcomings, one thinks instinctively of its haphazard and often reckless experimentation with psychotropic drugs—or, alternatively, its apparent indifference to the scientific mysteries still surrounding the simplest facts such as the correlation between blood chemistry and affective states and of the phenomena of sleep, dreams, hypnosis, and organic time cycles. And as for ideological gaps, here are the two obvious ones for starters: What are the grounds and the evidence for the acorn-oak analogy that is the root image of all the developmental theories? Plato's "innate ideas" I understand—and regard as unsupported by any experimental learning theory that has passed the minimum tests of verifiability. Aristotle's notion of entelechy I understand—and regard as promising if you alter his notions of causality. Likewise, Locke's *tabula rasa,* Piaget's biological calendar or Lévi-Strauss's "structuralism." All these make sense within their presuppositions and generate verifiable hypotheses as consequences and sequels.

But Fromm's human *optimum,* Rogers' self-regenerating person, Maslow's self-fulfilling achiever I do not understand—not in critical terms, at any rate—and this is not for want of trying either. They start with ideal assertions about the human potential, and they end with ideal assertions about the human achievement, all of which are infirmed by the most casual observations of the very same people they are talking about—not to speak of the rest of us. God forbid that I should disparage ideal assertions, having made a career of them; but I am unable to accept the transactional analysts' claims to the authority of experimental science or their indifference to the logical demands of coherence. A gaping hole in Gestalt theory is the question of the personal identity beyond the *Gestalt* itself. What or who is the self that is the personal unity of the personifications, or *hypostases* (such as the parent, adult, child)? In Freud's case, it is clear: There is *no* transcendental personal unity, Kant to the contrary notwithstanding. This seems to me profoundly mistaken, but at least not inconsistent. But in Gestalt theory and in transactional analysis, some sort of transcendental personal unity would seem logically to be presupposed. But as far as I know the literature, this has yet to receive any really scrupulous analysis or exposition.

Be this as it may, what is not in doubt at all is the resolute autonomy that is claimed for the human condition and the optimistic cast of the movement's general perspective. This is its real challenge to Christian pastors and to their theological interpretation of the human. I've tried to show that over two millennia now the Christian mind has in analogous cases avoided outright rejection or outright surrender. In this case, however, we can see instances of both reactions and their obvious inadequacies. The Gospel itself is a sort of human-potential movement; hence, to reject transactional analysis out of hand is both hasty and unwise. But we've seen more leanings on the other side: to a "theology" that is actually little more than an anthropology with ambiguous references to the numinous and the divine, or to the Void, or to some other euphemism for a nature mysticism. And it is also my impression that in this, the pastoral care movement has led the way. But if this is so, or even largely so, then we have one prescription for theological reform both within the movement as it has evolved and in an enterprise I have been trying to recommend to you: of developing a "new" pastoral theology that will try to accommodate itself to the secular wisdoms of humanism, naturalism, and human potential, and still reassert a Gospel realism about human bondage and radical dependence, about God's personal involvement in human salvation (and self-realization), about the moral self-restraints that are implicit in all the Christian imperatives that exhort us to love both God and neighbor—and to enjoy them both—forever.

CHAPTER
15

Of Human Bondage

"**M**an is born free, yet everywhere he is in chains." This famous outcry, the opening sentence of Rousseau's *Social Contract* (1762),[1] is not only a bitter condemnation of Western society but the iceberg tip of the romantic doctrine of the Fall and of original sin. For Rousseau it meant that the first humans were "noble savages," living happily in their natural and social equilibria until tyranny arose—and priestcraft to aid and abet it! Our original sin is ignorance and the unnatural constraints of "civilization." A later Romantic, mortally offended by the post-Revolutionary triumph of the bourgeoisie, had a slightly different version of the same doctrine of the Fall and of original sin. Primitive man, according to Karl Marx, lived happily in an economic Eden ("from each according to ability, to each according to need") until the entrepreneurial snake appeared to tempt him with the obvious advantages of "surplus accumulation." From this first sin of surplus accumulation—and consequent economic unbalances—came all our woes and their quintessence: human bondage (and of the proletariat especially).

I mention this to remind you not only of Marx's grim thesis, but also that this secular myth of a Garden of Eden, an original sin, fall, and bondage seems fully plausible to moderns who have plugged their ears to any truth about the *humanum* in the Genesis myth. Later, there was added the Freudian myth of total depravity, viz., the irrepressible libido (that can be restrained and civilized only to a degree) and an altered myth about a universal fall: viz., one's mismanaged Oedipal transition. At the very least, what this means is that modern men and women have no trouble thinking in terms of an innate human flaw, if it's put to them in immanentist terms. The biblical account has been discounted, not because it is mythical—so are Rousseau's and Marx's and Freud's accounts—but because it underscores the radical character of human involvement with the divine, the primeval nature of faith, of God's moral judgment against humanity's primordial recklessness, and of our radical dependence on God for any real restoration of lost humanity (*imago Dei*). All the various stories of how human beings came to be in bondage—alienated, unhappy and inhumane—point to a common human experience: that the untowardness of human existence has a history into which we have already entered, before we take up our own roles in the human tragedy and add ourselves into the shabby spectacle of human inhumanity.

The history of civilization *is* a history of repression, of somebody by somebody, of one group by another. This is the scandalous truth in *The Communist Manifesto*. Repression has ranged from the open brutalities of chattel slavery to the stable injustices of caste and feudal systems, to the subtler codes of class and status as in the civil hierarchies of Rome, Byzantium and Versailles, where breaches of protocol were criminal offenses. But remember, all the alternatives to civilization, e.g., anarchy, barbarism, have always been dreaded more than the constraints of morality. Indeed, this is the literal meaning of "morality": the mores of a society interiorized into individual and group consciences so that personal behavior may be controlled by the authority of society (and the gods) and by the internal restraints we impose upon ourselves, from our fears of punishment or hopes of reward.

The interaction of Christianity with these repressive moral-demand systems (based as they were on the essential notion of *ex officio* authority) has been ambivalent and ironic. Christianity began, of course, as an illicit religion (little enclaves of freedom in a brutalized world), but when, almost suddenly, they had the full weight of public morality saddled on them, they found no alternatives to moral compromise except monasticism. Here is where the paradox of the freedom of the Gospel and the demands of the moral law came to an agonizing focus—and to ambivalences that Luther and Calvin were later boldly to reject, only then to fall straightway into other ambivalences almost as baffling. Christians are committed to freedom, on principle—*veritas liberavit vos.* Yet Christianity has also been involved in the caste, class, and status systems of their environing societies and has regularly developed comparable caste, class, and status systems in the church itself.

Yet the fact remains that the overall impact of Christianity on the crude human stuff of feudal Europe was both gentling and liberating. Stop to ponder the ethical and sociological connotations of such quaint terms as *"gentle*man," "lady," "courtesy," "politeness," "fair play," *"noblesse oblige,"* "gallantry," etc.; and you can imagine the struggles of a religion of nonviolence, grace, and freedom with a society in which violence and excess were the accepted standard, celebrated in saga and orgy. If you know Sigrid Undset's *Kristin Lavransdatter,* or even *Ivanhoe* and *The Canterbury Tales,* you've some notion of the miracle of grace involved in persuading a man to be gentle or a woman to be chaste. Against this tidal force of concupiscence, gluttony, and lust for power, Christianity joined the secular puritans in trying to enforce the taboos and restraints of human bondage, inequality, and one or another form of a caste-class-status model of "law and order." It was assumed that the only kind of moral obedience that could be expected and enforced in such a society was rooted in *ex officio* authority, in taboos and codes, in the force of social approval and disapproval—e.g., Freud's description of society and the superego. It was presumed—and bolstered by much experience—that human bondage was somehow the price of human community.

And so the Gospel of Liberation and Justification, which has always been at the very heart of every version of the Christian message, was largely conceived of as an *inner* freedom and dignity and rectitude before God (whatever one's social situation) because of God's involvement in the human tragedy and the victory of his love over the bondages of sin, death, and social indignity. Here was true freedom in Christ, true equality before God, full and final justice and justification: when all inequities would be rectified and God's demand for righteousness finally and fully met. This is why justification without human merit was understood as the essence of the Gospel, and not just by Protestants either. "If the Son shall make you free, you will be free, indeed"; and this applied to the haughtiest and to the humblest (for in the final reckoning, it was the *Magnificat* that would win): "The arrogant he has put to rout, he has brought down monarchs from their thrones, but the humble have been lifted high. The hungry he has satisfied with good things, the rich sent empty away" (Luke 1:51–53).

It was, however, the essence of the Enlightenment, hence of all consequent codes of secular morality, that human freedom had to be won by human effort and uprising. And the history of these past two liberal centuries has been a history of the successive splendid victories of liberty over restraint, as far as *ex officio* authority is concerned, as far as customary morality, or the superego and the force of taboo are concerned. And if liberation is not yet a universal achievement, we in our time are closer to it than any generation ever before us. If equality is not a universal fact, few dare assert the dogma of inequality with any boldness at all. Elitism is now a no-no, at least as far as the liberated consciousness is concerned. Universal education, universal suffrage, religious freedom, ethnic liberation, women's liberation, sexual liberation, freedom of speech, press, public assembly, collective bargaining, a pregnant woman's private rights to dispose of an unwanted fetus, human rights, civil rights, freedom to act and dress and behave without let or hindrance—all the freedoms that people in earlier bondages dreamed of as equivalent to a return to Paradise—all these freedoms are almost everywhere granted in principle and achieved in practice to a degree never before recorded.

The triumphs of human freedom are very closely correlated with liberation from human indignity and injustice, but are not so closely correlated with human happiness. Freedom from arbitrary interference, arbitrary abuse, arbitrary restraints—yet freedom for what? For rich, joyous, fruitful, happy living—secure and serene, or exciting and rewarding—over long spans of time and involving total or even large populations? Any honest answer here raises the question about the human flaw in a very poignant way. For human beings still abuse themselves and misuse others in ways that are incredible to all of us who ever believed that *if* ever we were free and fed and secure in a secular, egalitarian society, we would be measurably less aggressive, predatory, victimized, and unhappy. What kind of animals are we, anyway, whose freedom and security have not brought us happiness and serenity? It cannot now be merely the fault of a repressive society nor of intolerable deprivations nor of external and arbitrary prohibitions. It cannot now be merely the maladjustments of our interpersonal or our object relations, or the penalties we incur in the games we continue to play. The obvious fact is that we are not yet free enough and that we are not likely ever to be free enough, for freedom is an insatiable aspiration. The tragic irony of every one of the great triumphs of human liberty (and they are great and to be celebrated) is the way in which, in every case, the victors turn into victims once again but to some new tyranny, some new injustice, some new stultification.

Freud was right, of course, about civilization involving restraint in all its cost-benefit calculations, as we shall discover all over again if it's a cold winter and if the world food shortage continues. For human bondage returns when there is any kind of conflict of massive self-interest, whenever and wherever survival choices have to be made (and not just because we are selfish and greedy either). Over on the other side, there is also a kind of bondage in intimacy, in any kind of really deep and abiding human commitment, "for better or for worse." Indeed, our chosen bondages are often almost as bad as the unchosen ones, for they point even more clearly to the deepest and most disturbing reality in all our experiences of freedom and bondage. For all of them—and this defines the human flaw in its very essence—are rooted in the paradoxes of the inevitable overreaching of our human outreachings and upreachings in their self-transcendence. Freedom to overreach comes with freedom to *reach* (out, up, within), and this brings with it the risks and reality of self-inflicted bondage. "The fault, dear Brutus, is not in our stars, "But in ourselves. . . ."[2]

As we have grown accustomed to understand ourselves as animals, we have also tended to underestimate our oddities as animals. For one thing, no other animal is so helpless and dependent for so long, with so many positive and negative options in its created potential. We are products of evolution, of course. But very much more immediately, we are creatures of culture. There has been no significant biological evolution in man for 50,000–75,000 years yet a literally unimaginable cultural evolution—all of it ambivalent! No other animals are so wildly variable in their herd mores (social morality); thus, no animal is so nearly at the mercy of its social upbringing. But even more crucially, no other animals are anywhere near to man in their incontinence and instability, in precisely those dynamics that set the human off from its animal matrix: (1) intellectual curiosity, (2) the hunger for freedom, (3) the need for conferred dignity (as distinguished from status fought for and won at some other animal's expense), (4) the love of loving and the need to be loved. Something of all these outreaches is evident in animate nature everywhere, but in humans their difference in degree produces a difference in kind. The hungers to know, to be free, to be approved, to love and be loved are precisely the distinguishing marks of being human. Deprive the human animal of any of them in any significant degree, and you have an unhappy, unhealthy, and even deadly animal.

In these human aspirations, our animal instincts serve us poorly and often deceive us cruelly. Nor will our prudence and self-serving cunning suffice: Rationality and enlightened self-interest finally fail us in real crises. Our granular frontex cortices are no better than thin veneers (i.e., late biological developments over our protopathic and autonomic nervous systems). The human being as an animal is a failure. Despite astonishing adaptability, he is designed to self-destruct under pressure, and to ruin the natural environment in the process. But if humans are so poorly designed as animals (measured by any of the canons of biology and technology), does this implicate their Creator, if any, in a botched job? Is the *humanum* one of God's misconceptions, a creation with aspirations that exceed actual potential? Did God on purpose make human beings with a congenital fatal flaw? Or, if you insist on a naturalistic premise, are humans the victim of evolution's most spectacular and tragic maladaptation?

Before we decide or dismiss these questions, let us look more closely at the conceivable alternatives. If there was to have been a truly human animal at all, it would have to be one with outreaches that transcend anything similar in any other species: intelligence, freedom, self-consciousness, joy, love—not one but all together. Every one of these human outreaches would also have to be incontinent on principle and socially productive in potential. Human intelligence, freedom, self-consciousness, joy, loving, all have the untainted potential of healthful coexistence, of maturation into the human potential; they are, precisely, those categories that, between them, include our truly human peak experiences. And they constitute, in an older phrase, our *justitia originalis;* our created and intended "righteousness," "justice," our truly human expectations and opportunities. Some stable and sustained mix of all of these—intelligence, freedom, self-consciousness, joy, love—is what every thoughtful human aspires to, what no sensitive human can fail to aspire to. This is the truth in the notion that goes by the term "eudaemonism."

Yet we also know that it is just precisely these specifically human outreaches that are so easily and regularly abused by humans, and that it is their abuse that is the root cause of unhappiness and moral evil of all sorts and in every degree. Abuse does not prohibit use, of course. But why the abuse, so regularly, so inevitably, so tragically? Why should an animal that was made to be free and happy ever be in chains, especially in chains of his own forging, or at least his own complicity? Why are human aspirations not like other animal aspirations, i.e., relatively stabilized, because generally self-limiting and satiable? This is the paradox that has given rise to all the various theories about the Fall and original sin (Genesis, Rousseau, Marx, Freud, etc.). Human beings, as it turns out with a dismal universality, abuse their human potential or fall short of it or find it tragically evanescent and bracketed by death. What is more, in the same process (or vice versa), they abuse the potentials of other human beings, often unknowingly or unintentionally. Injustice and inhumanity are universal data, and there is no good reason for them. They are not intended or necessitated by any of the primal acts of creation; they serve no intended or necessitated end of being or of the ideal good. Moreover, they cannot be fully rectified, or set right, by any act of human willing, or any human wisdom—even though they can and must be ameliorated as far as possible. This, as far as I can see, is simply the brute fact of the human condition. But why on earth should such things be?

Here the biblical view of human existence offers us a profound clue as to the sequence by which innocent outreach becomes sinful overreach. The driving force in every instance, so says the Christian tradition, is pride, which is what Christians have called the mother of all the other deadly sins. Now, the discussion of pride in Christian literature is immense, and I will not belabor its history for you. But this much ought to be obvious: Pride is a misconceived additive to or corruption of otherwise quite legitimate human aspirations. It is the organism's exaggerated self-concern that seeks (and supposes that it deserves) all available pleasure and avoids (and supposes that it ought to avoid) all avoidable pain. Pride is overreaching appetite of every sort, in any direction (gluttony, lust, aggression, etc.); pride is reactive resentment to thwarted outreachings (anger, "hurt feelings"); pride is the sense of merited, earned personal worth (not dignity conferred). Pride is the rationalization of self-love, it is self-righteousness with regard to our own excesses and our self-confidence as to what we deserve as our inherent rights.

The irony and tragedy of all this is that self-love is very close to self-respect. The line between deserved and conferred dignity is easily blurred—between ego-strength and self-assertion. So, given the barbaric state into which we are born and the tainted culture in which we grow up, it is no wonder that the innocent incontinencies that could make us truly and fully human actually turn us into those tainted abuses that lead us into self-induced bondage, self-chosen deviations from maturity. We may, in a measure, be liberated from all our shackles save our own self-will (and we cannot declare your independence on this score, since that would amount to self-abandonment, which happens not to be an actual option, not even in suicide). Suicide and catatonia are only apparent exceptions.

Thus, basic pride nourishes itself, and also generates dread: the dread of losing our hard-won dignity or of having it denied us, the dread of being punished or of going unrewarded, the dread of exposure to ridicule and rejection (since we are all phony enough to be vulnerable to anything that came close to total exposure). All of these are so many different modes of the primal dread of being abandoned, which is the taproot of all anxiety, which means that anxiety is endemic in all human alienation. Time was when anxiety and guilt were always yoked together. Now guilt is gone in our society or else is going (if by guilt you mean any sense of transcendental judgment). But anxiety remains, and goes on acting as the mainspring of most of our irrational or destructive behavior. Look at the list of subhuman, inhuman, antihuman behavior in its sociopathological context: aggression, rage, acting out, vandalism, brutality, self-stultification, etc. Then lay this alongside the biblical inventory of standard human vices: "fornication, impurity and indecency; idolatry and sorcery; quarrels, contentions, fits of rage, selfish ambitions, dissensions, party intrigues and jealousies; drinking bouts, orgies and the like" (Galatians 5:19–21). Now, whether or not you'd want to reduce or enlarge either of these inventories of inhumanity, is there any way to deny that each one of them, and all of them together, name prideful overreachings of innocent human outreachings? You might call them "sins" or you can call them shortcomings, as you like, and you still have the crucial fact on your hand that the tragic consequences of human incontinence are irretrievable human bondage, even for those celebrating their various liberations.

For if it is these insatiable aspirations of ours that make us truly human, it is their equilibrium that would make us fully human. Here "equilibrium" is another term for faith or trust or that crucial sense of being upborne even in our condition of radical dependence. Its paradigm, maybe, is the infant's sense of security when upheld in loving arms. But what could bring our aspirations into balance? The obvious answer, I should think, is that every human outreach has a moral norm that defines its proper limits, its valid means and ends. (1) In animals their intelligence, curiosity, inquiry are normed by survival and reproductive needs, and these strike a rough balance in anything like an adequate environment. In humans, these very same outreaches have to be normed by truth, or they become aids to cunning or cruelties and distortions. (2) Again, in the other animals, their freedom is normed by natural limits; in humans freedom must be normed by justice, which is not a natural limit, or it turns paradoxical and the freed human slides into some other, unintended bondage. (3) Self-consciousness is an animal phenomenon normed by their cerebral capacities. Human self-consciousness is a mystery and is either normed by a sense of social responsibility or it becomes either morbidly subjective or tragically self-centered.

(4) Joy in animals is a lovely thing to see (even though they do not seem to enjoy sex so much as they should, on any of our theories of sexuality—*post coitus triste,* and all that). But in humans, joy has to be normed by fellowship or it becomes self-indulgence. (5) In animals, love is *eros* and *philia* and is balanced off by seasonal rhythms and ruthless ecological curbs (as it is not in man); human love has to be normed by community or else it becomes possessive and the fuel of further injustice.

It is worth noting that none of these norms is immanent, innate, or self-enforcing. Truth, justice, responsibility, fellowship, and community are all self-transcending and society-transcending norms. Whence, therefore, could be their ground or final validation? Nature? Obviously not—not on any scheme of naturalistic ethics that we know. Society? No, not even on the most sophisticated utilitarian calculus! But something there is that rejoices in and encourages human outreach, yet resists and finally defeats human overreach. The wages of sin is (or are) death, said St. Paul. But there's an interim penalty that is tragic and yet somehow salvageable, or so says the Gospel, and that penalty is bondage. The overreaching of an outreach results in a sort of self-stultification. The overreaching intelligence turns into intellectual arrogance that slides into Faustian self-deception. Think how much our knowledge has gained for us and how many booby traps it has sprung on us! Overreaching freedom denies freedom to others—in the holy name of freedom (even if it is only the freedom of an erstwhile oppressed group). Self-consciousness without self-control turns into narcissism and self-deception. Joy that is snatched at or hung onto overreaches the limits of its *kairos* and turns to pessimism. Human love is forever overreaching itself—it is incontinent by nature—and thus always is throttling its own full and final potential with a finite existence, bracketed even at its best by death.

Over and over again, the Old Testament uses the metaphor of "the house of bondage" to recall Egyptian slavery and to describe the human condition in general. In Romans, it is "the spirit of bondage" into which men have fallen and in which they are subject to the dreadful powers of sin and death. This, then, is the essence of sin. But on the other hand, this means that the essence of salvation is liberation from sin's bondage. The human flaw and the spirit of bondage are paired metaphors—the human abuse of the human potential by overreaching the human up-and-outreaching basic elements in human nature. It is not necessitated, however universal it may be. There is no good reason why outreach, aspiration (the transcendental impulse) has to overreach itself. There are all sorts of good reasons why this is irrational and tragic. Hence the question as to who's to blame for this tragic, unnecessitated state of affairs is so elusive. If outreach is prerequisite to truly human existence, is God to be blamed for having created a creature whose human potential entails the risk of self-stultification? Is man, then, a cosmic blunder, an unnatural mutation? Any way you answer this, you have raised a prior question that leads straight into a radical ambiguity—what Scripture means by "the mystery of ungodliness." If man's original sin is chiefly in being human, then any notion of his salvation is at best a concept of amelioration, which is not really enough, at the end of the day. If original sin is a function of economic or political injustice or of the mismanagement of our interpersonal relationships, or if it holds the possibility of its own rectification, then salvation is self-restoration or social and political revolution. But this has never succeeded in anything more than upheavals and rearrangements of the patterns of our inhumanity and unhappiness, and there is scant prospect for any other outcome.

For human beings are, still and everywhere, in chains. Liberation has not been achieved by prosperity or political freedom; political freedom is not achieved by ideological mutations. Workers of the world, unite and arise—you've nothing to lose but your chains! Well, yes. But the tragedy of our time and of the human condition is that liberation does not come by self-assertion or even by deserving to be free. All human beings ought to be free. But human merit and desert do not avail to liberate. This is why we must be *liberated,* and this is a dreadful blow to human pride. Arise! Cast off your fetters, walk in the sun in freedom and in the joy of being fully human. Up to a point, yes. And we're all obligated to reach for, aspire to, just exactly that point. But our real dilemma lies deeper, in a paradox of aspirations and overreachings that corrupt each other. Oh, wretched humans that we are. Who or what can deliver us from this high tragedy? The only answer I can think of, not already infirmed by experience itself, is the purpose and power of whatever or whoever intended us to be free and joyous and loving to begin with. Is this any clue at all for any thoughtful pastor who is trying to help lost sheep find their way back to their true freedom in their Father's house?

CHAPTER
16

Oh, Freedom!

Christian pastors' loving care for their people is also their imperative to understand them as human beings sharing a common human existence and as persons: unique, individual identities, each a singular project. And this means that any *theonomous* view of their human existence must include the diagnosis we have just spoken of: of their freedom and bondage, of the radical human flaw that shows up in so many different ways but always in the same essential tragedy, viz., human outreach turned into overreach, use turned into abuse, freedom turned into self-stultification and inhumane behavior of one sort and another. Pastors must understand this human flaw as radical, inescapable, universal—yet not "natural" or necessitated or by God's positive design. It is the tragic entail of the risk of being human, God's tragic entail of creating human beings, our tragic entail of our own human aspirations. It implies no doctrinaire pessimism about human nature since it is, on principle, salvable. But it has no room for any doctrinaire optimism either, since it is also, on the same principle, damnable. Above all, it proscribes gnostic and moralistic views of our salvation (e.g., the notion of some secret wisdom that liberates the human potential to some predesignated fulfillment or the notion of some human achievement that surmounts the flaw by its own virtue and earns its liberation). Christian realism about the human flaw is cynical toward all human pretensions and claims to preterit perfection; it is perfectionist toward all human impulses to cop out and settle for subhuman or inauthentic existence as their doom; it is, in all relations, hopeful and loving because its chief reliance (i.e., "faith") is on God's grace.

Historically, the chief theoretical confusion here is in the clash between divine sovereignty and human moral agency, with polarities forming around each. The partisans of divine sovereignty (like other determinists) have found themselves pushed to corollary doctrines like election, irresistible grace, and the perseverance of the elect to go along with their doctrines of the radical human flaw, whereas, the synergists have always found it difficult (downright distasteful, actually) to talk about the human flaw as radical. What I'm suggesting is a pastoral theology (i.e., a theonomous view of the *humanum*) that fuses the residuary truth about original sin and total depravity (i.e., "the human flaw" and "our tragic bondage") with a frank and vigorous doctrine of synergism. This is the only alternative I can see, or conceive, to heteronomy on the one hand (i.e., determinism, natural or divine) and autonomy on the other.

Liberation from our primordial bondage is not, therefore, a simple human option, just as it is an undeclinable human aspiration. We cannot really wish to be unfree (if we know what we are saying or thinking); and we cannot gain our freedom by wishing for it or even striving for it. And by "liberation" here I mean what the classical vocabulary meant by "salvation" and what modern humanism means by "self-fulfillment." Self-salvation is a delusion, at any level that means more than amelioration. And it is one of the deficiencies of much that has passed for pastoral care and pastoral theology that it has either taught or implied one or another version of the gospel of self-salvation = liberation as a personal or social-ethnic group achievement.

This is why our various experiences of liberation have been so frustrating and so tragic. In his time Voltaire could point to the repressive society (both civil and ecclesiastical) and to the ignorance and inequalities they spawned and sponsored, and say, "There is the cause of our human unhappiness; there is the infamy, *écrasez l'infâme*" (erase the infamy). But then came the great liberations of the French Revolution, which turned out to be the liberation of the bourgeoisie and the intelligentsia but not the proletariat. The middle-class merchants and the high-domed intellectuals emerged from their life in the shadows of *l'ancien regime* (feudalism and its legacies). But it was in this liberation of the bourgeoisie that Karl Marx found humanity's worst enemy of all, now unchained and predatory. This is the bitter thesis of *The Communist Manifesto,* and its date is as ironic as its theme: 1848, when every country in Europe experienced a proletarian-democratic uprising and every one of them failed. Another irony of the great century of freedom was that the liberated bourgeoisie and the liberated intelligentsia fell into a mortal hostility that is still one of the most powerful and unhealthful impulses in modern art, literature, and culture. Pastors are often in the middle. Whatever their social origins, they are trained (typically) as a sort of quasi- or pseudo-intellectual to the tastes and values of the intelligentsia with their ingrained contempt for the middle classes whom they are often asked to serve. But in the process they also acquire middle-class tastes for material comforts that slide off into biting the hands that feed them.

Then, actually in our century, came the next great liberation: of the working class and the white proletariat. This was the liberation for which the Social Gospel was originally mobilized to serve, and it was widely advertised as the prelude to that peaceable kingdom of economic and political justice that would bless humankind. God forbid that I should disparage any such victory of freedom, and none of us would have it reversed. But labor's liberation has not brought human happiness with it, as every major strike and wage-price hike reminds us. Big Labor and Big Business turn out almost equally indifferent to the public good they both profess to respect and serve.

There have been the other bondages that have had to be liberated: chattel slavery and its substitutes in "white supremacy," colonialism, minority oppressions by insensitive majorities, women's lib, youth lib, liberation from constricting social mores as to sex and manners, taboos in art and literature. And now all these liberations are achieved—on principle altogether and partially in fact (there are no liberations that are not partial in fact, which is part of the point I'm trying to make). Today more of humankind is freer than in recorded history—and with what results? With freedom of speech has come pornography. With freedom of the press has come manipulation of public opinion. With freedom of assembly has come a widespread apathy toward constructive reform. With freedom of worship has come the decline of institutional religion. With freedom of movement has come tourism, good and bad. With freedom of exploitation (free enterprise) there has come pollution. With freedom of sex there have come antibiotic-resistant venereal germs and AIDS. The fact is that freedom is a trap: sometimes a tender one, yet always cruel because it is always self-deceiving. Time was when our pastoral task was to proclaim liberty to the captives, the opening of sight to the blind. And this is still a prime responsibility, especially to those who really are oppressed. But we had better understand, and help others understand, the ingrained ambivalences in every gospel of liberation; for being liberated from whatever has bound you up to now is at least to be involved in (and often bound by) the resulting situation, which never is, for any extended span of time, quite what you had expected or hoped for. It may be better or worse, but always different.

Good Christian shepherds are a very special kind of cynic, a very special kind of realist, a very special kind of comrade to others in the toils of their common humanity. They have long since moved beyond the utopian bedazzlements that once inspired their youth (or the false images of youthful heroes, if any, or the romantic uprushes of piety that turned them toward the ministry, etc.). Yet they are not at all pessimists or defeatists or doomsayers, any more than Amos was a doomsayer. Their ego strength has not been shattered, even though they get shook up more often and more profoundly than others less intimately involved in the joys and tears of human strugglings to be human. They will not put people down nor encourage them in self-detestation. Their main job is to help them grapple with their own discoveries of the paradoxes and ambivalences of their freedom without aggression or defeat, to help them realize that, even if they are victims and not truly free, their most radical plight is in themselves and that there is no hope of salvation in some magical transformation of their human situation—even though they can, and ought to, have all sorts of celebrations and satisfactions within the brackets of that situation.

Oh, wretched free man that I am! Who will deliver me from the ambivalences of my freedom? Well, there's always the hope of political change, and the pastor must be deeply involved in binding and loosing (i.e., guiding) the political consciences of people. But pastors will mislead if they point them toward some political utopia or counsel complacence with the *status quo*. Politics is no deliverance from the disenchantments or the frustrations of freedom. If we can liberate our neurotic constituents from their unhappiness, or the unhappiness they wreak in the world, we shall be serving them very well indeed, especially if, in the process, we help them avoid swapping off one enchantment for another. But therapy is not liberation from ambivalence; at its best it brings clarity and responsibility in recognizing and grappling with human ambivalence. Not even liberation is liberating from the bondages into which we bind ourselves.

Our salvation, our "deliverance" (if and when it comes) will have to come from beyond ourselves, and beyond all the ameliorations we can, and ought to, be making of our human lot. This is not to discourage self-improvement, self-enchantment, self-realization at any point, to any degree, short of self-deception! Salvation is not a transaction within or between ourselves and other selves. Such transactions may mean amelioration, but they are not salvation and the two had best not be confused. They may enrich our experience of meaning and value and so be religious, in Wieman's sense. But they do not secure the larger context of final meaning in and for our total existence, including death; *this* is what I'd want to save the term "salvation" for! That this security in the final meaning of our lives cannot be achieved by human effort (moralism) or by the abandonment of human effort (antinomianism) is the shock and scandal of the Christian Gospel. But it helps define the pastor's task. Until people have come to the point where they are properly shocked and rightly scandalized by this unwelcome reality that salvation must be given, and rightly accepted—not by right but in faith by grace—then they will go on spending their days and nights in one or another scheme of self-salvation. And in all of these schemes they are foredoomed to partial success and final failure. Faithful Christian pastors must find the ways and means to convey this understanding of human existence to their people, which is obviously impossible unless they understand it very well themselves and have found their way beyond!

We will be talking about this Christian confidence in "a way beyond" for the rest of the course, in various perspectives within an overarching *theonomous* view of human existence and destiny. But even now, in our effort to probe the paradox of freedom, there is another basic comment to make about it. This can be formularized rather simply, and then pondered more carefully over a long span of time and experience: "Freedom and self-fulfillment are justice. But in the nature of the case, human justice is never complete and perfect. It is never fully achieved and therefore never really saving or secure or healing (save, of course, always in an ameliorative sense)." Ameliorating, yes—and this is important in *any* view of the human predicament. But saving, no—in any sense that takes aspiration, perfection and transcendence seriously. The only freedom that would make us truly free is not our freedom from restraint—this is amelioration of an intolerable state—but the freedom to dispose of ourselves intentionally in some context of optimum meaning. Saving freedom is not freedom to be ourselves but to give ourselves, to bestow ourselves, to invest ourselves, to dedicate ourselves in meaningful oblations in love, zest, and joy! This means freedom to accept the brackets of existence and the specific individuality that is given each of us within those brackets, the freedom to live meaningfully in and through our own identities (not some ideal self we are not and never will be), the freedom to face and to accept our deaths in advance, and thus the freedom to go on living posthumously at the top of our powers as responsible persons with transcendent destinies, in faith, hope, and courage.

One of the ways in which the powers of sin and death exercise their tyranny over us is their proposal that our freedom (and freedom in humanity at large) is really for ourselves and our own self-fulfillment; indeed, that all our human hungers are to be satisfied by consumption and attainment rather than oblation. Yet any reflection at all on the human scene will show you that this is simply not the way things work out. Self-interested, self-centered focusing of intelligence or freedom or self-understanding, joy, or love lead to, and end in, self-stultification. Our human outreaches are, literally, projects; they look outward, upward, beyond themselves (without losing their subjective rootage, of course), and their meaning and value are always tied to their use, their disposition and dedication. All our animal needs can be sated in themselves (in various herd and gregarious participations—all aimed at the survival of the species and not the happiness of the individual). But none of our human hungers can be satisfied in this way or on this level. This is one of the grounds on which I keep stressing self-transcendence; all that we are and do that matters most point beyond ourselves. Out- and upreach are crucial metaphors in this view of what it means to be human and what it means to fail to be human. He who tries to save his life usually loses it (or loses its real meaning), and he who loses his life in truly human outreaches ("for my sake and the Gospels") comes close to saving it, or of having it saved for him. This strange text is not only the Christian prescription for the human role in salvation, but for all Christian notions of the stewardship of life, of calling and vocation, and of all Christian notions of "meaning and value," when life is viewed steadily and whole.

Saving freedom—the freedom that really would be free—is the decision (intentional and intelligent) to devote one's disposable gifts (intelligence, freedom, self-consciousness, love) in meaningful service and in joyful participation in the divine and human gladness in the world. We know all about unhealthful self-sacrifices, of lives thrown away or desiccated by meaningless or ineffectual renunciations and self-denials—neither intelligent nor fruitful, however well-intentioned or piously rationalized. We also know how unhealthful self-assertions overreach themselves and break against the jetties of counter self-interest— hard-driven, socially conditioned and either predatory or parasitic. Benevolence is freedom put to intelligent, loving use; hence, it is one of the truest and most truly human virtues. Gratitude is freedom's appropriate reaction to grace (to our awareness of the givenness of life); it is one of the purest and rarest of all the human virtues. Reverence is freedom's reaction to our awareness of the sacredness of life, and is one of the most cleansing and elevating of all the virtues. Freedom in its outreaches, then, is a prime and essential ingredient in what Wieman called "meaning and value, " and in their increase, which is one way of saying that freedom, liberation, responsibility are a nuclear complex at the very heart of true religion.

But freedom "from" must also become freedom "for," if it is to be real and at all lasting. Freedom must be turned outward or else it curves back upon itself and becomes self-indulgence (and that is what all too much of our freedom actually amounts to). The triumph of freedom is finding something really worth giving your life to and for, and then having the commitment turn out well (i.e., as a blessing and a source of blessing). This, often, has seemed a prescription for martyrdom or some other form of self-abandonment. Actually, there is all the difference in the world between self-abandonment and self-giving, for one is the fruit of despair, the other the source of the only lasting joy we humans ever really have. Pastors who understand this much about the paradox and mystery of freedom will be better pastors—and their flocks more faithfully tended, since they would be working nearer the grain of that truth that really can make us free: The truth that freedom is not an end in itself but rather in order to love and serve, as love and service are in order to blessedness (happiness), which is the end to which and for which God intended us, first and last.

CHAPTER
17

A Gospel for the Guiltless

From the beginning, we have been speaking of the collapse of the old linkage between anxiety and guilt and the old forensic metaphors of sin as crime, of God's wrathful but righteous judgment against guilty sinners. In that perspective the standard soteriological formula was repentance (confession of one's guilt), justification and pardon (by God's free, unmerited mercy prompted by Christ's atoning death), regeneration (the renewal of God's image and, with it, all our real human powers, in potency at least), and the consequent, maturing life in Christ (Christian discipline, growth, and triumphant death). All of this, at any given stage of life, was "salvation": here was the Christian ground of hope and courage, of joy and blessedness in this world and in the world to come.

The fading of this immemorial tradition was not so much the conscious rejection of the Christian message in its entirety as it was the collapse of that particular forensic law court-political model in which the Gospel had been set, from its Pauline origins down through its adaptations in the Roman-medieval legal and feudal contexts down to its Reformation focus on justice as imputation (an almost exclusively forensic metaphor), on down through Protestant evangelical theology and, with different context, in Roman Catholic theology to the present time. In this multiform tradition, there were twin constants: (1) the mystery of salvation has for its "scene" a law court and its principle of adversary proceedings; and (2) the leading characters in the legal drama were *ex officio,* i.e., their roles and authority (or rights) were assigned them by their office. If you have never heard a gospel sermon on "The Final Judgment," with the Father as Judge, the sinner as the accused, the Holy Spirit as prosecutor (with an open-and-shut case) and with the Son as defense attorney, who takes his client's penalty on himself, then you've never really understood the classical Protestant soteriology. If you've never worked through the exegetical tangle about *dikaios* and *dikaiosune,* etc., and the question whether they are chiefly forensic or ethical terms, you've never grasped the subsurface issue to the apparent battle of words about the imputation of Christ's righteousness in justification and its impartation. I pause only briefly to comment that *dikaios* belongs to a large group of Greek adjectives that can be made into verbs that imply the occurrence of the state described by the adjective. For example, *tuphlos* means "blind"; *tuphlow* means to *make* "blind"; *psychros* means "cool"; *psychrow* means to "cool off," etc. But then I would have to admit that the majority of Pauline experts agree that *dikaios* and *dikaiosune,* in its Pauline usage, is meant to be forensic. It is based on the metaphor of the law courts and the adversary models of justice. To be "justified," therefore, means to be acquitted (whatever the actual facts). It means that a verdict of "not guilty" and, therefore, "just" has been rendered. The dread of guilt expunged from the record, the accused now stands scot-free; he is "accepted in his unacceptability" (since everybody knows the evidence against him was clear and preponderant). Moreover, the officers of the court, and their authority to render such a merciful judgment without corrupting the law (i.e., because of a substitutionary punishment) is all *ex officio;* it is their office that gives them this arbitrary power. And they exercise it in arbitrary and selective ways: Some are justified and some are not, and this, of course, is what predestination is about. Nor do those unjustified have any justification on any just ground for complaint, since in the course of bare justice, "none of us would see salvation."

It is important to understand how basic this forensic-legal-trial procedures metaphor is, and how generally it has affected both Jewish and Christian ideas of soteriology and justice. The notion of God as Judge, of his will as law, of violations of God's law as crime (*lese maiestatis*), and of guilt as the natural dread of the consequences of the fact that we are in violation of God's law on some ground or other—all of this is the taproot of the old linkage between anxiety and guilt. Misery or misfortune beget anxiety—as do stress, threats, and apprehended dangers—and anxiety begets wishful thinking. And given a forensic-trial court perspective, anxiety begets guilt. Every time I see a police car, my glance at the speedometer is reflex; every time I run a yellow light and hear no siren, my sigh of relief is reflex; every time there is a letter on the desk from the IRS or a court or even an attorney-at-law, my shudder is reflex. I know, in my mind, that our system of justice is meant to serve justice; and I know that, by intention and comparatively speaking, I have been a law-abiding citizen for more than six decades; I have no criminal record and only three "moving violations" on my traffic record in more than fifty years of driving. But I belong to the generation—maybe the last one—that also knew that I was already guilty of something or other and that, if the court chose, it could condemn and sentence me (and would probably be serving the cause of justice, in some sense, in the process). *A fortiori,* there was never any doubt in my mind, since I can remember, that I was guilty before *God,* since he knew my heart—not only the sins I had committed but also the ones I would have, if circumstances and occasion had allowed. And I knew that his judgment would be just and right—and that it would amount to disapproval, rejection, and abandonment if I remained unrepentant and unconverted. This, of course, is what tortured Augustine in the Milanese garden, Luther in the Erfurt monastery, Wesley at Aldersgate. Guilt is the dread of a just condemnation by one who has a perfect right to pass such a judgment and to enforce it.

Now, it is precisely this forensic-legalist-law-court metaphor as dominant in our life view that has faded, or is fading—as the general idea through which we think our other ideas about justice and right and authority. If you want to find the watershed between this present permissive society and the repressive societies that preceded it, look for all those who first conceived the notion that justice, law, and law enforcement are all human-made, human-controlled and therefore with no other authority than political, cultural, social. For with the collapse of the divine origin and ground of the moral (and therefore the civil) majesty of the law went the guilt complexes that derived from transcendental notions of injustice, unrighteousness, and incrimination; this kind of guilt was the real solvent of the moral cement that had held society together, however tenuously. And now it becomes increasingly atypical of our instinctual feelings and our public and private consciences. In its place has come, instead, a sense of victimization and of self-righteousness.

The practical consequences of the fading of this basic forensic metaphor of guilt is now a psychotherapeutic commonplace. You cannot drive people to confess and any efforts to exacerbate their guilt feelings is either futile or counterproductive. Guilty by whose standards; condemnation by whose magisterial right and authority? We all know how haphazard and unjust our system of justice is—the court system, that is—and how it operates at different levels of equity for the powerful and the powerless. The majesty and probity and equity of the whole forensic system and our four branches of government (legislative, executive, judicial, and journalistic) are in tatters and shambles, although anyone who is greatly surprised by any of this is uncommonly naïve. The great organizing, controlling, life-balancing metaphors of the law court (the forensic view of damnation and salvation) have lost their organizing, controlling force, and with this has come a radical disintegration of an ancient (and still familiar) tradition.

Time was when the Gospel to the guilt-ridden was "you are pardoned and acquitted and reconciled to God through Christ's atoning passion, his vicarious substitution, his appeasement of God's deserved wrath against your richly merited damnation." "Accept God's acceptance"; "sin bravely; repent sincerely," "walk freely in the assurance of your sins forgiven." "I was sinking deep in sin;" "can my God his wrath forbear, me, the chief of sinners spare?"; "would he devote his Sacred Head for such a worm as I?" If you know the old gospel songs, we could go on indefinitely. And in most of them, this forensic image of sin as a crime, justification as acquittal, salvation as imputed righteousness is the inner, organizing principle. The Gospel was the certified truth that your sentence of death (just and merited) is erased, God's wrath appeased. God was in Christ reconciling himself to the world! "There is therefore now no condemnation to them that are in Christ Jesus, who walk not after the flesh, but after the Spirit . . ." (Romans 8:1). This was Good News indeed, and it still contains the very essence of the Gospel message. Those thus fully persuaded of their election and perseverance in God's grace could live and die rejoicing—beyond the reach of human intimidation and despair, even in the full quota of life's trials and in the face of death. Above all, they were not victims; they were of God's elect!

But what if there is no such sense of guilt, no such dread of damnation, no such expectation and hope in Jesus Christ? What if, singing that "Jesus paid it all" or that "the burden of my sins was rolled away," there is no life-changing sense of God's favor and love and assured salvation? Obviously, one's first surmise is that the old-fashioned ("fundamentalist") Gospel is down the drain and that your only real alternative is one or another version of moralism or amoralism: Jesus as moral example, among others, of humanity at its best or, alternatively, of self-salvation as the possibility of being as human as you can and as you are. The triumph of moralism is salvation as self-achievement. And, paradoxically, it is also the triumph of amoralism, for if there is no final negative judgment to be levied against our lives, then all that are left are the pragmatic sanctions in a world where the right and the good are functions of social, economic, and political power. And this is where we've finally arrived—or many of us, especially the young and the liberated. This is what Hobbes had in mind with his gospel of self-interest (although he would not have approved its actualities); this was the essential proposal of the deists and of Hume; this is the gospel of Voltaire, Marx, Freud, Fromm—and now of the new supernaturalists, since what they are really interested in is not a *theonomous* lifestyle but in what human beings can make of their supernatural powers and how they can apply them to human ends and means. This is what the talk of secularism has been about all these years—this basic rejection, at the root, of the forensic metaphor of divine justice! This is what the "Death of God" hurrah was all about—the denial of God as cosmic *Judge;* and this, as far as I can see, is where the theoretical implications of transactional analysis and other autonomous life views are pointed, even when their first and final presuppositions and implications have not been fully probed or fully stated.

We have spoken of Christianity's instinct for an eager acceptance of all possible secular wisdom and of its stubborn refusal to surrender its own essential convictions and abandon its distinctive mission in the world, of forming the human conscience in accordance with God's self-revelation in Christ and of binding and loosing consciences in accordance with the divine imperatives implied in that revelation. And I have already pointed to the weakness of what I see in the standard brands of contemporary pastoral care: their inclination to turn the movement into an ethical-culture society in which human concerns can be fostered by various forms of suggestive and supportive therapies all rooted in the premises of autonomy. In this they have the implicit sanction of many of the liberal, mainstream churches, where the Gospel is often more moralistic than evangelical. The situation is further complicated, of course, by the visible, powerful resurgence of new versions of the old stereotypes: fundamentalism, authoritarianism, pentecostalism, the Jesus People, the waning vitality of liberalism, the rise and spread of mysticisms of various sorts. The resurgence is stirring both the surface and the depths of the Christian mind and heart, even though it can scarcely be the wave of the future in its present form. But it is worth noticing that, even in these new revivals of the old gospel traditions, the forensic image is now subdominant, and in some of them, it is virtually absent.

This suggests the basic transaction by which the intentional, self-conscious Christian can receive the secular wisdoms of modern autonomy and reject the gospel that these wisdoms have proffered us as truly good news. We can ourselves, with no final loss, abandon the forensic image of divine justice as our basic soteriological metaphor and still reassert the primacy and truth of divine justice as the still-valid norm for human freedom and all the other human aspirations about which we have already spoken. The essence of the Gospel—that God's will is humanity's true joy and happiness—does not require a forensic model or paradigm, not even in the interest of God's sovereignty and of the final inviolability of his righteous rule (the kingdom of God) in the human community. What is crucial is the acknowledgment of God's justice, God's intention that men and women shall live and die in accordance with their actual human potential (divinely created). For people to live and die—forever—without achieving their created potential, and with no such prospect here or hereafter, is unjust; it is the essence of injustice. That this must be construed in juridical terms is not necessary, not now, at least, when forensic metaphors are more misleading than edifying. A gospel for the guilty is a true gospel when men and women are guilt-ridden, and we need not disparage its truth and relevance and power for those in that perspective. But what would be a gospel for the guiltless, for those whose consciences do not condemn them, for those whose self-images are self-righteous and self-excusing?

The place to begin is with the flat-out assertion that the gospel of autonomy is false and delusory—and for a very simple, very profound reason. It would be true if, and only if, humans were without a radical flaw; if, and only if, they were self-perfectible. But this is plainly contrary to every observable fact in human history and in the current human scene. The most obvious human reality we know and can observe is self-stultification and social injustice (in either order or in any of their mixes). Human happiness, at its best, is evanescent and episodic; it is tainted by the overreachings of our innocent outreachings, and it is bracketed and insulted by death and the pitiless natural environment that allows for both our lives and deaths without caring for our personal hopes and fears. There is much talk these days of hope, of futurism, of political transformations; and it all stills my heart and offends my critical reason. It has generated many brands of futuristic theology, of God at work on his project of achieving his divine potential, which makes us partners with him in becoming what we can become. Yet, laid alongside all the evidence of the human flaw and the dismal statistics of human performance (present and prospective), the promises of an autonomous life view are cruelly self-deceiving. If it is the case that the guiltless no longer need a gospel of forensic acquittal, it is also the case that the hopeless do need a gospel that promises something better than an epitaph that reads like Willie Loman in *The Death of a Salesman:* "He dreamed the wrong dreams and never found out who he really was."[1] Worse yet, if we ever find out on our own who we really are and what our prospects are, the tragedy deepens and the threat of final meaninglessness becomes as intimidating as all the old fumes of sulphur and brimstone.

For the human flaw remains. Our condition is still as ironic as it ever was—that the best this world can give is not enough for what we can and must aspire to, and our alternative is to settle for some quasi-human compromise, something less than full and real humanity. Those who feel no guilt are still trapped in blind, uncaring fate unless there's more to life than nature and society can offer us. For what kind of a Gospel is it to talk about human happiness in terms of partial, evanescent, death-bracketed values? This is to underrate (or maybe even never to *know*) what human happiness really is; it is to settle for partial substitutes for our deepest, irrepressible hungers. I may not be guilty of any crime that would deserve a loving God's rejection. But what is there to hope for if my outreaches never come to their final goal (even when they manage to avoid overreachings)? Is life's agony and ecstasy finally worth it all? Who will deliver me from this death of thwarted hopes, or hopes that are bound to be thwarted, even in their partial satisfaction?

Suppose we let the forensic, courtroom metaphor go, and turn, as so many of us have, to the therapeutic, clinical metaphor, what then? This is a decided advance in many ways, and is much to be welcomed and incorporated into our pastoral theory and practice. But there's no avoiding the fact that therapy, in any and all of its images, connotes amelioration, not total fulfillment. Therapy means the reduction of this or that symptom, the curing of this or that malady. It does not, and cannot, mean the determination of our ultimate concerns. It cannot fend off death. Its best good news is never better than a comparative judgment that your existential shortfalls are not so dreadful as they might have been. Beyond the courtroom and the clinic, the human hunger for happiness reaches out toward some sovereign power of caring that is neither a bloodless category nor a wishful dream. The good news we really need to hear is that "God so loved the world that he gave of himself that the world [we] might not perish [in some void of thwarted dreams] but have life, and that in all its human potential." There's nothing forensic here, and it reaches far beyond any sort of clinical autonomy. This is gospel for the guiltless who are nonetheless hopeless (or who would be if they really demanded the fullness of their humanity). The Christian Gospel is the message of God's love in Christ—"the power of God and the wisdom of God.... You are in Christ Jesus by God's act, for God has made him our wisdom; he is our righteousness; in him we are consecrated and set free" (1 Corinthians 1:24–30). Nothing forensic here—but great good news to anyone who knows all the other options. "God was in Christ reconciling the world to himself [which is the exact opposite of the classical substitutionary theory of atonement!].... For our sake [for the sake of our humanity] God made Christ one with us in our sinfulness so that we might be made one with God in his goodness" (2 Corinthians 5:19, 21). Here again, there is no forensic metaphor.

Jesus Christ "is the image (*ikon*) of the invisible God; his is the primacy over all created things. In him everything in heaven and on earth was created, not only things visible but also the invisible orders of thrones, sovereignties, authorities, and powers: the whole universe has been created through him and for him. And he exists before everything, and all things are held together in him. He is, moreover, the head of the body, the church. He is its origin, the first to return from the dead, to be in all things alone supreme. For in him the complete being of God, by God's own choice, came to dwell. Through him God chose to reconcile the whole universe to himself, making peace through the shedding of his blood upon the cross—to reconcile all things, whether on earth or in heaven, through him alone" (Colossians 1:15–20). This is gospel for the guiltless who are nonetheless aware of their radical need of grace and love and peace. "Even here and now, beloved, we are God's children. What we shall be has not yet been disclosed, but we know that when it is [disclosed] we shall be like him" (1 John 3:2). All of these are great gospel promises and they all point to the mystery of salvation beyond the heavenly courtroom or clinic and focus on a *theonomous* transaction of reconciliation that, on its human side, calls for two basic responses: repentance and faith. And the crucial agent in the transaction is Jesus Christ, without whose revealing and redeeming love, we could never grasp that level of meaning and value that transvaluates all of life.

We have already written out a valid prescription for the fullness of our human existence: intelligence normed by truth, freedom normed by justice, self-consciousness normed by God's true knowledge of us, joy normed by grace, love normed by community. My concern now is to stress that none of these norms can be self-chosen and self-applied. Human outreach does not discipline itself. This is the work of grace, which is to say, of God's love in action and on the human will and intentions. Human life must be lived in and by grace or else it will be lived gracelessly and death will find us, literally, hopeless. For all the elations of our autonomy, life outside grace is also life in which our overreaches are finally thwarted by divine justice, our best laid schemes fallen awry. Autonomous humanity is foredoomed to restless, hopeful, hollow triumphs—to all the paradoxes of aspirations forever skewed, victories that leave us victimized. The Gospel is the promise that we can live intentionally, following the inner leadings of the Holy Spirit, accepting what we are given to know of God's will—working, suffering, and hoping in the climate of grace, the atmosphere of love, which also and always means the forgiveness of our sins by the same love that thwarts their ever coming to success. And Jesus Christ is the guarantor and agent of this promise, not only in his revelation of God's love but also in his sharing in our human lot and opening out a way for us to share in his power and wisdom. His power is his victory over the power of sin and death. His wisdom is that God is all in all, and we can become all we can ever be only in *him.*

The Christian Gospel for the guiltless is not that Jesus Christ has appeased the Father's wrath but that he is, "for us men and for our salvation," the revealer, agent and living proof of the Father's unmerited and yet also unfaltering compassion. This is not to reject, or even diminish, the living truth in the grand articles of justification, pardon, regeneration, reconciliation. It is only to stress, more than the tradition has usually done, the fact that our Christian hope rests in God's calling us to participate in his goodness that is the first and final ground of our true happiness—to participate not only in the human potential but in the divine actuality. The human potential is for happiness (not peak experience but settled and uplifted joy). The divine actuality is holy love, accepting and calling even such overreaches as we are. Happiness and holiness are correlates and Jesus Christ is their bond: happiness that is the fruit of our love of God; holiness that is our love of God and neighbor. We love God for his goodness and our neighbor out of gratitude to God.

The formula for such a Gospel, for conversion from the self-stultifying life to the life of grace in the Spirit, is the same old one: repentance and faith. "Repent and believe the gospel," the good news that God is indeed the giver of life's meanings and joys and hopes, that life in his love is ultimately secure and can even now be serene, since its final meanings reach beyond life and death.

What is *repentance*? The best answer is the literal one: *metanoia,* a genuine, basic change of *nous,* i.e., our inner self-awareness, our inner intentions. What do you know about yourself really? And what are your real intentions? Are they self-interested, self-centered, self-righteous? To know the bleak, honest truth about your self-deceptions (your sinful *nous*) and to intend an honest change to something more authentic, this is *meta-noia,* repentance. Its stimulus and impulse is God's prevenient grace, the inner call and leadings of his Holy Spirit in your heart. And the fruits of repentance are new levels of self-understanding, which is to say, humility and self-acceptance. This is not a good work; it gains you no saving merit, no soteriological brownie points. But it does bring you into a lifesaving truth about yourself and this is the threshold of new truth about God and God's intentions for your human potential.

And what is faith? Neither orthodox doctrine nor submission to external authority of any sort. Rather, it is the twin awareness of God's reality as the Encompassing Mystery in which we live and move and love, and of a willing, radical trust in God's upholding power and unfaltering care. It is the willingness to be upheld in God's love and to be uplifted by it to our potential. Faith is our awareness that our existence is from, in, and to God and our being glad to have it so. Faith is the human acceptance of *theo-nomy,* and anything less or other is faithless.

Notice that we've been talking all this while with no reference to the old forensic images, and that we have been consciously including the best intentions and achievements of all authentic therapy (within its limits). But this *is* the good news:

"God is on our side" (Romans 8:31). Then what can separate us from the love of Christ, save unfaith or self-righteousness?

> Can persecution, hunger, nakedness, peril, or the sword? "We are being done to death for thy sake all day long," as Scripture says; "We have been treated like sheep for slaughter"—yet, in spite of all, overwhelming victory is ours through him who loved us. For I am convinced that there is nothing in death or life, in the realm of spirits or superhuman powers, in the world as it is or the world as it shall be, in the forces of the universe, in heights or depths—nothing in all creation that can separate us from the love of God in Christ Jesus our Lord. (Romans 8:35–39)

Nothing that I know about any and all the contributions of psychotherapy to deliverance from our unhealthful guilt complexes and self-defeats cancels or even limits this *theonomous* view of the human potential and its achievement, in Christ and in the body of Christ. In these terms the Christian gospel is still alive and well and was never more desperately needed by guiltless people, those whose very guiltlessness has added to their final desperation.

CHAPTER
18

The Pastor and the Hallowing of Life: The Sacral Community

Thus far in this course we have been concerned with (1) a historical perspective on the changing images of "The Good Shepherd," (2) a revised "diagnosis" of the human flaw and of the prospects of any and all the versions of human autonomy that have been suggested, and (3) a summary revision of the Christian Gospel—now for the guiltless generation emerging, guiltless because of the fading of the forensic metaphors that guided the older traditions. We have spoken of the values of the newer therapeutic images of human self-understanding and also of their final inadequacies. The gist of the Gospel is still grace, the grace of our Lord Jesus Christ. But the "salvation" offered by that grace is not now so much from the fear of God's avenging wrath as a positive recognition of human beings' essential hopelessness: not plea bargaining but the hope of a meaningful existence. Modern men and women may not feel guilty any longer (and if they do, it's usually for a wrong reason) but they still feel anxious, and well they might, for doom is writ large in the banalities of ordinary, "successful" living, the futilities of virtue, the overreachings of pride and lusts, the betrayals and disloyalties of all earthly trusts, and the inexorable sentence of tragedy and death passed by the nature they have come to worship.

Given (1) this historical perspective, and the creditable (if also spotty) track record of Christian shepherding in times past, (2) a diagnosis that denies autonomy as a prescription for human happiness, and (3) a reformulated gospel that speaks to human anxieties if not to guilt—what then? Where do we go on from there? Well, obviously, we go on to a delineation of the Christian life, to an attempted prescription for meaningful, joyful living in and through the grace of God in Christ that a pastor can believe and communicate, and in terms of which he and she can get on with the essential tasks of (1) ameliorating human needs, whatever they are with whatever resources the pastor has, or can muster; (2) being a person for others (any others and not a select few); (3) serving as a representative of faith and a conduit of love; (4) joyfully sharing the ministry of grace; (5) sustaining the roles of both participant observer and involved participant. Good pastors are those most likely to be "there" in times and circumstances of human crisis, not only the one to whom others may go (as they can, in principle, to other professional helpers), but one who goes to others in some appropriate way and to whom others turn because of pastoral initiatives and significant presence.

I would be deceiving myself, and you, if I pretended to have a set of recipes for all this: either a rounded-off theoretical analysis of the Christian life and ethos or a budget of how-to-do-it techniques (success stories) guaranteed to turn mediocre ecclesiastical functionaries into bluebirds of gospel happiness. As a matter of fact, if candor is of any help in such matters, I've already run out the string of my fairly confident expertise. These last four lectures are, therefore, ventures past my own fields of history and theology, and they will, perforce, have to be experimental in an almost amateur sense. There's no alternative, for me, to this effort to talk theology-ethics-and-practice in problem areas where I've more opinions, convictions, dreams than confirmed practical experience. This is actually the case with all theological education that isn't already obsolescent in its own time. For if I'm even half right in my thesis that the moral and theological climate is changing on us beyond easy recognition, then it will be perennial principles that will survive and not even good current practice. Indeed, it is fairly clear to me and other observers that most current practice in pastoral care and pastoral direction is already outdated.

Let us begin with the reiteration of our basic problem, viz., that secularism is now the dominant mindset of modern man, that the modern world has been almost totally desacralized, and that the insatiable human hungers for happiness have been bracketed within the limits of this *saeculum,* the human potential, and human responsibility for human destiny. Yet autonomous man is still unhappy, discontented, and at least as anxious about his human future as he used to be when he was also guilty of classical distortions of the human past. The phenomena of victimization and self-righteousness (the hallmarks of true modernity) are still with us, and no longer correlated with any of the older patterns of oppression. The liberated amongst us are not visibly happier than the rest of us, and their self-righteousness is, if anything, more oppressive.

This brings us to another basic premise in any new and newly relevant pastoral theology. The *humanum* is, and always has been, a *eudaemonistic* creature. Humans have an inbuilt tropism for happiness, and the highest good they can perceive and recognize is the most powerful incentive in every moral decision. They cannot choose to be unhappy, as a conscious choice between two live options: happiness and unhappiness. They do not ever choose the evil because it is evil, but only because it is the lesser of two evils or an indirect means to some greater good (or some more immediate good that seems attractive at the time). Freud's *Lust-Unlust Prinzip* goes deeper than even he realized, and reaches out much further into the mysteries of divine being and human being. He saw it focused in its biological substratum—the tumescence and detumescence of genital tissues, physical pleasure and pain, satiation, depletion, repletion, etc. This much is so in a thousand different correlations (including psychopathological ones where the inflicting of pain is a pleasure, or the suffering of it). But the hunger for pleasure in the human reaches out beyond concupiscence to the paradox of self-denial and self-sacrifice on terms that are not instinctual or reflex. All the unique human virtues are more profoundly eudaemonistic than deontological. "Duty," without some happiness involved in its doing, becomes "grim duty" or routinized duty or resented duty. The "ought" without joy leads to frustration, discontent, unhappiness.

There was, and still is, a close and essential correlation between the forensic images of justice and the ethics of "ought," and duty. The law can be defined as duty—as what the law-abiding citizen ought to do—and violations of any legitimate law or betrayals of any legitimate lawmaker could be defined as a threat to the moral fabric and equilibrium of society. The force of taboo and of customary morality lay in its interiorization, the inner conviction of the ought, the right, one's duty. Two things moved Immanuel Kant to awe: "the starry heavens above and the moral law within." What does one do when the starry heavens are obscured by man-made smog and the moral law within is analyzed into man-made values that you've taken in, or been taken in by?

It is hard to realize how modern and how superficial that bromide is that "you can't legislate morality." Of course you can legislate morality (the Code of Hammurabi is proof of it before the Pentateuch) when the lawgiver(s) are acknowledged to be just (or legitimate) and when there is a social consensus as to right and wrong. But if law is a human construct and morality is a human convention, then of course you can't legislate morality, and law enforcement is felt to be unjust (i.e., discriminatory) by its victims. And it is to this that we have come or are coming. This is why the "Puritan work ethic" is scorned by its parasites; this is why so many of us are in contempt of court (not just this court or that but of the legal process in general), why politicians doing each other in awaken our gladiatorial emotions that have little to do with justice or the public good, why the policeman's lot is not a happy one. But humans still seek to be happy; they are bound to and by the deepest urgings of their nature and the highest leadings of the Spirit. The Beatitudes sound visionary to most of us, but they touch one of the deepest chords in our human being: the hunger for blessedness, happiness—*makarios*!

Still, humans are unhappy, unblessed. Their curiosity and intelligence take them pretty far but not far enough. Our freedoms, old and new, are exhilarating and frustrating. Our joys are often real and memorable, but they come and go, in an existential medium that is often profoundly joyless. Our loves are often noble yet so far short of a just, peaceable human community that we can never be more than ambivalently happy, even as we mumble something about the Lord making us "mindful of the needs of others." For there is something that vetoes our human quests for happiness when they are sought or grasped on the wrong terms, when they are primarily self-interested or predatory or inappropriate. For there *are* happy people in the world (not "perfectly" happy, not "constantly" happy but basically and essentially happy) in and through its turmoils and tragedies, in and through their own trials and tribulations. Not many, maybe (percentage-wise), but enough to establish the possibility as a fact: This hunger for happiness is not a species psychosis. And the correlations between happiness and any of the other human aspirations (intelligence, freedom, self-consciousness, joy, love) are not very high. Bright people may be unhappy, and liberated ones and highly self-conscious initiates and joyful eager lovers, too—all finally unhappy and deeply discontented. And happiness is not merely subjective, either; it is not the absence of pain.

The real correlations with happiness (or vice versa) are with the norms of our distinctive human outreaches: with truth, justice, fidelity, generosity, community. In short, to fall back into confusing and offensive rhetoric, happiness is linked with holiness. Only the holy are happy, and those truly holy are happy as a divinely ordained consequence. And this is one of the oldest traditions in Christian ethics—and one of the best. But before you groan and tune out, stop a moment longer to ask what "holiness" means. And the answer is astonishingly simple yet astonishingly relevant to anyone looking for an alternative to the forensic images of salvation, faith, and good works. Holiness is twofold: inward and outward. Inward holiness is our love of God above all else and of all else in God. Outward holiness is our love of our neighbor (i.e., every other *humanum* to whom we have any access). And these two together make for happiness, happiness that is real, that lasts, against which the gates of death and hell will not prevail.

Thus it is that the agenda of the Christian life is not how to be happy though human but how to be happy by becoming holy. For what shall it profit a man if he lose his sense of guilt and still feel hopeless? What is the profit in liberation if it curves back upon itself in frustration, resentment, and unhappiness? Why turn away from the fleshpots of technology only to fall into ecstasies that wind down into disenchantments? What is the final good of all these futuristic hopes with which we console ourselves if the brackets of our existence are themselves random and meaningless? The single valid plot in the theater of the absurd is the undeclinable human pilgrimage in quest of unattainable human happiness.

We have already mentioned that anxiety generates magical thinking. To this, I would add that it also generates scapegoating and judgmental thinking. Anxiety makes children fall into tantrums or despair; it also stirs parents into solemn imitations of Jahveh: "I told you so"; "How stupid, wicked, or unlucky can you be?" Imagining a game-free life is itself a game. It may be the first game we learn to play and the last one we give up. The pastor's main concern in a world where anxiety levels don't go down much (or else rearrange themselves in new mixes) is to get clear and keep clear the radical distinction between worship as magical thinking and worship as participation in the holy, between the human potential as a possession, and the human potential as a gift and a promise, under the conditions of one's human responses to the Encompassing Mystery, the Mystery that is beyond our manipulation, the Mystery that is loving, gracious, deeply involved in the human enterprise and its agonies.

The seedbed of all religion is the idea and the sense of the holy: *numen, mana,* the gods, God, *die Umgreifende.* There is a quarrel whether human anxieties generated the idea of the numinous, (which would have been an impressive feat of a half-simian imagination, or whether what turned a simian into a human was the discovery of the *numen tremendum, fascinans, agitans,* etc. But that the sense of the holy is aboriginal, universal, and profound is undeniable. This sense of the numinous and its linkage with dreams points toward the taproot of religion: animism. Yet the great watershed in religion has always been the line that divides off worship as magic (however sophisticated and subtle) from worship as participation: celebration and incorporation into the divine life on terms stipulated and provided by the divine, not by our selfish interests or our rites and spells. And it is just this sense of the holy that needs most to be recovered in our time. We need a new agenda for the resacralization of life, not as sorcery (as in the new supernaturalisms) but as a whole new mindset and heart orientation toward that true holiness that makes for true happiness: the *humanum* as holy, human life as hallowed and to be hallowed—all over and throughout.

To speak of the hallowing of life as the chief agendum of the Christian life, personal and social, is certain to awaken all sorts of ghosts in our minds that you may have thought were safely laid to rest: "pie in the sky, by and by," "otherworldliness," acquiescence in present miseries and injustice in hopes of a final rectification on the "Great Gittin' Up Morning," etc. This is the sort of religion that is the opiate of the people—and the placebo of the neurotic. Why have we fought and won the battles of secularization, of demythologizing, of autonomy if we are now to be told that our salvation and happiness depend on something as pious-sounding and otherworldly as sacralization and the hallowing of life? Part of my answer is already on the record: The vaunted boasts of secularization and of demythologizing are clearly and vastly overrated and, in fact, delusory. If our human hopes are bracketed by this *saeculum,* we are foredoomed to unhappiness, for happiness is the fruit of human satisfactions of our human outreaches, and these are never full nor final within the *saeculum.* Only if our existence is given meanings that are valid within and beyond the *saeculum* can it ever be claimed, in death's retrospect, to have been truly meaningful or happy. Autonomy is not a guarantee of happiness, and not even a valid precondition of it.

Another part of our answer, though, might lie in a fresh and more adequate understanding of what "hallow" and "hallowing" really mean, what the sacralizing of life would actually amount to. Let's start with a familiar blind spot: Hallowe'en. In our flat and washed-out imagination, we've forgotten what a moving and disturbing myth there was that on the Eve of All Hallows, the souls of the departed were turned out of heaven and hell, on parole, for a revisiting of the earth and the revivification of the ties between the quick and the dead. And then came All Hallows itself, the renewal of our awareness of the human community in time as well as space. There are churches named All Hallows and churches named All Souls, and there are those of us who haven't realized that these are exact synonyms, or that the Church of Humanity would not be a misleading paraphrase. For purge the myth of its literalism and of its brazen dualism (spooks and ghosties and things that go bump in the night), and the essence of "hallow" and "hallowing" is simply the recognition of the human in its transcendental outreach, in its spiritual upreach, in its participation in the divine (and vice versa).

The hallowing of life is another way of calling for its rescue from a single, linear, materialistic vision of it. It is the enterprise of transvaluing all of life in terms of our awareness that all of it is holy, sacred, suffused with transempirical, metahistorical, supernatural dimensions, dynamism; that there *is* more in heaven and earth than Horatio's flat empiricism ever dreamed of. The hallowing of life is the perception of it as more deeply spiritual than we had thought; it is the ensouling of life and society; it is the recognition that human meanings and values focus in human persons and that human persons are sacred. And what does "sacred" mean? It means something quite ordinary that has been given special worth (*dignitas*) and meaning and conferred status by God's approval of it, by God's designation of it as of value to him. This is what it means to recognize and value human life as an end in itself and not ever as a means only, and this is the only ground on which justice is ever done to the weak by the strong. Only the hallowed life has any immunity from predation; only the hallowing of life is the full intent and meaning of love.

I would, therefore, suggest that the pastor's task may be defined, at least one way, by this agendum of the hallowing of life, for this is really what it will take to humanize life, at its highest and best, and to secure it against the ravages of time, meaninglessness, the lapse into the subhuman. Salvation is the transformation of life's values—our faith and hope and love— from ourselves to God, the acceptance of our worth as a gift (and sacred because it is God's gift), the awareness of the holy in all others as well as in ourselves, the joy and happiness that comes from an assurance of God's love in a hallowed world whose interface with the infinite is a function of hallowed and hallowing lives (humanized and humanizing lives at their highest and best). This is the way to stop the world, to gain real power, to find the peace and joy that the unhallowed world cannot give and cannot take away. This is not a new supernaturalism, and not the "Old Gnosis" either. And I do not believe in ghosts or witchcraft or satanism.

My concern is for our blinded eyes to be open to the *numen tremendum* (moving, disturbing, exciting, awe-full). I'm concerned for the loss of reverence and awe, for a recovery of the holy as dread-full and yet also comforting, reassuring, sustaining. We know how our primal anxieties persist and proliferate in life: the dread of falling, the dread of constriction, the dread of loud noises, the dread of neglect and rejection. Anxiety is the primal font of all sorts of defense mechanisms, of all sorts of games and of neurotic deviations out of happiness. And anxiety can never be eliminated or anesthetized, save at our peril. But there are constructive uses of anxiety—healthful reminders of our finitude, healthful motivations to avoid unnecessary pain and to accept all gains and advantages with gratitude, stimuli to compassion and to deeper fellow-feeling. But all this requires a hallowed life as context. In an unhallowed life self-interest is bound to be the highest value: enlightened self-interest, of course—just as the Nazarenes speak of "sanctified pride."

The tragedy of anxiety comes when and because it threatens life's meanings, values, and happiness. When I'm anxious and foreboding, when all reasonable prognoses indicate disaster or the probability of some grave shortfall, when I'm stricken with grief or loss or pain and a grim prognosis—how can I then be happy? Lightheartedness will help, if the trouble is minor; and Stoic fortitude if it's worse. But neither of these is real happiness, and there is a profound difference between lightheartedness and high-heartedness. Happiness is a function of meaningful life and *that* is a function of a hallowed life (life of the human spirit in and through the Holy Spirit, a grace-full life in and through the grace of our Lord Jesus Christ). The happy life is possible only in an existence hallowed, secured, and conserved by the God of All Hallows, All Souls, of all the human creatures that seek their full humanity in his love and providence. If life is sacred, then it can be hallowed—and happy, in and from and by God.

But there is no meaningful nor happy life apart from a hallowed and hallowing community, from communities of shared reverences, shared enthusiasms, shared celebrations, shared joys and sorrows, shared sacraments—outward and visible signs of the holy (inward, invisible but far more real than anything else we know). In this sacral community, the pastor is chief celebrant, not because the pastor has the most to celebrate for himself and herself, but because the pastor is the representative in any given local community of the universal community of the

Holy People of God. This is the meaning of ordination: the church's authorization of certain persons to act representatively for the whole sacral community. In this sacral community the good pastor is therapist: the symbol and agent of liberation from all the stultifications of joy, and the agent of all sorts of ameliorations of all sorts of human unhappiness.

The church is the hallowed and hallowing community, the community of grace, the family of humankind, the People of God, the Mystical Body of Christ. In its sacral and sacralizing fellowship, people may be redeemed from banality and routine (dehumanization) and "saved" for both the tasks of living and dying, in joy and hope and happiness. "Come, ye blessed of my Father [you happy ones]; inherit the kingdom prepared for you." And this begins here and now, and has already begun for all the really happy and faithful souls (my own life within the church of All Hallows, that is). Since the holy life has no threat of cancellation by transience and time, it can be (and *is*) happy, in the only final sense of happiness.

The hallowing of life is our recipe for happiness in life and death; it is the process by which life is transformed from its chief concern for human self-attainment within the death-bounded brackets of the *saeculum.* It is the opening out of life's frontiers to those real ecstasies that come in those high moments of joy and inspiration that show up psychedelic trips for the transient episodes they are. And it is the basis for all we can ever learn of the art of holy dying and the intense ethical commitment that goes with it.

CHAPTER
19

The Pastor and the Hallowing of Life: The Good Pastor and Life's Occasions

The theme of these last four stanzas in my Ballad of the Good Pastor is that meaning in human life comes from its significance—what it signifies or what is signified by it—and that the primal and ultimate significance in life is in its radiance of the holy. Meaning is focused on the holy: the aura of a beautiful sight, the thrill of an illuminating insight, the heart-catching seriousness of another's tears, grief or agony, a sunburst of joy, the glory of God in another human face. Meaning is awareness, discernment, involvement; and this always comes from beyond or above or "out there," even when it is registered deep within. Meaning comes with our awareness of something interesting outside ourselves, even if we are ever so intimately related to it. It means attention to something interesting besides ourselves, or of ourselves as involved in something interesting outside ourselves. Even the act of self-awareness, when truly meaningful, is a sort of extroversion, a recognition of ourselves as significant (i.e., as a sign-event of something more to which we are vitally related). Narcissism is finally meaningless and boring; selfishness is narcissism in action—and just as meaningless in the end.

Meaning is, therefore, awareness of and attention to the holy, to the holy as the sign-event of human self-transcendence and to God as the ground and end of our true human identity, the source and consummator of our fully human potential. And this means that the hallowing of life is more than pious thoughts, more than religious observance. It means, literally, the intentional relating of life to the holy, the encompassing Mystery in which we live and move and have our being. And every intentional response to this relationship, every conscious acting out of our awareness of the holy, is an act of hallowing and of being hallowed, of humanizing and being humanized, of participation in the divine and in the joys and sorrows of the happy life. It is the essence of the pastoral task to understand this enterprise of the hallowing of life and to be endlessly resourceful in leading one's people into some comparable understanding appropriate for them.

In any such understanding, the crucial distinction is between routine, on the one hand, and occasions, on the other—between *chronos* and *kairos,* between time as flow and time as event. The vast bulk of our human existence and our experience of it is routine, is flow (directly from the future into the past, without pause), the daily round, the domain of the habitual. Days on end go by without "occasions," without any sign-event. Passing time gets piled high with drudgery or gets emptied into the sinkhole of boredom. Even so, routine itself may be a sign-event of sorts, and it does have positive, human uses. Routine is our enmeshment with nature, in the orderly processes of the determined and determinate. Heartbeat is routine; so are respiration and metabolism, and we are truly grateful for their steadiness, especially in retrospect when they've fallen out of whack. Diurnal cycles are routine, and all our seasonal rhythms; and so are schedules and timetables. Routine is the domain of cause-and-effect, of linearity, of statistics and predictability of rule making, rule keeping, of habits, of inertia and momentum. And over it all presides the clock (the sign-event of time's flow) and the schedule (the sign-event of our partial freedom). Chronicity is another word for finitude, yet another reminder of the brackets within which all life's meanings are cast or canceled.

The ways in which we cope, or fail to cope, with routine is an accurate measure of our mental health and, even more importantly, of the quality of our lives and their meanings and values. For routine can be hobbling; it can be boring, frustrating, intolerable. But this is almost exactly what we mean by "meaningless." We speak of "killing time" when what we really mean, of course, is killing life. "Time on our hands" is life "on our hands": either to be hallowed or to let pass through us as through a dispirited conduit. Routine is the equivalent, in human experience, of mechanism in the natural or technological order, and it has the same valence, i.e., it is good or bad according to its output, values, and final end.

Which means that if routine can be meaningless, it can also be meaningful. It can be, in fact, liberating, just as creative idleness can be. I'm deeply grateful to my reflex neural system when it goes about its business and doesn't bother me in the process. I'm grateful for what few steady habits that I've acquired or managed to hold onto; for meetings that begin and end on time; for traffic lights in synchronization; for machines that hum and people I can count on; and for all the useful things that get done in the world when I'm not there and without my having to worry about them. There is such a thing as meaningful idleness—like lying on the grass of a Saturday (after it has been cut!) and watching the clouds and sky and the birds; like chitchat with friends, like sleep and dreams. There's even creative idleness—like listening to a Beethoven string quartet or to Ariel Ramirez' *Creole Mass*.

An "occasion" is an event in time but it really is out of clocktime. It is a "moment" in the NOW, an episode of self-awareness that can't be caught on a stopwatch. While it lasts, an "occasion" is an experience when time no longer flows through us. It is a moment when the "world" (in Don Juan's phrase) is "stopped" by the experience itself and in our awareness of it. Occasions are extensions and expansions of consciousness; they are elating or depressing. They evoke memories (glad or sad, but significant either way), and they leave memories. Above all, they are reminders of life's outreachings, upreachings, inreachings—of our human aspirations (intelligence, self-awareness, joy, love), of our humanness. A great occasion is a time of discovery, of self and other selves, a time of challenge, of "rising to the occasion" or of blowing it. Occasions are creative and humanizing when managed well; they are temptations to self-deception or self-excusing and rationalizations. An occasion is a *kairos,* a fullness of time, an intensification of our humanity, a passing glimpse of "what it's all about."

This is why it is so tragic for occasions (or what might be occasions) to go unrecognized, to pass without our noticing or responding to them. No one can say how much boredom in the world comes from our blindness to all the potential occasions that come our way, but it must be immense. When "Wow" becomes "Ho-hum," your capital stock of meaning is reduced by just so much. But, by the same token, it is equally tragic for occasions to be routinized and stylized, to have the spontaneity and interest squeezed out of them and so have their meanings impoverished. This is how worship is so easily flattened out, occasions turned into routines. This is also the danger of ritual, of routinizing occasions and still pretending that they are real occasions!

All the great personal occasions of life—birth, birthdays, holidays, parties, marriage, trips (actual or in the mind), sudden turns of life's direction, grave illness, death; or great social occasions (catastrophes, war, sky-lab, Superbowl, etc.)—all these are climaxes or crises. A climax is the culmination of a process that decides what it's really all about, what it adds up to, whether it's been worthwhile or meaningful. A crisis is a parting of the ways, a moment after which nothing can ever again be quite like it was before. Climaxes and crises are disruptions of routine, and transvaluations, as well. Even more, they are little windows into Mystery, shutter-snapping glimpses of what really is beyond grasping or reporting. They are actual experiences of our conscious participations in the holy—fleeting, of course, but supremely important all the same. For occasions, whether stately or seasonal, expected or unexpected, planned or surprising, are given and they are sacral sign-events: outward and visible signs of God's inward and invisible grace. Whenever we ignore them or misread their signs, life is diminished. The sign of the holy is always that sense of "beyondness" or "withinness" that betokens mystery, that fascinates and solemnizes and warns us away from grasping or snatching or trying to manipulate, that invites us to understand and enjoy or to be comforted and sustained, "amidst the encircling gloom."

This applies to the positive occasions of life and to the negative ones as well. One of the good pastor's most important priestly functions is the improvement of his and her gifts of discernment of true occasions and of his and her understanding of their signification, positive or negative. "This is an occasion; let's celebrate it," or "This is serious; let's think it through" are appropriate reactions to a *kairos,* and blessed is the one who can tell which is which (in his own life or in the lives of others) and react in tune with empathy. This is where the difference between the truly grace-full pastor and the well-intentioned bungler shows up most clearly.

Some of us have inventories of positive occasions, and a good pastor had better have a whole calendar of them. The birth of a baby is old hat to an obstetrician; it is an occasion of profound meaning to the active participants, with meanings at several levels and various significations. It's a climax and a crisis, and it matters a great deal (then and thereafter) how many of its meanings are hallowed and for whom. It's an utterly natural thing and yet genuinely holy. Many lives can be enhanced, and more than one life can be decisively hallowed and humanized if the occasion is prepared for, experienced, and then celebrated in and with a due and proper sense of the holy. The quality of love bestowed on a human infant and experienced by it leaves an indelible mark on the emergent self and its later potentials for growth and maturation: One loves as one has been loved. Unhallowed lives pass on the plague of original sin far more directly than any such thing as seminal transmission. This, of course, is the meaning of infant baptism, which is meant to be a formal, public hallowing of new life and of its new home and family by the church as a family of families. But this sacrament all too often amounts to a liturgical cop-out—as if it could take the place of, instead of symbolize and sacralize—an occasion that the church (and the good pastor) has had a crucial stake in all along, before and after.

This principle that all occasions are made for hallowing (and for eucharistizing) could be spelled out in endless detail. Sundays are occasions and when they are not hallowed, the whole week flattens out (as whenever any long stretch of time goes uncelebrated in the Spirit). Birthdays are occasions, "Thanksgiving" is an occasion, and Christmas, and the turnings of the seasons, and all significant endings and fresh beginnings. Falling in love, getting a new job or a merited raise, finishing a book or term paper, getting an award, an engagement and a marriage, a sudden focusing of confused ideas into an illuminating insight, graduation, a peak experience, a ringside seat at a great historical event (or maybe even a part in the cast of characters). This list could go on and on and would vary with each individual. But what is common to them all is the impulse to celebrate them and the opportunity to sacralize them, i.e., to glimpse the full scope of their human signification, all the way back to their origins in mystery and all the way on down the road toward the final retrospect. This is the essence of the Holy Eucharist, our thanksgivings for that Self-Given Holy in our midst and in our hearts.

Occasions and their celebrations are inherently communal and inherently sacral (oriented toward the holy). The positive ones are not only happy times; they are clues as to what makes for happiness, joy, and lasting significance. This is why they call for pastoral and sacramental ministrations—not to dampen the joy and elation of the event, but to relate the occasion to the encompassing holy—not so much by solemn palaver about the encompassing holy as by representative presence and representative actions that are grace-filled, gracious, affirmative, and illuminating. For pastors who help to celebrate an occasion are not there on their own, and not just with their own wit and wisdom. First and last, they are there as the representatives of the sacral community. The meaning of pastoral presence is not merely to do the right things gracefully at the right time and not just to say the proper things in the proper way, but to convey the love and concern and blessings of a loving, concerned, and blessed community. This also means—and sometimes this is the hardest part— that pastors have already done their job (or are doing it) in bringing the congregation to the point where it is itself blessed and a source of blessing. Good pastors, then, are wholehearted and graceful celebrants whose frequent and repeated celebrations never sag into bare routine. They are effectively "present" because they really understand how meaning comes to life, how it is tested and tempered in life's crucible, how it is sustained in joy and sorrow and in the face of death. They rejoice with those who rejoice because they love life (and trust in the love that sustains it), and they weep with those who weep because, again, they love life and mourn its loss, its diminution, and its tragedy even as they continue to trust in a love divine that is stronger than suffering and death.

It goes without saying that life has its full measure of negative occasions (sometimes more than we can bear, it seems). These, too, are times when routine is upset—sometimes shattered—as by accidents, grave illness, traumatic loss, sudden reversals of fortune, the expected but all too sudden sign-events of age and relegation—all related to the finalities of dying and death, grief and mourning. These things happen, to us and those we love and those we ought to love, and they, too, are apertures on mystery: on that grim mystery of evil, those negations of the joy and happiness that all of us would prefer as a steady diet. These negative occasions are reminders of our finitude, our sin. They are sign-events of those surd factors of mischance and bad luck in life that wreak havoc with the stabilities of our routines. There is some evidence that the so-called accident-prone people in the world have somehow come to prefer accidents to boredom and ennui; in their disordered way, they provide more excitement and attention than routine ever does. But, above all, a negative occasion is dangerous, because it is anxiety-producing and therefore generative of magical thinking and self-centered preoccupations. It is a temptation to unfaith and self-pity, to a surrender to the powers of sin and death, i.e., their power to persuade us that evil has the upper hand and the last laugh. In this way, they are invitations to the corrosions of bitterness, rancor, or despair. A negative occasion always involves a loss—losing a job, losing a love, losing face, money, time, or vital powers, and, finally, one's own self-control and consciousness. This is why they must be preeminent concerns of the good pastor and the crucial test cases of how far life's sorrows may be hallowed. For the Christian message is not only about holiness and happiness, but also about God's grace in and with our travails, sorrows, and the fear of death.

For some, such times of stress and trauma are moments of a discovery, when we test how deep and strong our faith is or may become in the deathless grace of God. For negative occasions can be hallowed, and as they are, our confidence in life's final meaning is deepened and undergirded. For every such occasion literally cries aloud for presence and intelligent understanding from others. Sorrow borne alone is unbearable. And if the pastor is, literally, a man for others (the effective representative of a truly sacral community) he can be of unmeasured service to the unhappy, to the distressed, the upset, the downcast, the discouraged, the sorrowful, the fearful. The pastor is one who is there, in a representative, upholding, helping role—and who will be there when the crisis is past but its wounds not yet healed—as a graceful witness to grace with genuine sympathy in the midst of anguish and real serenity in the face of death. If heartbreak and illness and death can be hallowed—in principle and in hope—then the Christian case is made, viz., that all of life is hallowed, human, sacred, participant in the divine mystery of grace, and therefore not finally bounded by its brackets of time and space, birth and death. This is why we need to know more than we do about the psychopathology of heartbreak, and illness and dying and grieving; for these are universal and inescapable and call for insights and convictions that link us with God's providence and care at a deeper level than emotional and social adjustments or readjustments can ever do.

Illness, of course, is an insult to the body but, more and worse, it is an insult to the *humanum* and its *dignitas*. It is regressive—to a state of dependence on others (whose own schedules and agenda are also disrupted and whose care may be marginal or perfunctory—or, alternatively, smothering and spoiling). People react differently to pain—with different thresholds and tolerances to different kinds of pain—but all with anxiety and self-pity. The literal meaning of anxiety (*angustia*) is a narrowing of the way ahead, a throttling of one's options (of freedom and self-determination). Illness is both an experience of this and a sign-event of the tenuous hold we have on our health and strength and self-sufficiency. Illness is, literally, undignified; it reinforces the dread of desolation and abandonment that we all bear with us in our psyches. Illness is, moreover, a temptation to resentment or to self-indulgence. We know people who try to deny the plain facts of their situation, or who complain of it or want it whisked away by some medical wonderworker (which is one reason doctors nowadays are regarded as priests once were: as shamans and sorcerers). On the other end of the spectrum are those people who "enjoy poor health," who wallow in sympathy and attention. In either case, the ego is working overtime and one's interests are turned inward instead of being drawn and pointed outward.

But illness can be hallowed, and always by the same prescription: "This, too, is of grace," and therefore may be managed with some measure of style, which has been defined as "grace under pressure." And we can be helped to this by gracious, graceful people, among whom the good pastor ought always to be included somehow (if only in spirit and by intention). Pain and loss are not to be sought or welcomed, but their sacral import ought not ever be ignored or denied, for it is often in our weakness that we discover the source of our real strength; it is often in our despair that we are reminded where our real hopes are focused.

Pastoral ministry to the ill is an art of infinite delicacy, of one-to-one compassion. For illness is not an entity and, besides, it is the personal meaning of illness rather than its symptoms with which the pastor is primarily concerned. The doctor's business is to ameliorate symptoms, restore organic and emotional equipoise, and prolong life. For most of us nowadays that is what we mean by health. The pastor's business is to support and reinforce all that rational therapy can do, but also to add a dimension of concern that the doctor, as such, does not, the concern of the sacral community. Obviously, good doctors are also good pastors, and it is their personal interest and love that often is as curative as what else they do. But the pastor is "there" to communicate his own love and God's and to hallow the sickroom by an incarnation of concern, which is, of course, an intelligent mix of interest and love. Here, the excesses to be avoided are overdone solicitude, fake assurance, and intrusive piety. When Mrs. Outler was last in the hospital, she had the usual quota of clerical visitors but only one who offered prayer as the climax of the visit—gracefully—and she was grateful. But there is, and ought to be, no rule for this. I've a friend who has an inoperable pancreatic cancer, and he'd rather be prayed for than with. All I ever offer him, when parting, is some fairly offhand reference to God's love from which—as he knows now, better than I—nothing can separate us. What matters here is that this illness has been, and is being, hallowed; it functions as a sign-event of human weakness matched by sure trust and confidence in God's unfaltering love.

Death and dying and grief and mourning are the negative occasions that say it all: the *humanum* is mortal and it is dreadful and tragic that this should be the case. Death is the unhallowing of life, its literal dehumanizing, and this is why it is so traumatic, why all cultures have tried to sacralize it by solemn rituals of various sorts. In our culture, death, because it is such a blatant put-down to our secular pride, is treated as impersonally as possible as either a natural event or as a nonevent, to be cosmetized, solemnized, and managed with a minimum of stress and confusion. Death must be prepared for; the art of dying must be cultivated, funerals should be triumphant; one's pastoral ministrations to the grieving must be a summation and recapitulation of all one's pastoral ministrations in life and illness. For the dying, the crucial thing is human dignity, awareness of divine grace, and serenity born of faith.

All occasions are episodes, all are assertions of the human potential, all reminders of its limits. They are soul events, spirit events. They are suffused with mystery, infused with grace. They are holy moments and their hallowing redeems routine from tedium. But they all are transient, too. Thus, we must learn to accept and enjoy them gratefully and to let them go gracefully. Where have all our good times gone? What do they mean to us now? What do our memories teach us about what we have to hope for? Here, it all depends upon how fully and genuinely our lives have already been hallowed, how naturally we have come to live and move in the climate of grace. This is how we come to learn that all the meanings and joys that we have cherished, all our occasions are also cherished and conserved in God's cosmic treasury. They all contribute to God's enjoyment of his creatures and to their joys in the Lord. All occasions are and ought to be holy days, and all our holidays should be occasions for love and grace.

CHAPTER
20

The Pastor and the Hallowing of Life: The Hallowing of Raptures

The hallowing of life, finding the holy in all of life, in all our human occasions, includes the hallowing of our highest and deepest experiences, those outreachings that pass beyond our normal ranges of consciousness and meaning—inward, upward, outward (all spatial prepositions that only faintly suggest transcendence, ecstasy, rapture, reverence). But as we move into this area for exploration, I remind you of a basic premise of all talk about the hallowing of life: Transcendent mystery and love are actually immanent and encompassing, that they suffuse the whole range of our awareness and yet exceed that range at both ends— of rational clarity, at one end, and of ecstasy at the other. This is why any sort of swap-out between normal and paranormal experience is deceiving: It presupposes that one or the other is the truly real, that the holy is to be conflated with paranormal or, alternatively, the abnormal. The first of these is the basic premise of mysticism, and all sorts of otherworldly nostrums—the ground on which the mystics and romantics have always tended to depreciate normal experience. This is why they find it so easy to cop out of the human struggle for justice. And it is also why most of us feel tempted to agree that paranormal experiences— ec-stasis (i.e., standing outside one's normal consciousness)—

are inherently superior, that almost any kind of a "trip" is bound to be better than stagnation in the Dullsvilles of routine, duty, and rationality. Every generation has had its mystagogues, eager advertisers of paranormal experience by formula: induced ecstasy, mystical visions, cosmic consciousness, samadhi, satori, psychedelic trips, etc. And every generation has had its quota of self-centered, self-indulgent devotees, people who believed in the human management of mystery, by various techniques and exercises: triggers that launched them into orbit (sex, drugs, yoga, ESP, biofeedback). Ticket sellers for excursions into the infinite have always found a brisk market, and nowadays all the more so when there are so many new psychedelic agents and so many new techniques (new to us, mainly) that give us promise of being loosed and let go.

For my part, I am no more concerned to depreciate paranormal states of consciousness than I am willing for the mystics to depreciate normal consciousness. It seems to me equally important to insist that both normal and paranormal are both loci for human meaning and value, that neither is intrinsically more hallowed than the other, in and of itself. For ecstasies readily deceive us. Mysticism and antinomianism have always run hand in hand. "Peak experiences" often slide backwards into depression; "stoned thinking" is no passport to perduring meaning. Most of the new supernaturalisms are variations on old recipes for human autonomy.

There is nothing wrong in our hunger for ecstasy. Our memories of rapture color all our subsequent experience, and so do our expectations of raptures still to come. And there is nothing wrong with any of the exercises and techniques that aid in probing and expanding our effective states, unless they create psychobiological addiction or encourage social irresponsibility (i.e., unless they are unhallowed).

And this is my main point: Our humdrum *and* ecstatic states do not come unhallowed or hallowed, in and of themselves. Both have to be hallowed—by our conscious, willing recognition of the givenness of the holy in them and by the application of the same moral and social norms to the human consequences of paranormal as to normal experience and behavior. Our ecstasies must be hallowed, i.e., offered up to God for God to validate and justify. Our raptures must be brought under the same theonomy as the rest of our existence.

There is an ancient quarrel between the moralists and the mystics, between ordered liturgy and spontaneous rapture, between the guardians of the status quo and those whom Max Weber taught us to call charismatic. At issue is the question of public and private norms of behavior, for Weber defined the charismatic as "one who acknowledges none but his own inner constraints and controls." And it may be that these polarities have neuropsychological groundings of one sort or another. At the very least, it is the good pastor's business not so much to take a stand on one side or the other, but to try to help referee the issue by insisting that the hallowing of life requires of the moralist, the rationalist, and the public defender a vision of the holy that rebukes moralism, rationalism, and devotion to the standing order, whereas (at the same time) the ecstatic needs to be reminded that ec-stasis may as readily be demonic as holy.

Again, there is an ancient issue between those who think of ecstasies as given (what we might call "ecstasy by faith alone") and those who think that they can be self-induced and managed (ecstasy by works-righteousness). This is as profound—yet also as fruitless—a quarrel as that between the solifidians and the Pelagians. For the real issue is not whether human agency is involved—of course it is, in every human experience, normal or supernormal—but the terms on which such peak experiences are understood, sought, received, assessed, and woven into the fabric of unfolding life.

The hallowing of life's paranormal dimensions is, therefore, a crucial aspect of our larger pastoral enterprise since they don't come, and are not self-induced, with an infallibly holy quality of their own. There *is* a distinctly human need for ecstasy, rapture, expanded consciousness. We need our minds blown from time to time; we need reminders that the world is *wonder*-full. We need mind-stretching heart-lifting episodes; or, alternatively, times of profound relaxation and inner quietude. There is a numbness of the heart that is worse than paralysis. And the hallmark of paranormal experience is ec-statis, being carried "outside" ourselves, or deeply "within" ourselves, depending on your sense of spatial metaphors.

We have the endless task of fixing and adjusting our life's agenda and its priorities. There is the overplanned life that can be shattered by the disruptions of the unforeseen. There is the nonlife of drift and happenstance that never comprehends what is going on until it has, in fact, gone on, with no profit gleaned from hindsight. And the pastor is caught up in this same maelstrom, in the conflicts between his/her own agenda and those of the people whom she/he serves. How can the noncharismatic pastor minister to, or even tolerate, the charismatics who may be about, with their tendency to pray *for* him? How can the charismatic pastor minister to the noncharismatic without feeling "holier than thou," and conveying that feeling? There is, of course, no easy answer; and for some of us, the strain of trying to be all things to all people in order to save some, perchance, wears our patience and grace-full-ness thin and we succumb to the temptation to "specialize," and so cease to be pastors in any fully authentic sense.

The crux of the matter, as I see it, is whether or not we are convinced that *ecstasis* requires hallowing, and that our pilgrim journeys into cosmic consciousness must finally be normed by the same sign-events of love and grace that norm all human existence at every level, in any life space. For seven years, at Duke, I lived as neighbor and colleague to Joseph B. Rhine, and so have had something of a ringside seat at the contest over the data and interpretation of ESP and of telekinesis. The problem never was whether there is something "real" in the alleged data of parapsychology, but rather whether and how it can be quantified and made a matter of verifiable and manageable public knowledge, i.e., to allow for precise and regular predictions. All the parapsychologists have ever achieved, according to the general verdict of their academic peers, is the sort of gross statistical generalizations like those of insurance actuaries: important for any calculations of percentages; negligible for individual case procedures.

I have long been interested in psychoneuro biology. It was in graduate school that I first discovered Hughlings Jackson and his distinctions between the successive levels of neural stimulus-responsiveness, from spinal ganglia to the granulated frontal cortex of human brains. Two years with Clark Hull at Yale prepared me for B. F. Skinner and for the impression that Hull and Skinner illustrate the difference between the professional and the amateur scientist. None of this, of course, has made me a scientist, in any strict sense. I'm no qualified judge of the speculations now being bruited about in the current psychobiological investigations. But it has taught me a sturdy skepticism as to any claims made in the name of experimental science as to what is known or knowable about an identifiable personal agent in neural activity of any sort and on any level. Biofeedback is a fact—in some sense of facticity or other—but its implications for the metapsychological questions of "self-hood," "personality," "personal agency" are metaphysical questions and just as systematically obscure (as far as scientific knowledge is concerned).

The fact is that the range of voluntary (epicritical) control over what have been heretofore classified as involuntary (autonomic) processes has been extended and may be extended further. This is important, and we've all a stake in the progress of these inquiries and their translations into practical results. But we pass from physics to metaphysics when we raise the question of the self (which or who?) that is presupposed in the basic phrase "voluntary self-control." This is the crux of the question about "cybernetics" and its human implications. "Kybernos" means "governor," and the prior question in any computer process is who programmed it, who is asking it the appropriate questions as guide to its data processing—and who assesses and uses the printout. Whatever one's faith in the future of computer technology, no one that I know of has yet conceived of a self-programming, goal-oriented, self-assessing, self-correcting cybernetic system that comes equipped with emotions and self-transcending aspirations—with id, superego, and ego, or whatever myth you choose.

What would it take to verify or infirm these notions of a grid of positive correlations between neural processes and human self-actualizations? Well, several things. For one, we would need a verifiable demonstration that the brain not only affects feelings, thought, and image making but actually generates them. Second, it would take rigorous empirical explanation of the agency that is involved in the correlations between activities in the medulla and the cortex, and in the integrative transactions of the corpus callosum in the interplay of our cranial hemispheres (remember Descartes and the pineal gland). Finally, it would take something like a "Turing machine," computers that could do more than receive, exchange, and retrieve information from each other. It would take computers that could make moral, political, human decisions in situations involving multiple options of radically different valences. Till then, it is important to keep sharp, skeptical watch on all alleged conflations of psychology and metapsychology. This is not to disparage metapsychology (the vast bulk of what goes under the label psychology is *meta*). I'm only pleading that metapsychology be assessed on its own grounds without invoking the currently impressive authority of laboratory or clinical science. There is much wisdom here, as in all imaginative inquiries. But science asks for more, or less, and the fissure between science and wisdom has not yet been bridged, despite scientists who are very wise and wise men/women who are amateur scientists.

The pastor's problem, of finding the holy in the extraordinary, focuses on two main questions: (1) What are the limits, if any, of extensions of "normal" consciousness, and what are the optimum means of pushing consciousness to these limits? and (2) what is the expanded consciousness conscious *of*? The answers to (1) are multiple and ambiguous. Nobody knows what normal consciousness is or how far it is affected by genetic predeterminations, by body types, by socialization processes, by cultural mores, religion, or whatever. Its extension, therefore, is a comparative affair and forever recessive. Moreover, human consciousness always includes concurrent awareness of process (orderly and regular) and of events (disruptions of what has come to be understood as process). Process generates a sort of psychic equipoise (as in sleep); events generate excitement (psychic stimulation). But what is an event for one person may be a nonevent for another; besides, there are variations in the modalities of psychic excitement and its social and moral context. This was the basis of the old "scientific" theory of the four "temperaments," or "humors"—sanguine, melancholic, choleric, phlegmatic. But the human organism needs excitement (ec-stasis, actually) as much as it needs homeostasis—but neither at the expense of the other. And this gives us a rough rule for the choice of indicated and optimum means for seeking, inducing, or preparing for paranormal experiences. Any means that threatens the organ's biological homeostasis in any acute degree or over any protracted period is contraindicated, and we will not stop now to argue out the comparative harm of caffeine, nicotine, alcohol, cannabis, LSD, amphetamines, etc., or megavitamins, either. At any rate, there are limits to the expansion of consciousness, if at no other level than blood-chemical adaptability. For a pastoral theology, however, the second question is more basic. What is it that we are conscious of in a paranormal experience? This is an ancient epistemological battlefield (littered with corpses and philosophical weaponry), but the issue is fairly simple (even if also insoluble): Is there a perceivable world out there or is consciousness a subjective experience that constructs "the world" and then extrojects it as if it were objective? Obviously, in all experience there is a mix (over an immense continuum) of perceptions and imaginations, for we have neural end organs and we are inveterate image makers. But are our "perceptions" (actually *per*ceptions) of a real world (*cosmos*) or are they all illusions (as we can prove that some of them are)? Are our imaginations purely subjective, or are they also in some sense archetypal and universal? Are reason and intuition functions of hemispherical polarities, or are they different inlets to the interfaces of Being? If expanded consciousness is self-consciousness, what is the self of whom it is conscious; and is there any consciousness that is conscious of that self as that self is not conscious of it? Is cosmic consciousness a consciousness of the *cosmos,* and if so, is the cosmos conscious? Either way, is cosmos finite or infinite, and how would who know?

In the Christian tradition, i.e., of Christian mysticism, there is a salutary modesty about these paranormal experiences and their hallowing. St. Paul reports an ecstasis of his in 2 Corinthians 12:2–6, of being caught up into the third heaven (delta waves?) or paradise, and of there receiving ineffable wisdom and truth. But, lest he become a habitual tripper, he was also given a thorn in the flesh so that "the power of Christ" might be given him in his human weakness: "My grace is sufficient for you; power comes to its full strength in weakness." St. Augustine reports two ecstatic visions (*Confessions,* VII and IX) and uses both as confirmation of the Holy Spirit's inward, illuminating, uplifting action. Other raptures and peak experiences followed but were never "methodized." And so with thousands and thousands of other Christians, great and small. There was Thomas Aquinas whose life of prayer and reflection was lived out in a constant climate of grace, and whose final ecstasy reminded him of the shortfallings of his intellectual aspirations. One of my favorite churches in Rome is Santa Maria della Vittoria (even if the "victory" was over gallant Protestants), and its showpiece is Bernini's sculpted "Santa Teresa in Ecstasy." I've spent hours trying to fathom this extraordinary hallowing of the paranormal, trying to sort out Bernini's baroque extravagances from his authentic vision, always being reminded that the ecstatic saint is about to be reminded of her humanity (her creaturely finitude), as indeed she herself tells us in her report of it!

The same goes for all the extraordinary gifts of the Holy Spirit: gifts of healing, of discernment, of prophecies, of tongues, of handling venomous snakes with immunity, etc., and for cosmic consciousness. All of these—and they can serve as symbols for paranormal experience in general—are experiences not of self-consciousness but of the Spirit. They are encounters, not with a void, but with an inner presence of the holy that is not different in principle from the outer presence of reality in the perceived world. Good pastors must be aware of, and sensitive to, and concerned with charismatic gifts—their own and those of others. If they speak in tongues, they must not only be patient and loving toward the rest of us; they must show us how we, too, can hallow our high moments without imitating theirs. If they are the non-rapturous kind, they might bethink themselves of how to find their way further into the Mystery of Grace they profess and proclaim; and must, in any case, be grace-full with and gracious to those they serve who have "higher" gifts still. The pastor as charismatic must find a vital balance between rapture and "self-possession," between worship as routine and worship as transfiguration. Most of all, the pastor must himself and herself be an interesting, exciting person with at least an occasional aura of the Spirit.

I would rather think of charismata and all paranormal experience as divine gifts rather than as achievements. They may be prepared for, expected, appreciated with gratitude and joy and love; but they are not self-induced, or if apparently so, not ultimately. The holy is in us and with us and for us, but not at our beck and call. Spiritual techniques and exercises, transcendental meditations, yoga, prayer, and worship are all available means in our quest for life's highest, deepest, fullest meanings. But their common aim must always be to put ourselves at the Spirit's disposal and not to program Pentecost. For the holy is the Living God who is calling us from our tumults into his peace. And I would rather think of hallowing of our peak experiences and life's daily round and its great occasions in the same terms. Both kinds of experience call for pastoral ministration aimed at reflection, radiance, rapture, and reverence. I'm not concerned with their order or priority but with their integration, that they concur together in a life that "is hid with God in Christ."

Reflection is the distinctively human capacity to be a participant observer of the world and of our involvements in it, the power to understand and adapt behavior and insight in accordance with reality. If the *genus homo* is *sapiens,* this is what makes him so; and God has not given us minds to let them be stampeded by passion or bunkered by logic. To think that we can park our rational functions at some threshold of the noumenal is to mistake what being human really means.

Radiance is the outward and visible sign of an inward and invisible glory. It's a tricky notion, for it teeters on the edge between exhilaration and vanity. It has its pompous side (fame, acclaim, praise) and all of this is tragically transient (literally, "vainglorious"). But there's another side to glory, a more truly human, more healthful side, that can and should be hallowed. It comes clear as soon as you stop and ask what you mean when you report a sight or sound as "really glorious." The obvious answer is something radiant, vivid, thrilling: a sign-event of the Spirit's presence and your recognition of it. Whatever that something is, it shares common traits: a radiant flush of the spirit, a sudden sense of being hallowed, an experience of being spellbound, almost literally, for a moment at least. What matters is that human life should, from time to time—and in its literal sense, "spontaneously"—be visited by these gifts of radiance and delight, for this is the earthly analogue to God's own glory, reflected as that is in our *imago Dei,* however besmirched. This is at least in part what the Bible means by the human. All creation is finite; only the human is inspirited: God breathed the breath of life (personal identity) into the prefabricated human clod, "and he became a living soul." This is the final ground of the dignity and sanctity of human personality, and it defines our task of sacralizing the world and hallowing all its heights and depths.

Raptures also belong to those heights and depths, and we have spoken of the problem of how far they may be induced and how far they come as God's unmerited gifts—of vision, of joy, of transfiguration. The Christian experience, by and large, reports that the faithful and hopeful and loving are more often overtaken by raptures than they ever manage to induce them; and this would fit all else we know of grace and of our radical dependence. The main point to rapture and charismatic phenomena of all sorts is that they are not the holy in themselves (and even less do they identify us as holier-than-thou) but are sign-events of the holy, intimations of that Holy Mystery that is life's constant context.

Reverence is our habituation to the holy, our habitual response to its manifestations, the sense of awe that is neither terror-stricken nor ecstatic. For ecstasies, raptures, trips come and go. Reverence may become the steady disposition of a life, the *inclinatio* of a human spirit. It may be a sense of awe in the most ordinary experience when properly attended; it may be an awareness of mystery in great occasions; it may be the still center of a busy and distracted life. But always it is love: love of God and love of God's creatures. Reverence has little to do with solemnity and nothing at all with humorlessness. It can be jaunty or serious, lighthearted or earnest, indignant or serene. But always it is loving, always hallowed; therefore, always supplying all life's events with their meaning, interest, and final value.

"For if you are led by the Spirit [and this is what St. Paul means by charismatic experience, in any of its contexts], you are not under the law. . . . This is because the fruits of the Spirit are love, joy, peace, patience, kindness, goodness, fidelity, gentleness, self-control. There is no law dealing with such things as these. If, therefore, the Spirit is the source of our life, then let the Spirit also direct our course" (Galatians 5:18, 22, 25).

This is the only way I can think of—or have ever seen verified in human life and history—to get beyond a materialism that degrades human life, a moralism that shackles it, a nature mysticism or pantheism that finally negates selfhood to a true Christian humanism in which our participation in the holy and in the hallowing of life is also our joy and happiness and peace.

CHAPTER
21

The Pastor and the Hallowing of Life: The Hallowing of the World

We come now to the end of this course of lectures, with much said and much left unsaid, with what I hope are at least a few fresh or more inclusive perspectives on the pastor's calling, office, and tasks. We have had a swift survey and assessment of his heritage, and a critical evaluation of some pastoral resources from the contemporary human sciences and the modern arts of healing and helping. To this we have added a reformulation of the Gospel in terms that tried to take account of the fading of the forensic image and the final inadequacy of all merely ameliorative or cybernetic therapies. Finally, I've been urging the thesis that our role in our salvation here below is the hallowing of life, the recognition and grateful reception of God's gifts of human wholeness, holiness, and happiness. Now, we have one more dimension of hallowing to speak of—the hallowing of the world, or the pastor's task as prophet and catalyst of social change.

But before we tackle that, there are some cautionary comments to be made in case I've left the wrong impression of how I see the relation between pastoral theology (the sort of thing we've been struggling with in these lectures) and pastoral practice (the sort of thing we struggle with "out there" in the congregation or the clinic or the community). On the one hand, I've been frankly critical of the currently fashionable image of pastors as cut-rate therapists for people who are both mobile enough (psychologically and socially) and docile enough (psychologically) to consult them. This is not to depreciate competent therapy at bargain rates in a society overrun with ambulatory hysterics in one degree of unhappiness or another. It is only to doubt the actual competence of much of what passes for pastoral counseling (shockingly thin in its theories, shockingly overconfident of its techniques and rituals). But more, I have wanted to stress as earnestly as possible my conviction that pastoral ministry is always an active search, a constant initiative and, above all, a presence—in the church, in families and small groups, and in the community at large. The Christian pastor is not a private person; he/she is a public representative of the Christian community, a sacral person—called, ordained, and accountable. One of the minor scandals of our churches is the tragic superficiality of both theory and practice in the business of ordination and accountability. Don't tell *me* that you hold yourself accountable to God and not to any old church; for if you tried any analogue of *that* in business or teaching or the law (or even at home), anybody at all familiar with the symptoms of paranoia would begin to think of how to get you to a shrink! And don't tell me that you've science on the side of your newest therapeutic nostrums either; for if you get far enough in your alleged scientific analyses as to use any such terms as "reality," "myth," "symbol," "self," "human," you must then show your credentials in metaphysics and meta-psychology, not to mention theology, over and beyond anything that can rightly be called "scientific."

But there is an equal danger on the other side—and all the more so since I myself have been talking so much, with so few alleged case histories (or verbatims) and at what some would call a "mentalistic" level (or worse). It is, therefore, at least plausible to infer that I regard the pastor as some sort of answer man for some, if not all, questions troubled people are entitled to ask. In the old days, seminaries had courses called "Christian Evidences" in which all conceivable objections to Christianity were raised and summary answers provided. In our own time there have been people like Edward Thurneysen in Europe and John Sutherland Bonnell in this country who made their reputations for listening to a person's story and then choosing a suitable short homily from the file of suitable short homilies on most conceivable troubles and delivering it to the admiring soul who was often grateful for having had his problem so well understood and so summarily solved!

One of the few things we know for sure in counseling is that good advice does not amount to good therapy, and that the inquirer must clarify and choose his options in the light of his own development, self-understanding, and insight. Even this commonplace is tricky, however, for what is crucial here is not giving or withholding "advice," but offering the other person genuine freedom to react in terms of his and her own clearest and best judgment (even if that turns out doubtful or wrong). The illusions of talking-cures are very real, and the temptation to talk about problems as if they were thereby being dealt with is analogous to all those moral or political statements that churches and groups often produce as if they were moral or political acts.

My purpose in these lectures, therefore, has not been to offer any model of question-and-answer techniques for thoughtful pastors, but to lay out a perspective, a mindset (*Lebensanschauung,* if you like), in which pastors can understand themselves and respond to their pastoral challenges and opportunities accordingly. Good shepherding is an *art,* entitled to seek and utilize whatever scientific and theological resources we can muster. It is the art of seeing, loving, hearing another person (or persons) with self-evident respect, genuine attention, and goodwill. It is the art of responding, in word and deed, so that some sort of constructive option appears to the other as his or her own. It is not so much a matter of easing tensions as of opening up new and meaningful choices, not so much a matter of praise or blame as of insight, not so much a business of "delivering your own soul" but of registering your intelligent concern. It is important, in therapy and in social analysis generally, to recover the past in perspective and transvaluate it; but the aim is always a more open future.

Even so, the art of good shepherding is an art that depends upon vision (as all arts do, really), and my concern has been less with theories or techniques than with vision. For the most ominous limitations I see in all the human sciences root in their limited or distorted visions—of God and humanity, of the human flaw and the human hope, of what Jesus called "the abundant life," the life of meaning, serenity, courage, and joy that he came to bring.

It always helps mightily if the pastor can preach—solid, lively, trenchant proclamations of the Word of God in Christ. The pulpit can no longer rival the news commentators, the talk shows, or the ad writers; but preachers have at least the chance (actually the duty) of being the medium of a message that commands their own attention as well as the attention of their hearers. Every now and then, in a good sermon, I realize that the preacher and I are both attending to a message beyond us both; that I'm listening less to him/her than to what the preacher also is striving to hear. This, indeed, is what I mean by "a good sermon," and it is possible for almost any pastor (eloquent or not) who really is willing to be a medium rather than trying to communicate his/her own self. It helps mightily, also, if the pastor is a good liturgist, and here again the same principle holds: liturgy is always a means and never an end in itself. There is no liturgy to end liturgy making, and so the traditionalists are wrong in principle. But innovation, or development, in liturgy must be judged on honestly functional terms: Does it (or will it, sooner or later) serve the People of God to glorify God and to enjoy him? Otherwise, it can become an avenue of pastoral narcissism (and this can happen with traditional or "contemporary" forms).

And it helps mightily, still further, if pastors become good counselors, within the limits of their competence, and without any special awe or envy of their psychiatric brethren whom they need more as allies than as models. It rarely occurs to a really sophisticated pastor to be in awe or envy of an internist or a dermatologist, which suggests that we have invested shrinks with something like a priestly aura. There is no great harm in this so long as we realize in what appalling disarray contemporary psychiatric theory and practice is, and so long as we do not redefine our own callings as being deacons to such priests!

But the pastor is more than preacher, priest, counselor. If *all* of life is to be hallowed, i.e., to find its secure and safeguarded meaning in the holy, then the pastor must accept and understand his and her role as *prophet,* with some kind of moral authority (representative and not personal)—the so-called power of the keys, of "binding and loosing here on earth what is bound and loosed in heaven." Now, obviously, it is both superstitious and arrogant to think of our power as involving the dispensing or withholding God's grace or even the means of grace. That's the heresy of sacerdotalism; of all clerical delusions, this is the most demonic and destructive. But there is a power that a pastor may— ought to—feel free to exercise (obligated to exercise), and that is the power to challenge, prod, and evaluate another's appeal to conscience, and in this sense to bind and to loose such appeals. Now, before you denounce this as insufferable arrogance of another sort, the very idea of anybody challenging and evaluating your conscience, consider this: What one feels as his/her conscience may seem so near the very center of that person's being that it is inviolate. Yet this may be terribly self-deceiving. Time was when most of the worst crimes against humanity were committed in good conscience by conscientious men and women. Even now, when their superegos (or parents) are so nearly negligible for the rising horde of psycho- and sociopaths, there is still the terrifying fact that deeply inward impulses are as often demonic as they are truly human. What this means is that consciences must be challenged, prodded, and evaluated; but not just by other consciences susceptible to the same distortions as our own. We need our consciences opened up to the imperatives of God's righteous rule in human hearts and lives; to the divine imperatives of love, justice, and community; to the shame and wastage of hedonistic and undisciplined living; to alternatives of self-control and authentic self-development; to opportunities of self-oblation and service.

We cannot, perhaps, make folks feel guilty anymore, and that's just as well. But if we have nothing more to confront their experience with than our own, they've every right to ask, "Who are you to be telling me what's what?" Suppose, though, without any presumption of self-righteousness I could open your mind and heart to a Christian alternative; suppose I could reinterpret your notions of religion and theology in what Seward Hiltner calls "dynamic" terms (i.e., psychologically illuminating and credible); suppose I could get you to consider your personal and social relations in moral terms, i.e., of the right and the good and the eventual. In this sort of genuinely interpersonal exchange the spontaneous affect of your conscience would have been altered significantly. In one degree or another, the transaction would have bound you more closely to your sense of ought and outcome, if you are a libertine; or it would have "loosened" your inhibitions with a new sense of Christian freedom, if you're still shackled by false scruples. Thus, one can appeal from an unformed happenstance conscience to an informed conscience and whenever that happens, you're in business—the pastoral business of responsible ethical decisions in moral behavior, personal and social.

It is not enough to have a sacral community in which our routines and occasions and raptures are hallowed, although without something like this, we are in sad, subhuman shape. The world in which all this takes place must also be hallowed. And whenever we speak of "world," we must always distinguish "nature" and "society" even though they are mutually independent, what Duns Scotus called a *formal distinction.* For there is a sense in which nature is easily hallowed. "The groves were God's first temples," etc.; we know the nature mysticism that the Romantic poets celebrated, the residue of the animism that is humanity's first religion and that gives the ecology cause the religious fervor it has. We can find meaning and joy in natural beauty, and we can salvage meaning and joy even out of our contests with nature's impersonal furies: the cold and the heat and the jungle. Even so, we must see through and beyond nature to nature's God; and even there, till we have seen his heart in Christ, we can have no assurance of love's final power. This is the ultimate pathos of all nature mysticism, the melancholy that is its shadow side.

Hallowing human society is another thing altogether. It is the most difficult, the most imperative of all our human tasks. For we can be truly human in almost any context where grace abounds and faith is real, but we can never be fully human in a subhuman society until we and all humankind are holy and happy and human at their best. "No man is an island," and ". . . never send to know for whom the bell tolls; it tolls for thee"![1] But how shall we answer its summons? The two polar alternatives (conservative and radical) have been (1) the salvaging of personal life from a noxious society and so reforming the society by so much from within; and (2) the radical, rapid changing of society and so creating a more humane and habitable environment for the persons in it. Now, it is interesting (and not altogether insignificant either) that the pastoral care movement in general has been a largely conservative affair, in terms of social action. Along with its psychiatric models, it has operated on the premise that if you can change the lifestyles of enough individuals profoundly enough, *that* will change society. Changed humans will humanize society. This is yet another secular analogue to pietism: Convert enough people to true Christian faith and they will Christianize society. Psychiatrists (and pastoral counselors) may be ever so permissive, but they share the conservative, *laissez-faire* cast of modern culture and the essentially conservative tendencies of institutional religion. One of the incidental reasons for the partial eclipse of the pastoral care movement (as a nostrum in place of the traditional pastoral enterprise) is the rise to prominence of yet another nostrum: the current version of the "social gospel," viz., the so-called "theologies of liberation." Their premise is that you've gotta be free and fed and powerful before faith, hope, and love are anything better than opiates to ease the pain of oppression.

Presently, we must consider a third alternative for the pastor as good shepherd, viz., as advocate and leader of a permanent, conservative revolution. Right now, it is enough to notice the significant correlation between psychotherapy (and pastoral counseling) and the social classes they serve best, viz., the bourgeoisie, the intelligentsia, and the beautiful people, who tend to have their personal psychiatrists as dukes once had chaplains; whose essential problem is banality, *anomie,* self-stultification (in all their anguished symptomatics). For such people as these and their needs, the pastor has to find a way between the rival temptations to become a genuine tame cat and a fake prophet. He/she must find how to offer people personal self-assurances within a society in anguish or else to summon them to a revolution aimed at overthrowing the system, even as the rebel is demanding support and protection *from* the system!

But there *are* insatiable human hungers for a New Jerusalem that are as authentic as any other: "a new heaven and a new earth" with no more human degradation or tears. This was the Gospel that Jesus brought: "The kingdom of God is at hand; repent, believe, participate." The righteous rule of God is immanent: take up your part in it and play it to the hilt. Jesus refused to raise the people in revolt and yet he radically undercut the heteronomous control of the Establishment (on account of which he had to be disposed of). The Christian revolution is no mere overturning of one party in power by another, but the radical independence of every person to act in the light of his and her informed conscience, which seeks the public good in a hallowed community. Or it is at least a community in which freedom is normed by justice, where powerlessness is redeemed by God's sovereign power in the interest of justice and humanity.

The essence of human anxiety is powerlessness, and that on two levels: (1) impotence to determine the terms of one's own existence, and (2) impotence to secure one's gains and advantages against loss, degradation, and death. When another race, another class, another ruling group can determine my station in life and its duties against my own legitimate interests, I am oppressed and humanity's true joys are being denied me. The outrage of it all is that this sort of thing has happened to whole races, to whole classes, and to both sexes. The cause of women's liberation would seem to me somewhat less ambivalent if the evidence of mutual oppression were not so obvious. Women have been and are oppressed, but they also arrange two-thirds of the funerals (often of poor suckers who had housed them in the suburbs while *they* were fighting life's losing battles on the expressways and in the downtown canyons).

Oppression, as such, cannot be hallowed; it has to be resisted, to be overcome, which means that the cause of liberation is a clear, straightforward imperative for every Christian pastor and all who bear Christ's name. Of course, life can be hallowed in and despite oppression, since "stone walls do not a prison make,/Nor iron bars a cage"[2] for truly free spirits. But we must never accept that as an excuse for tolerating the status quo, or the denial to any of God's children his and her share in the determination of his destiny. It is in this sense that the Christian revolution, God's kingdom on earth, the peaceable kingdom here and now, is a permanent, endless enterprise and imperative. It is a *theonomous* revolution, seeking for all persons what God wants for them and not necessarily what they want for themselves. For self-centered people seek power for itself, either to wield or else to use in self-defense. And whereas in the conventional revolution there is a sort of fixed quantum of power that the have-nots take from the haves ("dog eat dog"), the Christian revolution is less interested in power than in dignity and the freedom freely to serve, freely to inquire, freely to enjoy self-chosen community. The Gospel will always seem to the Machiavellis and Nietzsches of this world as a slave morality because it does not cherish power for itself, and is always and regularly corrupted by any power that is not put directly to use in significant service ("service" here is merely another term for fruitful, productive, creative living), with the needs and rights and dignities of others always included, always cherished. This is the proper qualification to Lord Acton's aphorism about power corrupting and absolute power corrupting absolutely.[3] Power is like the manna God provided for the Israelites: Put directly to significant use, it enables; cherished or wielded for its own sake, it stinks (of pride), and prepares for the inevitable tragedy. Power needs power to maintain itself, and this need of survival readily becomes a justification of any necessary means. This is why every political system is inevitably corrupt, though none needs to be so corrupt as most of them are. A politician, a political party, a nation all feel they must survive, and so feel justified in whatever means that look promising at the time. As Freud noticed in *Civilization and Its Discontents,* nations like persons have death wishes. *Thanatos* is working overtime in America just now.

In the Christian revolution justice is a condition, *sine qua non*—justice understood in the classical sense of "to each his own," to each person his and her inalienable rights to life, liberty, and the pursuit of happiness. But justice is not enough. And whenever it becomes an end in itself, it helps to distract the real end of human society, which is happiness. The happy society would be one that took the natural inequalities of human beings for granted in mutual acceptance and respect and hallowed them all in zestful work, joyful play, fortitude, and compassion in pain and faith and serenity in the face of death—for every child of God.

In the Christian revolution, it is less justice that is confidently proposed as an achievable goal than that injustice may be identified as an insult to love and must be renounced whenever it is thus identified. Pure, full, precise justice, in any positive sense, is, of course, unattainable for the very simple reason that it presupposes what no human has, and human societies even less: omniscience and omnipotence. Who knows positively what is fully just for me, now, in this case? Answer: someone who knew all its antecedents and contributing circumstances and who could foresee all the consequences. And for that, I have no nominations except God. But even supposing there was someone who knew enough to know what really was just and right as, for example, between the rival claims of the ecologist and the industrialists; what would it take to enforce his or her just decisions? Answer: there is no such human power on which any of us can rely with any final confidence.

Thus, the perfectionist demand for nothing short of justice is forever being thwarted, and any society oriented toward justice as a feasible and expectable goal is on its way to tyranny. The Christian revelation aims at something different: more paradoxical, more dialectical, and far more self-disciplined. The monks sought this in their vows of poverty, chastity, and obedience: self-subordination to a higher good. The Protestants transferred this monastic ethic out into the world, which made it the real "Christian secularism": Poverty becomes thrift and industry, chastity becomes fidelity in love and marriage, obedience becomes productive service. In his Standard Sermon on "The Use of Money," John Wesley oversimplified this with his famous threefold rule: Gain all you can, save all you can, give all you can (all your surplus accumulation). The early Methodists bought numbers one and two and rationalized on number three.

But the only kind of revolutionary ethic that liberates the revolutionary before, during, and after the revolution is an ethic of inner freedom, which is to say, of intentional self-giving in a meaningful cause. In the eyes of the Christian revolutionary, *laissez-faire* as a lifestyle is dehumanizing, for inevitably it serves the strong (whoever the strong may be) and oppresses the weak (whoever the weak may be). In *laissez-faire,* power is wielded to augment itself. But by the very same token, collectivism is equally dehumanizing (or more so), for it involves the oppression of the private will (the individual) by the collective.

The crucial distinction between all conservative and all radical revolutions is simply this: the agenda of the victors for the vanquished. In the American Revolution, there was freedom enough for all, in principle, and freedom for many in fact. In the

French Revolution (and Russian and Chinese and Ugandan and Chilean, etc.) there was scant freedom for the vanquished even in principle. This raises a difficult question for the liberationists of our time: What is your agenda for your erstwhile oppressors? And here, it seems to me, is where the Hebrew prophets and the Christian teachers of righteousness agree in stressing the choice of a conservative revolution. Revolution, yes, as an endless process of endless liberation, for freedom is never fully won and is never secure even after victory. But conservative, too: to conserve all the human values that possibly can be, to turn all power to human uses and the public good, not to be ministered unto but to minister and to give one's life as the price of significant human service.

If I do not mistake these comments for a comprehensive political ethic for Christians, you need not either. Their aim is not to summarize a political theory, although there is one implicit in them, viz., a politics of minimum politics, i.e., a minimum range of coercive power, and a politics of persuasion. Rather, they have been a prelude for a concluding unscientific postscript on hallowing the world in which the struggles for justice and peace and dignity are still far from won. And here, far more than in any, of our own conventional self-conscious preoccupations, the Christian revolutionary—or the good shepherd, to subside into calmer language—can find meaning in the *imitatio Christi;* here is where the cost of Christian discipleship is the most obvious, the most difficult, the most rewarding. The texts are legion, but three can serve for thirty:

1. John 3:16–17: God loved the world so much that he gave his only Son, that everyone who has faith in him might not perish [meaninglessly] but have eternal life. It was not to condemn the world that God sent his Son into the world but that through him the world might be saved [hallowed].

2. 2 Corinthians 5:19: God was in Christ reconciling the world to himself.

3. Romans 8:32, 31: If God did not spare his own Son but gave him up for us all, will he not also, with this gift give us all he has to give? And if God is for us [in this way and to this extent], who is against us [that matters in the end]?

Can you imagine that if God knew as much about the world as we do, he would think it still worth saving—or even within reach of salvation by anything short of a wholly unwarranted divine *fiat*? I should think it unlikely, wouldn't you? Yet, it is just this disbelief that reminds me how far I have sunk back into a satanocratic view of the world, that sees it under the rule and power of Satan, of demonic, selfish, destructive forces against which the peaceable, nonviolent, rational, and loving don't really have a chance. Wherefore, fight fire with fire, power with power, self-assertiveness with counter self-assertions; root for the underdog to turn top dog, for a while at least. This is the unhallowed world, the world abandoned and thought to be abandoned by God. In which case, we can depreciate the world or flee from it or try to squeeze out our joys before the curtain falls: "Ah, take the Cash, and let the Credit go, / Nor heed the rumble of a distant Drum."[4] This treats the world as desacralized, truly secularized. In such a world, we are excused from trying to reform the irreformable, or to attempt to save what is not worth saving. And I must confess that the pietist in me, and the mystic and the cynic, all agree that this is the way of wisdom, the way of withdrawal, of escape, the mystic flight.

But Christian secularism is different from all autonomous views of "The Secular City." For it says that the world is hallowed because God has hallowed it—not by wiping out its troubles, but by entering them in dead earnest and with a self-sacrificing love that revealed what moral power really is and what it really is for. It says, furthermore, that this is the way that we may imitate Christ and participate in that "love divine, all loves excelling" that we sing about. Thus, Christian faith sees and knows how and why and to what end this world has been hallowed, and therefore what has already hallowed our lives in the world and will go on hallowing them forever: the love of God for this world (this same wretched world), which calls out our love for all our brethren for whom Christ died.

Again and always, the Good Shepherd comes into this anguished world, and into our hearts, that we might have, he says, life abundant. Good pastors are those who find their self-identification, norm, joy, and final meaning here. They convey this Gospel to all their flocks (to all of them in all their needs), that in this world, hallowed by God's ungrudging, suffering, serving love, we, too, may seek out our pilgrim's way as disciples of Christ, whose ungrudging, sacrificial love to us hallows all our efforts to make this world safe and habitable for all his people.

PART 5

Second Look at a First Book

Introduction

Outler prepared this lecture during a time of reconsideration of his major constructive statement on the subject, his influential 1954 book, *Psychotherapy and the Christian Message*. Some of his revisioning of that book is more than hinted at in this selection, and even more is expressed explicitly in the next. In this particular piece, offered to the Lutheran Theological Seminary in Columbia, South Carolina, in 1968, what will be of particular interest is the "agenda" Outler envisions for developing a comprehensive theological anthropology, and the approach he takes to the issue of mind-body interaction in the context of considering psychedelic drug use for generating quasi-religious experiences. His discussion of this latter topic, to be sure a matter "hotter" in the 1960's counterculture than it is today, is nonetheless worth careful attention for the light it seeks to shed on the psyche's connections with neurological and physiological processes.

CHAPTER

22

Psychotherapy and Christian Faith

It might be helpful if I began this lecture with a summary account of how I got in this business in the first place. It began back in 1929 when scarcely anybody had even touched the question of what the theoretical interrelations of psychotherapy and Christian theology were or might be. And in 1932–1933, I wrote my senior B.D. thesis at Emory on "Psychotherapy and Pastoral Care." In graduate school at Yale I picked up the equivalent of a Master's Degree in psychology in the Institute of Human Relations concurrently with my Ph.D. in patristics—a faintly preposterous combination, as the professors in psychology and patristics both agreed. When I went back to Yale to teach historical theology, I continued my work in psychotherapy, and in 1954 published my first "own" book on *Psychotherapy and the Christian Message.* Since then, I've neglected the field and am only just now returning to its theoretical reassessment after nearly fifteen years of "distraction."

What then are my credentials for talking psychotherapeutic theory? To be honest, none that are very impressive, as a psychotherapist—except the practical qualification of pastoral counseling as a marginal enterprise in a very busy schedule. But then, I've never been interested in psychotherapy as such—that is, as a prime and singular profession. And this is what I keep on trying to explain. The clue is that double major in psychology and patristics and my subsequent work in medieval scholasticism. For first and last, I am a theologian—a dilettante, maybe, but a theological dilettante! And my liveliest intellectual curiosity throughout the years has been focused on the question of Christian faith and secular wisdom. Hence, my interest in patristics, where Platonism was appropriated and transformed by the Christians in the construction of the Christian doctrine of God. Also, my interest in medieval scholasticism, when the newly discovered Aristotle helped Christians to develop a doctrine of nature that supported the Christian doctrine of grace, in a fashion that could rightly be called "scientific" then and now. And, finally, my interest in modern psychology, which is the humanistic distillate of the modern life sciences and behavioral sciences, where what is at stake is a Christian doctrine of human nature that can match the biblical revelation of the fullness of the stature of humanity perfected in Jesus Christ and the critical self-understanding of modern man as to his place before God and in nature. For there can be little doubt that the overwhelming dominant issue of our time is the problem about human beings themselves: our nature, identity, possibilities, and destiny; and from the Christian point of view, the urgent and open enterprise of what we might call a theological anthropology to lay alongside the secularized anthropologies that are being developed in such great profusion by our psychologists and philosophers. This is the nub of the quarrels about "the death of God": "God is dead; long live man!" Yet it is also the pedal-point motif of the Second Vatican Council: *Dignitas Humanae.*[1]

When so many diverse minds converge so intently on so critical an issue, it is an omen and portent. Is it, therefore, only fanciful to guess that we are at the beginning of a major movement in the direction of a Christian dogma of man (i.e., a consented problematic as to his "nature" and human reality)? If such a dogma were achieved, it would faithfully have to reflect the integrity of the entire Christian revelation (our flawed *bonitas,* our self-transcendence and radical incompleteness, etc.). To be about man, it would have to be faithfully "secular" and, quite literally, "catholic." In such a process, we might actually hope to see the sub-Christian rivalry between God and humanity eased and sublated into a truly Christian notion of the *vincula amicitiae* between Creator and creature, between heaven and earth, between humans and nations.

Some such prospect would suggest a place on the time line of doctrinal development for this outstanding item of unfinished business in the history of Christian thought. The dogma of the Triune God came first, and even those most confident that they have got "beyond Nicea" are struggling still with the problems that Nicea set in train. Then came the Chalcedonian dogma of the coordination of divine and human energy systems in Jesus Christ and—despite its bad press since Schleiermacher—I know of no modern essay in Christology that has more accurately stipulated the unevadable Christological issues. It is arguable whether there is a consented problematic about sin and grace, and also how far Lateran IV, Vatican I, and Vatican II have brought us toward a possible agreement as to the basic questions defining a suitable dogma about "the church." But the case is plain to all that we never have had, and do not now have, anything close to consensus in the area of theological anthropology.

Here, then, is where modern theology really has its work cut out for it: a doctrine of human being that is emancipated from the psychological models of "Christian Platonism" (including those implicit in "process metaphysics") yet also liberated from the pseudo-empirical models of Marx, Freud, Pavlov, Pareto, et al. It would be a fruitful sublimation of the frustrations of our new iconoclasts if they could get themselves variously involved in the constructive tasks of psycho-anthropo-sociological theory and practice. But not, God forbid, in terms of any of the theoretical options currently available. For if "man" has finally become our chief and proper study, it cannot yet be claimed that this study has come to anything like valid summation anywhere at all. On every hand, there are exciting and promising breakthroughs—molecular biology, reflexology, chemotherapy, learning theory, mass motivation and mass communication theory, ethnography, anthropology, etc. But they have not yet been added up into any magisterial theory of the human being as person or of society as specifically human. So far, our vastly increased knowledge has simply increased the complications in the project of producing a reliable account of the known data of human consciousness.

Consider what an adequate *summa anthropologica* would call for: verifiable correlations between psychic states and blood chemistry, between thought and neural processes, between biological individuation, sex and personal haecceity, between appetition and value, between self and society, between "the savage mind" and the "modern," between human bondage and freedom, between the human possibility and the human good. All these will finally have to be integrated within a feasible program for an individual's becoming and being fully human in the face of pain, tragedy, and death in a world in chronic catastrophe. And when we turn from this very partial inventory of an optimum agenda to a coolly critical assessment of even the best recent efforts in anthropological reconstruction (Freud, Jung, Heidegger, Sartre, Lévi-Strauss, Jaspers, Erikson, Mayo, Koestler, Adler—and who else?), one can only wonder at the hypocrisy of those who reject traditional theology as incredible without passing equally bleak judgments upon the glaring insufficiencies of modern anthropology for the purposes of human self-understanding. Van Harvey has reminded us of "the new morality of knowledge," which requires critical and funded warrants for all our professions of faith.[2] Applied to *theo*logy, this new version of Occam's razor has cut the lashings on an abundance of dispensable baggage. But if it were restropped and applied, without indulgence, to the bristling dubieties of modern wisdom about *anthro*pology, what would be left? The truth is that secular humanism is in at least as parlous a shape as Christian humanism—and both for the same reason: our common and abysmal ignorance of the final reality of the human subject.

Any Christian dogma about human beings would naturally involve the coaptation and synthesis of the wisdom of the human sciences and the Christian views of humanity's origin and end in God, which is to say, the general problems of the psychology of religion, sociology of religion, religion and psychotherapy, etc. Here, again, we are in an area preeminently "modern" yet ironically barren of significant results in terms of really fruitful personality theory. The literature in psychology of religion and Christian nurture is inexplicably sparse, that in sociology of religion inexplicably irrelevant. In the crucial joint inquiry into "psychotherapy and a Christian doctrine of man," the bright promises of significant theoretical progress (David Roberts, et al.) have not yet been fulfilled.

Any soaring hope for imminent achievement of an adequate doctrine of human being is grotesque. And yet the enterprise is undeclinable, if only because it is one of the few irresistibly fascinating topics left us in our overstimulated urban culture. These difficulties are overwhelming. The distortions of three millennia of dualism and authoritarianism die hard. And, in their dying, new mutations in "human nature" are happening to befuddle the vision and judgment of the best observers. The most evident signs of this are the phenomena of displacement in all conventional moral-demand systems based on customary morality and conscience. They have taken away our superegos, and we know not where they have laid them. Yet the question of moral self-control is the utterly crucial issue in the current crises of humankind.

Here is a real Pandora's box opened wide—and no good fairy yet to tidy up the confusion. But at least one thing is clear: These new developments are theoretically awkward for every one of the anthropological models of the past, including those of the materialists. One can readily see what the notion of one's blood chemistry, as the vital medium of human self-consciousness, does to all the classical body-mind dualisms. But it also undercuts the antithetical notions of classical behaviorism, of the conditioned reflex sort (even in its sophisticated form, like those of Joseph Wolpe, Clark Hull, and B. F. Skinner). The already known effects of chemotherapy raise awkward theoretical questions for the orthodox Freudians (e.g., the new case histories of schizophrenics), but they don't ease the pain for the ego and social analysts with their greater stress on the peculiarly human dimensions of illness and health. And now comes the faintly cultic vanguard of psychedelics, and the fascinating vistas of the alteration and expansion of consciousness—of benign *ecstasis* by means of psilocybin, or mescaline, or peyote. This has occasioned the first firings of Harvard professors for academic hocus-pocus and also "the miracle of Marsh Chapel," in which several theologs and theological professors ingested psilocybin and reported "the deepest religious experience of their lives." And there is Walter Phanke's Harvard dissertation on "Drugs and Mysticism: An Analysis of the Relationships Between Psychedelic

Drugs and the Mystical Consciousness" (1963). The issues here are extremely tricky and "explosive" because of the powerful neurotic need of hysterics (who comprise so large a fraction of our population) to convert the anxieties and tensions of their normally discontented lives into acceptable equivalents—psychosomatic illness, narcotic additions of one sort and another; and now, all this and heaven, too!

My immediate interest is not in settling the matter of drugs and religion but only to make two comments that get toward the nub of the matter as far as the body-mind problem is concerned. The first is that if mystical experiences can be had by deliberate psychopharmacological intervention, the place of "mysticism" in the hierarchy of religious epistemology and ethics is rendered newly dubious ("programmed" spiritual exaltation). My other comment is to the same effect: In the instances of psychedelic *ecstasis* thus far reported, there is a striking noncorrelation between the chemically induced religious experiences and the observable changes in moral, social, and human dispositions and habitudes. *Ecstasis* may be exalting; it is not normally ennobling: Neither heroin nor LSD make people more loving, more responsible, more constructive members of society. Indeed, there is a profound antinomian cast in contemporary psychedelic teaching, which has its echoes in other forms of mysticism, too.

But our query just now is about the implications of all this for our image of humanity and of the nature and function of the human psyche. So to complicate matters just a mite more, I ask what we are to conclude from the fact that subcutaneous injections of lysergic acid can create a temporary but full-blown psychotic break (indistinguishable, symptomatically, from the "real McCoy")—and that we don't know what the long-term effects of repeated experiments of this sort would be? What are we to conclude from the fact that with our present pharmacopeia, we can depress and elevate our moods with some precision and with relatively innocuous, short-term, side effects—and that the frontier for this sort of thing is just opening up? And, finally, what are we to do with the psychological and moral problems generated by the increasing success of organ transplantations (kidneys, eyes, hearts)?

We need not pretend to medical or physiological expertise in these matters or wait until the details are solved in order to identify some important psychological, philosophical, and theological corollaries of these current analyses of the internal human environment:

1. The first, and most obvious, is that psychophysical dualism, parallelism, isomorphism are all dead as models for personality theory. You cannot separate the psychic from the somatic in any grossly obvious or consistent fashion so that they vary independently of each other.

2. Yet it also follows that the psyche has no physiological locus, no neural center. All little-man-in-the-head notions of the self or of self-consciousness, and all topographies or typologies of the psyche, must be recognized for the mythological projections they are. The relations of thought and the brain, of reason and the cerebrospinal cortex, of emotion and the optic thalamus—and of these to the homeostasis or variations in blood chemistry—all of this has become curiously "porous" and theoretically unsatisfactory. Inner states of consciousness and of self-consciousness—of the most intense and exalted kinds, "existential" in the truest sense— turn out to be functions of an organism's blood chemistry. But of what is the organism's blood chemistry a function? The right, but inconvenient, answer would seem to be: one's inner states, as (1) when "fear" or "appetite" affect endocrine output. But "fear" and "appetite" are code words for tissue states whose "causes" are also organic; or (2) when one "decides" on a pharmacological interference in his or her own body chemistry; or (3) when someone else "decides" on such an intervention. But to say that psychic reality is dependent on blood chemistry and that blood chemistry is dependent on somebody's psychic reality is circular and logically intolerable. It reminds us that the Hebraic psychology was closer to the mystery of selfhood than the Greeks ever imagined when they insisted that a man's life is in his "blood" and that out of "the heart" are the issues of life.

You might think that this would give the behaviorists aid and comfort, but for the fact that there is no clear relation between capillary diffusion and conditioned reflexes—and there is a clear relation between capillary "accidents" and the disruption or cancellation of synaptic configurations (especially in one's powers of recall and identification, etc.). No, the behaviorists are, it seems to me, in serious trouble as far as basic theory goes, unless they can come to terms, really, with the physiologists, the neurologists, and the geneticists. So far as my knowledge goes, this has not been done to anyone's real satisfaction.

All this adds up to a clear challenge and demand for a widespread and active collaboration among Christian theologians, historians, behavioral scientists, pastoral counselors, and all who work closely and effectively with people in the joint effort to probe and reformulate the structure and substance of a Christian anthropology. We have two Christian insights that bring real promise to this sadly underdeveloped task.

One is the biblical concept of *imago* and *similitudo Dei* as the ground for a doctrine of human personality as a specific and unique enterprise in creation. In effect this says that the human organism and its processes are wholly organic and "natural," a creature that comes to be and passes away, but that the emergence of a human self in that organism is a mysterious creative project of God-Creator, which is not a part of the organism but rather *is* that organism ordered according to a specific personal intentionality. Here is a unique self-consciousness that is not an awareness of objects or of introspected feelings but rather a consciousness of consciousness for which there is no identifiable physiological process or ground. The other Christian insight is the orthodox Christological formula of Chalcedon, which, in addition to confessing Jesus Christ as *homoousion to patri* (as sharing in the utter Mystery of the Father) goes on to balance that by the striking phrase *homoousion hemin*—sharing in our own mystery of being human—of sharing our stresses of psychodynamic development, yet without sin (since we, too, were not created to be sinful *on purpose*).

But what is this *homoousion hemin*? This, I suggest, is the convergent point between theology and anthropology, the Christological prism that we have turned to since Pentecost for God's self-revelation but not so fruitfully for God's revelation of the human self. Christology is, then, the clue: What matters about Jesus Christ is not his historicity and not his inner self-consciousness nearly so much as his human character, the imprint of his human personal identity on the people who knew him and whose memoirs we have in the Gospels, Acts, and Epistles. It is a character of which at least the following is true: A man of radical openness to God (faith), of love as personal essence, of radical obedience, of utter confidence and undying hope. This is the surface of the human mystery in its full and authentic reality. This is the human possibility; this is what it means to be, or to become, fully human.

But if the *homoousion hemin* is the true mirror of human nature, it is also the first premise of the *sola fide, sola gratia, sola gloria Dei.* For Christ's human nature is proof that human beings do not, even at their sinless best, achieve their own salvation or perfect themselves by their own endeavors and aspirations. " My will is to do the will of him who sent me. Why call me good; there is none utterly good but God!" And so we come back to the heart of the Gospel: "By grace are ye saved through faith; and that not of yourselves: it is the gift of God; Not of works, lest any man should boast. For we are his workmanship, created in Christ Jesus unto good works [the human enterprise] which God hath before ordained [providence] that we should walk in them" (Ephesians 2:8–10). This, then, is why I continue to be vitally interested in psychotherapy, why I'm interested in Christology, why I regard an adequate theological anthropology the utmost desideratum of our theological epoch. For Christian truth is always in an interplay with human wisdom, and there is the constant imperative that we bring that wisdom captive to Christ, to be redeemed by him and to be applied as a boon and blessing to humankind.

Introduction

A t the invitation of Dr. James Hall, a prominent Dallas Jungian analyst, Outler set about the task (which he reported privately to be one of his most arduous in memory) of reassessing his 1954 book, *Psychotherapy and the Christian Message,* from the hindsight of thirty years. Most North American pastoral counselors and pastoral theologians, in the Protestant tradition at least, regard this book and David E. Roberts' *Psychotherapy and a Christian View of Man* to be two of the most important mid-century efforts to establish grounds for a continuing dialogue between Christian caregivers and secular psychotherapists. Sadly, the kind of dialogue Outler envisioned did not materialize. The discipline of pastoral care and counseling continued to take its cues from the latest fads in psychotherapeutic theory and practice, eschewing comparable attentiveness to theological reflection on the human condition, even as psychotherapy itself moved perilously close to a state of captivity by psychopharmacological and psychobiological models of mental disorders. Ironically, Outler believed, where the dialogue continued at all, it aroused far greater interest among secular psychotherapists than it did among pastors and pastoral counselors! This reconsideration of *Psychotherapy and the Christian Message* is important especially for the attention it pays to the work of Carl Jung. Jungian analytic psychology was not dealt with at all in the earlier study, and the engagement with Jung in these pages is unique in the Outler archives. In his articulation of a fascinating agenda for further dialogue between Christian theologians and Jungian analysts, Outler suggests more than just a general outline for a new book on *Psychotherapy and the Christian Message.*

CHAPTER
23

Psychotherapy and the Christian Message Revisited

W hy should I call your attention to a book that was begun more than thirty years ago, that has long been out of print, and for which there will be no updating now? (Even though, like old Simeon, I keep waiting for someone else to do a proper sequel.) The answer to this is: perspective. It would be an illusion to suppose that there is anything like a general *entente cordiale* between current psychiatry and orthodox institutional Christianity. But there is a general working relationship between psychotherapy and pastoral care. Of the more and more mental health professionals who also work within the context of organized religion, Karl Menninger has asked *Whatever Became of Sin?* and has sought to enlist the clergy in doing something about that.

In 1930, when I began, there were no guidelines, no agreed agenda. Men and women working in the uncharted spaces between religion and psychiatry (Anton Boisen, the Wieners, et al.) were lonely pioneers typically alienated from historic Christian faith, on the one hand, and ordinary congregational life on the other. Pastoral psychology, pastoral care, and clinical pastoral education began to develop in the wake of, and were dominated by, the unfolding patterns of psychiatry, psychoanalysis, and analytic psychology. Biblical, historic Christian faith was rarely normative; indeed, was increasingly ignored and discounted as a baseline. Instead, the ranks of psychiatry, psychoanalysis, analytical psychologists—and pastoral counselors—were filled by people repelled by their childhood experiences of religion (in Judaism and Christianity) and who had found their "liberation" in "scientific psychiatry," Freud, Adler, Jung, Fromm, Horney, or Sullivan. Moreover, the basic change in the psychological climate that W. W. Auden had attributed to Freud had already begun to affect us all: libido, id, ego, superego, complexes, archetypes, introversion, extroversion, sexuality, and dream interpretation were already household words, cultural commonplaces. There were theologians deeply influenced by Freud and Jung (for instance, Reinhold Niebuhr more by Freud; Paul Tillich more by Jung). But few psychotherapists were influenced on a theoretical level by the challenges or resources of Christian theology rooted in the *fides historica*. What theological interests that were in evidence derived from the nonevangelical liberal moralisms of the Ritschlian school, romantic pietisms à la Schleiermacher, or the mind-wrenching defiances of existentialism (Heidegger, Sartre, et al.).

Dave Roberts, Seward Hiltner, and I set out to remedy this—Roberts and I more from the theological side, Hiltner more within the psychiatric and psychotherapeutic community. Roberts' *Psychotherapy and a Christian View of Man* was a pioneering effort that gained the grudging respect of many psychiatrists and did a world of good for many Christian clergy. It emboldened me to risk a lance or two on a broader theological front, and *Psychotherapy and the Christian Message* was the result. The basic idea, intention, and agenda of the book still seems a feasible project: (1) to begin with a hearty appreciation of the positive contributions of modern psychotherapy in all its forms to any wisdom about life, interpersonal relationships, and respect for persons; (2) interpenetrations of biology, psychology, and spirituality in human existence; (3) neurotic behavior not meaningless; (4) the art of listening and hearing in therapy; (5) the concept of psychodynamic development; (6) moralism as self-defeating; (7) a critique of pathogenic religious ideas and expressions; (8) the omnipresence of endopsychic conflict; and (9) the sovereign virtue of love (variously conceived). This appreciation of the aims and achievements of psychotherapy in general praxis was then followed by a sort of debate between what I understood to be the then reigning psychotherapeutic views of the human quandary, the human possibility or potential, and the wise and good ordering of human life—and what I was prepared to expound and defend as an orthodox Christian view of each of these: human quandary, potential, and agenda.

It is important to remember how confident, in 1950–1954, the *credo* of the Enlightenment was, and how certain it was that orthodox Christianity was already archaic. The credo: (1) Human nature is not depraved; (2) the end of life is life itself; (3) human nature, empowered by reason and intrinsic wisdom, is capable of perfecting itself and also the good life on earth; and (4) the means to this are liberations from ignorance, superstition, oppression, and indignities. The signatures are Voltaire, Rousseau, Feuerbach, et al. But a large roster of new names has been added, from Freud to Werner Erhard—and very few avowed dissenters. But each article in this credo (religious as it is as a devout humanistic faith confirmable only by a lifetime whole commitment) is antithetical to biblical religion's view of sin, salvation, and human fulfillment. Hence the debate over real issues that still run deep. Hence, the conflict about "ultimate concerns" since the naturalistic religions of human self-salvation are as transempirical as any other sort, and are now in process of nonconfirmation in as disheartening a fashion as Christianity ever was.

What Roberts and I had hoped for was a redefined and substantive debate in which our theological ideas would be analysed and appraised in much the same fashion (and spirit) as we had done with naturalistic and humanistic psychotherapy. That way, we hoped, the Christian message would get a hearing and would convince, or at least intrigue, those who were disposed to be convinced so that the question could then be raised: Does modern psychotherapy require an agenda of self-salvation? Is some sort of hyper-Pelagianism, or some sort of impersonalized "Gnosticism" ingredient in modern psychiatry—or is it only a part of its cultural origins and circumstances? If the latter, then a Christian psychotherapy might become possible—as Christian Platonism had been and as the current armistice between empirical science, duly limited, and Christian faith, newly modest in its claims, has begun to be.

The results were a brush-off. There were few complaints of my summaries of psychotherapeutic theory along with some praise for the theological passages (from Jews and Christians), although one reviewer recognized in my statement of the doctrine of grace and free will "a sort of genteel, Erasmian Christian humanism—with little of the rugged force of Augustine, Luther and Calvin." Well, yes . . .

The psychotherapists weren't about to learn enough about Christian theology to argue with this version of it. They already knew enough to warrant their judgment that Christianity is pathogenic; their waiting rooms were full of people whose emotions and views of life had been crippled or hobbled, stultified or disabled by "religious" superstitions, illusions, delusions, and worse. And so the idea of a debate between peers about the weighty issues of the human quandary (there *is* one, whatever its etiology), the human potential, and the ordering of life died aborning; the Enlightenment credo was reaffirmed; and pastoral psychology continued to develop within the terms of the anthropological and soteriological models supplied to it by a humanistic psychotherapy (which, even at that, was far more humane than the so-called "scientific psychiatry," with its lobotomies, its EC therapies, its tranquilizers, its complacent warehousing of "incurables," etc.).

Psychotherapy and the Christian Message, then, was a tract for the times, but for the wrong times. But it was not a wholly fruitless exercise. The cause to which it was devoted, a serious consideration by psychotherapists of more sophisticated versions of historic Christianity than they had upchucked in Sunday school, and a more appreciative understanding of the *vis medicatric naturral* by theologians, has continued to inch forward and there are now more genuinely interesting and hopeful prospects on the horizon than before. I was, therefore, pleasantly surprised to find that the book's agenda is still feasible; many of its insights and formulations are outdated, but much of what I would still profess as Christian faith and hope is in that little book, in one degree of maturation or another.

A second look, however, has revealed some deplorable flaws. It bears too clearly the marks of an opening dialogue between strangers (deaf strangers at that)—and, therefore, a great many more oversimplifications than I had realized at the time. The crucial flaw in the book is its habit of pitting one camp (psychotherapists as a category) over against another (Christian theologians as a category). This, as I can see now, only contributed to the schism I thought I was trying to overcome. Equally interesting, in retrospect, are the book's omissions: some due to a notable lack of clairvoyance; some conscious and deliberate even at the time. Even in 1950, we were past the dawn of psychobiology and psychochemistry, but I simply failed to foresee the possibilities of correlating blood chemistry, amino acids, and enzymatic interactions with affective states. I had no clear picture of the psychological implications of psychotropic psycholeptic drugs—and no theory as to why imipramine or amitriptyline hydrochlorides could alleviate depression (when they do). I knew about Sir Charles Sherrington's pioneering work in brain neurology but not of its extensions by Eccles, Sperry, and others; and I still am far from clear as to their philosophical import.

There was no way in the early 1950s, short of prophetic vision, to foresee the radical cultural transformations in the 1960s, which still go on in so-called developed societies: the shattering of societal taboos from anxiety and guilt, to anxiety without guilt (in the traditional sense), from acquiescence and accommodation to assertiveness of a pandemic sense of victimization. In the book I had quoted Nietzsche's anguished triumph about "the death of God," but had not imagined the destabilizations that would follow in contemporary theology when non-genius types would make like midget Nietzsches. I took Freud seriously, and also the neo-Freudians; I would have been dumbfounded to think that three decades later I'd be reading an account of the radical confusions of "Psychotherapy in the '80s" in *Newsweek,* or its casual reporting of the eclipse of Freudian doctrine (it would have been more accurate to report how far Freud's basic concepts have become commonplace and therefore no longer identified with his name). In 1950 liberalism was still dominant, the West was still dominant, the social gospel still on the upswing, and the future of the middle classes (the economic base of both institutional religion and psychotherapy) looked secure. Now, all that has changed, and we are looking at a rising generation of "born conservatives."

This will have enormous cultural repercussions in society in a future of diminished expectations.

There were, however, two notable and deliberate omissions in the personnel for the dialogue I was proposing: Carl Rogers and Carl Jung. In Rogers' case, it seemed clear to me that here was a *praxis* suited to a limited class of psychological disturbances (however large the number of people in that particular class) but without a distinctive theory to support it. It was, in effect, a program of assurance and reassurance, devoid of a credible etiology or teleology. It was, as I thought (then and still), not worth arguing with at the level I was interested in; and the Rogerians I knew (including Rogers) were not even mildly interested in such a debate. Why should they have been, since, in their view, the Christianity I represented was already discredited by sophisticated moderns. The other omission was serious, but it seemed unavoidable at the time because it called for a different sort of discussion based on a radically different view of psychopathology and psychotherapy. This, of course, was Jung. It was not that I hadn't tried to understand Jung or that the general body of his system was not already in place. Indeed, I had heard his Terry Lectures at Yale on *Modern Man In Search of a Soul*[1] and had met him (in a wholly formal fashion) at a dinner following.

But how does one debate theology with Freud and Jung together—as if on two fronts? For Freud, the crucial question about religion was its legitimacy: If religion is an "illusion," what is the future of rationalizations about that illusion and its misunderstandings? For Jung, the crucial question was adequacy: How to conceive of religion, in its bewildering manifold expressions, so that it could be made to serve the cause that was always first, last, and central in Jung's entire career, individuation—the attainment of a single, homogeneous being, in a stable equilibrium between self-ego, the personal unconscious, and the collective unconscious. Freud had never encountered Christianity in a fashion that persuaded him. Jung had encountered it, at home, and had been repelled by it. Jung's *Answer to Job*[2] had just appeared (in 1952), and *Aion*[3] was already in translation. In them, as in the Terry Lectures and everywhere, really, there were clear overtones of an active rejection of Christianity, but no argument about it and no explanation. Freud had cast off his Judaism without much struggle; Jung seemed in some sort of emotionally

276

charged endeavor to displace the Christianity that repelled him with a more adequate syncretism that would include the best in all religions (with, however, precious little from Christianity). I think I understand this now; I didn't then. Even then, though, it was clear that it would take another book to deal with Jung, and I wrote a paragraph for the introduction in which I almost committed myself to some such task. But there were many other and usually more exciting things to do (which may have contributed something to contemporary ecumenical theology in our century, but not much to psychotherapeutic doctrine).

There were emphases of great positive import in Jung, even as I saw him then. First and overriding was his insistence upon the legitimacy of the transempirical and the supernatural (of "religion" in some sense) even in psychiatric and psychological doctrine. Freud was reductionist; Jung was expansionist. His hostility toward orthodox Christianity was coupled with a confidence that something better was at hand. But this was (and still is) a welcome relief from the claims of the reductionists, the behaviorists, the technocrats—not only in medicine but in society at large. It makes room for parapsychology, metapsychology, new understandings of myths and symbolic transformations. It marked a move from the Freudian topography (id, superego, ego) to a more complicated map of the mind, with psychological type and combinations of feeling, thought, sensation, intuition within types.

Freud had seen dreams chiefly as diagnostic, apertures onto an otherwise inaccessible unconscious. Jung saw dreams chiefly as didactic: "messages" from the collective unconscious to the conscious person, shedding new light on persona-shadow, anima-animus aberrations and tensions and, therefore, new wisdom about one's personal decisions and valuations. This enlarged the repertory of human resources for self-understanding by a great deal. Freud saw the way to wisdom as an emergence from obscurantism to reason, from id and superego dominances to clearheaded, illusionless self-determination. Jung saw the way to wisdom as a return to the human center, to those archaic, chthonic wisdoms of humanity preserved for us from prehistoric times in archetypal images, myths, and alchemical speculations. Freud wielded Occam's razor ruthlessly: the simplest explanation is the truest. This meant the reduction of all possible paradoxes. Jung saw opposites everywhere, in *complexes, coincidentia oppositorum, coniuncta oppositorum,* syzygies of anima and animus, all the paired opposites that fascinated the Gnostics, and dualists of all sorts.

It has not been surprising, over the years, to see the Freudian star wane (leaving, however, an indelible imprint on modern consciousness) and Jung's star wax. In various combinations, with a medical base, Jungian theory has led to more intervention in therapy based on less doctrinaire models than orthodox Freudianism, and to a sort of encouragement in a science-oriented society to feel and think about the pervasive mysteries of human experience (and in theory, about the Encompassing Mystery). Jungian psychotherapy is, in principle, open to further insights from biology (blood chemistry in particular), to neurology (brain, mind, and human spirituality), and on the other side, to philosophical questions about ontology, epistemology, axiology, and ethics. It is open to Eastern religions and to secular superstitions. And it is sensitive to the deepening crises of civilization on this planet, with more hope for its future than any of the visions rooted in the grim realisms of Freud's *Civilization and Its Discontents.* Most of all, the concept of individuation is both axial and radial. It was never fully developed by Jung nor, so far as I am aware or can judge, by any of his followers. Here, as I would suggest, is where the future of Jungian psychology lies.

But there are serious difficulties in Jung for an orthodox Christian theologian, however ecumenical or however eager for a fruitful alliance between Christianity and analytical psychology. The first of these is a question: Was Jung's hostile attitude toward Christianity (and Judaism) a function of his own experiences, at home and in his time, or was it a matter of principled rejection and therefore ingredient in the Jungian system as such? In 1954, I couldn't tell. With *Memories, Dreams, Reflections,*[4] the picture came a good deal clearer and opens the way to an "analytical" explanation still not altogether satisfactory. Jung's attitude toward his father was chiefly negative and his doubts about his father's faith and understanding of that faith were vivid. Carl's description of Johann's Catechism classes is harsh and hostile; his description of his own first (and last) communion is scornful in a way that none of his description of other mysteries in other religions ever is; his *Answer to Job* echoes his rejection of his father's professed faith in God's goodness. But should Christianity as a whole be judged on such a basis? One of the important clues here has not been noticed, so far as I know, by historians of nineteenth-century thought or by Jungian theorists. It is Jung's memories of sneaking a look into one of the few unconventional theological tomes in his father's library; he had rejected "the traditional conceptions" out of hand and never thereafter considered them seriously. The book, he tells us, was Biedermann's *Christliche Dogmatik,* published in 1869. This was Alois Emanuel Biedermann, a maverick Hegelian idealist, dedicated to abstractions of the loftiest order, the sort of rationalist who had already driven Søren Kierkegaard bonkers. If young Carl was seeking an unconventional Christianity, he had other versions of liberal Christianity besides Hegel and Strauss and Biedermann; he calls it, however, "drivel."

The other side of this same coin (of parental influences) was young Carl's attraction to what he perceived as the chthonian religion of his mother. While his father's church became, as he said, a "place of torment" for him, he was also discovering, with what he recalls as his mother's approval, that the lakes, mountains, trees, and flowers far better exemplified "God" than men did. Christianity, he concluded, was "a diabolical mockery," but Goethe was an inspiring alternative (he felt more at home in *Faust* than in John's Gospel) "somehow connected with animals, trees, mountains, meadows and running water," an alternative that displaced his father's religious views.

All this is natural enough, of course. In Jung's case, however, he left Christianity (and Judaism) where he had found them early in adolescence: as incredible, boring, morally and intellectually offensive. He learned to live sympathetically with other religious myths; he became uncommonly sensitive to other symbols and their transformation. He was deeply moved and heartened by the papal dogma of Mary's bodily assumption into heaven in 1950. But the Christianity he knew about closer to home never counted for him. Religion, for Jung, was no illusion; but the Judeo-Christian tradition was, in his eyes, a sort of travesty. Reading Jung's autobiography sometimes reminds me of long talks I've had with Paul Tillich in New York, Cambridge, and Chicago, when he would rhapsodize about the beauties of the Schwarzwald, of the sacral powers of running water, his sense of oneness with sea and sand on the North Sea beaches on holidays, and when he would deplore Christianity as he saw it in vulgar practice.

A Christian theologian has another question for Jung and Jungians, and it picks up on Freud's famous appeal to Jung to stand firm with him (Freud) against the "rising black tide of occultism." There are differing interpretations of this incident, but these would not change the question's more crucial form: How far was Jung's interest in the occult, in alchemy, etc., a dimension of his wide-ranging curiosity—and as a resource for still more instances of basic and universal images, symbols, and archetypal themes? Or how far was this intended to be an essential ingredient in Jung's system? Put another way, is it possible to be a credentialed and loyal Jungian and confine one's interests in the occult to the dimensions of cultural curiosity? Ditto for alchemy and magic? This matters, not only to *de*mythologized moderns, but to *re*mythologized Christians as well. Judaism and Christianity, from the beginning, have cast a wary eye on occultism, spirit-possession, witchcraft as threats to monotheism, as temptations to the human manipulation of divine power, as the Faustian spirit prepared for self-defeating pacts with Mephistopheles. My friend, John Wesley, believed devoutly in witchcraft, poltergeists, and synchronicity: I would not argue, however, that this belonged to the essence of Wesley's Christian faith.

Another question to Jung: Is his blunt and unnuanced rejection of God as *Summum Bonum* in *Answer to Job* a well-considered judgment in axiology or is it an outburst of outrage at what he regards as a human portrayal of God in terms that he regards as shoddy? The passage is puzzling; it is almost as if Jung were reading the text of Job as God's *verbi ipsissimi,* responding to him, *coram Deo,* with a stern rebuke. "To believe that God is the *Summum Bonum* is," says he, "*impossible for a reflecting consciousness.*" Two difficulties here: (1) It would follow that all those who have professed belief in God as *Summum Bonum* (a large company) were not "reflecting consciousnesses"—and that would be an astounding charge to make; or (2) is this a denial of the claim that *God* is the *Summum Bonum,* or, rather, that there is no *Summum Bonum,* only a *Proximum Bonum?* This, too, would be an astounding claim. I am less interested here in trying to adjudicate these questions, but to recognize them as theological questions, which Christians have had some experience in pondering; which only means that the debate should go forward in appropriate terms. In any case, for such a discussion, Jungians will have to qualify as theologians and theologians as analytical psychologists.

Another line of question to Jung. More than any other psychologist, he has helped to make God talk permissible among sophisticates without being suspect of fideism or pietism. But is it essential to his system that God be regarded as radically impersonal and unitarian? Jung tells us how he came to discover a collective *a priori* beneath the personal psyche. This idea, he began to realize, postulated something of an altogether impersonal nature underlying the psyche. Elsewhere, he attributes transcendence to this impersonal nature and occasionally refers to it as God. Moreover, he never refers to God in personal terms that would make prayer, in a Christian sense, appropriate. That Jung believed in an altogether impersonal spiritual force or power is one thing (and it goes without saying that such a belief is wholly legitimate). Moreover, that many, if not most, Jungians share such a belief is wholly in order. But is it ingredient as an essential element in the system, over and beyond that axial structure of the psyche and the crucial steps "on the path to the center" (which is to say, individuation)? Could a Jungian believe in a personal God? If so, in what terms? What in Jung's theories could be revised or accommodated to a religious tradition like Judaism or Christianity without striking a fatal blow at the goal of individuation and the archetypal structures that guide and sustain the way to it? Obversely, what elements in historic Christianity would have to have been accommodated, and in what way, to allow for an adequate doctrine of individuation and its archetypal matrix? Does individuation require a naturalism, or a Gnosticism?

Much depends on what I regard as the great unfinished task of the Jungian system: an adequate map, inventory or categorical ordering, of the archetypal system. Jung tells us of his discoveries of Schopenhauer, Nietzsche, and Kant. But more and more I have come to think that Jung's endeavor to explore the collective unconscious by proving its archetypal images and themes was a parallel endeavor to Kant's heroic undertaking (in *Critique of Pure Reason*) to deduce the dynamic structures of knowledge, a map of the knowing mind and its inherent categories. We remember that it was David Hume's *Treatise of Human Nature* that had wakened Kant from his dogmatic slumbers and alerted him to the defense of the rudimentary claims of empirical science. To do this, he had to show that we are knowing selves with a universal and "transcendental" structure in our minds (which organizes all incoming information in intelligible combinations of rational categories), that all sense impressions that rise to the level of thought and conceptualization can be combined and made intelligible by the transcendental categories of the human understanding. This is valid knowledge: What can be so categorized can be conceptualized, formulated, and evaluated by "pure reason." What cannot be so categorized is excluded from the domain of *pure* reason and left to generate the confusions, paralogisms, and obscurantisms that pass for common sense among most of us most of the time. That theological statements fell within this limbo of paralogism was, in Kant's view, simply a part of the price to pay for establishing the ground of a rational, universal knowledge. Christian theology has been arguing with Kant ever since, and I must confess that the argument has been both uncomfortable and genuinely fruitful.

Is the analogy fanciful that Jung was prompted to his explorations of the archetypal kingdom by the challenge of Freud to reduce the rich flowering of the human unconscious to libidinal energy and to reduce libidinal energy to sexuality as a bottom line? For Jung, the human underground—chthonian, mythopoetic, shadowy—was far more romantic, more inventive, more numinous than that. Here was a *depositum* of all the memories of mankind, long before the dawn of rational consciousness, deeper and richer than the reductionisms of modern empiricism, science, and technocracy. It retained all the archaic flavor of primitive mentalities—the primal urge toward etiological and celebrative myths, toward primordial images—and this as an incremental process that has gone on through millennia of cultural evolution and all over the world. Here is a shared structure, not of neatly catalogued categories of the grids and structures of the mind (as in Kant) but of endlessly repeated themes, images, and reenacted myths that belong together and are shared by all: thus the notion of the *collective* unconscious. Experience, to Jung and to Kant, is not a simple interaction of the knowable and knowers; it is always an interpretation of raw data by means of the primal quaternity of sensation, thinking, feeling, intuition.

But how far does the analogy between Kant's transcendental deducation of our mental categories and Jung's map making of the human imagination run? Kant claimed that his map of twelve categories was exhaustive. Jung makes no such claims about his catalogue of the archetypes—and none of his followers has that I know of. Yet does not the Jungian system call for a complete and intelligible inventory of the archetypal contents of the collective unconscious, either in terms of their accessibility—from the most readily accessible to the most inaccessible? Or in some other schematism that allows for a critical judgment upon the rival claims of various interpreters of the manifestations of the contents of the collective unconscious? Jung tells us much (almost all we know) about these archetypes but always in some noncategorial sense. There is, of course, The Shadow, the most easily accessible of them all—the dark side of every light, the snake in every Eden, the dramatic flaw in every hero, the fly in every ointment, etc. But is The Shadow more or less archetypal than The Wise Old Man, the Chthonic mother, the Anthropos, the Syzygies of Anima-Animus, crucifix, mandala, wheel, flower, Uroborus, t'ai chi, etc.? How many archetypes are there, and how are they organized, integrated, evoked? Are they like Plato's *eternal elements*? Or like Mircea Eliade's myths of the eternal return?

You can see that if I knew Jung better, I might have a better answer to these questions. But I hope you can see that I also have found Jung and the Jungians enormously stimulating and challenging and that I wish I were not past the time for an updated version of *Psychotherapy and the Christian Message,* focused this time on Jung rather than Freud. There is much in Jung that seems to me to resemble Paracelsus (whose last name was *Bombast*) and Jakob Boehme, who drove my friend Wesley up the wall. Although it is clear enough that, for Jung, the process of individuation, the essential agenda for human life, presupposed autonomy and self-salvation, I am not yet convinced that Jung's vision of individuation and his dimmer view of socialization might not be even better served by a clearer sense of *theonomy,* a frank avowal of radical dependence (if only in the sense that Schleiermacher understood it), an assured, unanxious trust in the upholding power and love of God. I do not assert that this is the case; my real concern is to raise the right questions with and for Jungians and to suggest new or extended horizons and agenda for their reflections (memories and dreams) and for their dialogues with thoughtful Christians.

There are two reasons why I have come to think that Christian theologians (even in the biblical and historic traditions) and Jungian theorists could find important consensus on what is accidental and notional in Jung's system and in Christian theologies (as we know them). One of them is that Jung's mysticism has an interface with Christian and Jewish mysticism; it is will-mysticism and not unitive or absorptive mysticism, and that is a crucial distinction! The other is a quite curious business. Every now and then, Jung will use the term *Gnade*, "grace," in one context or another—never defined, always as if it came spontaneously to his mind from way down (and way back). It is more of an accent point than a dominant theme, but it's repeated often enough to catch the eye of the Christian theologian. For whereas Jung's references to and usages of Christian theological terms generally reflect his anti-Christian bias and ignorance, his usages of this central, crucial term "grace" are invariably right, as far as I've checked them. Jung uses "grace" to mean "the gift of love," "an unmerited gift" from beyond, an unmeasured and bountiful good will. Grace, for Jung, is always supernatural in its source. It is almost as if, in all those foments in church, in childhood, and all that repugnance for his father's faith, the Christian notion of grace had stuck in his heart, and had remained a part of his personal unconscious. So, what if, in a way not yet noticed clearly enough, "grace" turned out to an archetype, as Christian faith has also said it is? Unless this is simply an amateur's amateurish reading, it would open many vistas and at least set the stage for meaningful explorations that might help us all. That, of course, could mark a turning point in the unfolding dialogue between the Christian wisdoms about life and death and the Jungian wisdoms, too.

PART 6

At Career's End

Introduction

The years immediately following Outler's formal retirement from full-time teaching at Perkins School of Theology (although he remained a very real presence on the campus from 1974 to 1979 as Research Professor of Theology, Emeritus) were heavily devoted to completing the long-awaited editing of the "Standard Sermons" of John Wesley. During this period of extraordinarily tense and intense scholarly effort, Outler found a special quality of relief by immersing himself in the discussions swirling among an uncommonly erudite and creative group of scholars and professional persons committed to exploring the relations between science and religion at the frontiers of both disciplines. In the 1970s the group founded the Isthmus Institute in Dallas, Texas.

Outler delivered the following address to Institute members on January 21, 1984, as part of a symposium program. It is included in this volume for several reasons. First, the response to it was one of the deepest in many of his colleagues' memory. Second, it represents one of his last and most carefully considered treatments of a theme foundational to his theology and pastoral work across his long life. Third, it examines profoundly a polarity at the very center of pastoral ministry today and offers a way through the deep distresses of a graceless society whose illusions about power's manageableness have led us only to fratricidal conflicts and inconsolable alienation. For the pastor, the pastoral counselor, the psychotherapist, and all whom they serve, it *is* grace that has brought us thus far, and grace alone that will lead us home.

CHAPTER

24

Power and Grace

$\mathbf{A}$s a theologian on our program, I am inclined to begin with the radical paradox that, perennially, has prompted theological reflection, viz., the human condition as we know it, with our near total immersion in nature and natural processes yet also with our partial consciousness of this immersion and, thereby, our partial transcendence of it. This sort of awareness is not shared by the other animals, so far as we can tell; and it includes self-consciousness, our powers of image-making and language, our translinear rationality, and our further awareness of a whole set of infinite aspirations, all bracketed within unsurpassable limits—finitude, transience, and death. One thinks of the psalmist and Karl Jaspers in almost the same connection. On the one hand, we are, indeed, "fearfully and wonderfully made." On the other hand, we are also aware (at least occasionally) of being encompassed and engrasped by an infinite Mystery—the Mystery of the Holy, the Numinous, some sort of Ultimate Environment in which we exist as radically dependent, yet also with a sense of belonging, of being "at home." Thus, the core question of religion is whether this *Umgreifende* (this engrasping, surpassing Mystery) is benign and self-disclosing and, if so, on what terms?

Current philosophies of science, in conscious contrast with the classical traditions of "modern" science, with their versions of a closed universe, have come to see the physical universe as open to transcendence and thus not being fully self-explanatory and self-sufficient. This means, among other things, that human selfhood is not merely epiphenomenal, that human behavior cannot be reduced to behaviorist terms, that arguments for the reality of Universal Mind and Spirit (from design, purpose, and moral freedom) can no longer be dismissed as mere paralogisms. The scientific method, within its operable limits, still yields the highest level of empirical certainty and control that we have. But we know now that its uncertainties are not just provisional but inherent. This allows us to take our intuitions of an Ultimate Environment seriously without fear of obscurantism, and so to conceive the world process, with *natura* and the *humanum* within it, as existing within a transcendent Ground and End. But this, in turn, allows for religion as a cluster of our human symbols of and responses to this Ground and End.

What we have not heard very much about is the shadow side of the *humanum,* our radical propensities for alienation and *mis*behavior, our no-win struggles for an optimal human order, with freedom from imposed stultifications and freedom for fulfillment. Here we are, born to know ourselves, and yet also so deeply confused in our successive identity crises, young, middle-aged and old. Born to be free, we are so easily entangled in webs of frustration. Born to grow up to the full stature of our humanity, our maturation is so often arrested or deviated. Born to equanimity, as finite creatures with infinite horizons, we live anxiously in swirls of chance and stress. This is not the fate of ordinary folk only, or of the misfits, but of our brightest and best, of those least threatened by the desperations of which Pascal spoke. This, then, is what I mean by alienation: the not being "at home" in a life matrix designed for meaningful life. Ah, but was it well-designed for such ventures: what with all the perinatal traumata with which human life begins, what with all "the slings and arrows of outrageous fortune" along the way, what with the unavoidable pathos of transience, tragedy, and death? There are no easy answers here: One can only point to the human record (and to at least a few clues in one's own experience) of truly meaningful life under less than optimum conditions. What this record suggests is that it is not required of us, in defense of honesty, to deny that "life has meaning, that it means well" and that the finding of that meaning is an irrepressible human need and impulse.

Tragedy comes when, given all these paradoxes, the *humanum*-under-stress turns to coercive Power (in whatever forms available) as a coping strategy. It is as if we thought that power over others could make us more secure in ourselves. The tactics involved may be aggressive or wheedling, or any of the thousand ways of enlisting others to our advantage, as perceived or defined by our cultural milieus. Power, in this sense, need not include all forms of causality and therefore does not extend to natural regularities (like gravity); though magic does pretend to have power over such regularities, which is why it is so fascinating to so many people. What I have in mind, in speaking of power is rather like what Augustine spoke of as *libido dominandi*—the lust to dominate other people (or its psychological inversion, the willingness to be dominated, of "going along to get along"). Power, in the sense we are using it here, is a code word for our scramblings for higher rungs in any given pecking order, our efforts to fend off the world or else to grasp it as a prize. Power is that cluster of chosen antidotes for the dis-ease of the *humanum*-at-odds-with itself and with the humane values in the Ultimate Environment. Power is the multifaceted enterprise aimed at the achievement of human order and freedom within the conflicts of self-interests.

We have ancient disharmonic memories stored up as residues in our archetypical images and themes: primeval innocence and aboriginal turmoil. They focus on the radical ambivalences in all issues of order and freedom. There is the Genesis myth of Adam and Eve: lured by the bedazzling promise that knowledge of the right sort would open a way beyond their human condition. "You shall be as *gods*" was the promise (viz., immunity from the indignities of finite existence). There are also those stories about Cain and Abel, about Joseph and his brethren, about Moses and the Pharaoh, and on and on. Concurrently, we know about pecking orders as normal and normative in ancient Ebla and Ugarit, about the splendid tyrannies in Babylon and Nineveh. There were all those brilliant ideas of divinized monarchy in the ancient Near East, those splendid failures of democracy in the

Mediterranean world. There were those magnificent self-deceptions of the Roman visions of *Lex et Pax*, which had, however, to be enforced by heavy-handed legionnaires! Thus, our myths and digs and documents say pretty much the same thing: From time immemorial, and in the name of order and rank, men and women have been willing to inflict and to suffer horrendous measures of inhumanity. And they tell us something else besides: Something in the human spirit is indomitable, that the *humanum* cannot be reduced to an item in nature—not by domestication, not by misery, nor even by slavery. History confirms Kant in its own strange way: The *humanum* cannot be treated as a means only and remain human.

Even so, the sorry history of so many assaults on human dignity provides abundant reasons for what Unamuno spoke of as "the tragic sense of life in men and peoples." And it forces us to see the consequence: Those who wield power inhumanely are diminished thereby in their own humanity. Plato dreamed of a well-ordered society in which the wise would rule, the rulers would be wise, and the ruled would be glad to have it so. But the price of the ideal republic was a more static and hierarchical order than the *humanum* can tolerate, especially when a mudsill of slavery is taken for granted. Machiavelli taught aggressors to be clever; Hobbes encouraged them to be candid; Adam Smith absolved them with the assurance that their enlightened self-interest was, indeed, a mode of true benevolence; Karl Marx justified them in the name of the humane impulses in the historical dialectic. It was left to George Orwell to cry, "Pox," upon inhumanity as such. Yet here we are, now finally in 1984—The Year of Big Brother's Epiphany—and how stands the human prospect? What have we learned in four millennia that has led us to discount the power syndrome and its symbols of pyramids and pomp? Indeed, have we not seen how readily the ethos of power is borrowed and accommodated by religious hierarchies as well as civil and military and economic?

Such a record, however, has an instructive counterpart in any just view of the *humanum*. There were the Hebrew prophets who spoke, in God's name, for justice and mercy above the whims of kings and priests. There was Socrates, serving his country more nobly than Pericles by being gadfly to the high and the mighty and by scorning, in life and death, all attempts to intimidate or corrupt his humanity. More importantly, there have been the nameless multitudes who have neither bowed to oppression nor fled the imperfect world because of its imperfections, who lived and loved and held the world together even as the swaggerers were fretting their humanity away. These were the men and women whose energies were more devoted to being at home in God's world than to being recorded in the annals of violence.

Now, of course, our stock of kings has run out. In their place, however, we have updated models: tyrants, tycoons, and juntas. We have no divinized cult heroes, but still no end to our thirst for glory (or notoriety). The powerful among us want no less power: the powerless will no longer accept their fate as tolerable. The result is a fulminating epidemic of victimization (and the paranoid sense of being victimized) in nearly every society over the globe, and this deepens the sense of human malaise. High in a pecking order, there is a dizziness and a fear of falling (not only the fear, but the prospect); for those low on the world's totem poles, there are all those countless affronts to dignity that cauterize the human spirit. In the flood of the tracts for our times, the bases for hope would seem to be the discovery of still more clever uses of the power that we have and the avoidances of power abused. But these strategies assume that all that is needed for solving human problems is a proper under-standing of them, plus earnest exhortations to each other to get our acts together.

What often goes unnoticed in all this is that there is an inexorable nemesis of power even if it does no more than invert the old pyramids, reverse old pecking orders, let underdogs have their turn at being top dog. Power takes its own revenge upon the powerful and prompts them to a triple self-deception: a false confidence (1) that one's power is one's very own; (2) that it has been attained by one's own merit; (3) that enough of it might cancel one's radical dependence. None of these notions is true. The facts are that (1) all power is on short-term loan; (2) all claims to intrinsic merit lead to rationalizations and ingratitude; (3) the paths of glory *do* lead but to the grave—and not only to the grave but to a fair amount of irony and indignity along the way. Reliance on such deceptions blinds us to the Mystery in which we do actually exist and on which we depend, more radi-cally than we are willing to acknowledge.

This is the point to a strange story about Jesus that appears in all three Synoptic Gospels, in different versions (a sign that it left a deep impression on widely different groups in the early Christian community). As the disciples began to believe in the actual prospects of a messianic kingdom, the question of their pecking order in it began to gnaw at them. James and John (Luke reports that it was their mother who took the initiative) made their brazen bids for preeminence early on (provoking the others less to disapproval than to jealousy). Taking them where they were, Jesus tried to lead them to a radically different view of power. "You know," said he, "how the *archons* of this world love to lord it over their underlings (and you can translate *archons* as "top dogs"). You also know how the *megaloi* (literally, "the big shots') love to be kowtowed to." Luke adds how they also demand compliments and "strokes" from their lackeys. But, Jesus insisted, it shall not be like this among you. Those who would be great in this community may become so only by becoming servants. The measure of greatness (of real success) is preeminence in service. He reminded them that he himself was among them as one "who had come not to be ministered unto, but to minister."

Here was a great reversal of the power syndrome, and it has been easy enough to rationalize it away over the course of religious history. Indeed, it has been more often honored by profession than performance. The worst of the Roman emperors claimed the title *Euergetes* ("Benefactor"); power-hungry churchmen have proclaimed themselves *servi servorum Dei* ("servants of the servants of God"); Uriah Heep discovered that humility was a good way to get ahead. The fruit of this hypocrisy is all too familiar: Altruism is professed by many very powerful people, as part of their game plan. But if there is one thing clear after all these years, it is that a recourse to the power syndrome (or to its masochistic counterparts) is self-defeating as a strategy for overcoming alienation. It does not function as advertised. It does not alleviate our alienation in and from our immediate environment, much less the Ultimate Environment. Domination cannot command loyalty; it cannot confer dignity and respect, cannot stave off estrangement. It cannot, even in its altruistic modes, ease the aches of meaninglessness or end what Thomas Hardy spoke of as "the long drip of human tears."

Stoicism was an answer to this realization that the power syndrome does not work humanely, but it will not work for us. Fatalism is not credible, even to the Jacques Monods and B. F. Skinners of our contemporary world. Yet self-abasement is no better than self-advertisement. Neither is hedonism nor epicureanism nor conformity. There is a tyranny of custom, and there are penalties for failure and much energy locked up in clothes and folkways and trendy ideas! We really were not made for ourselves or even for nature, and our lives are unstable, way down deep, until they have found an upholding medium on whose buoyancy they can rely so that even as they are tossed about by the waves of life, they are still sustained by its deeper calms.

What high religion suggests, with all its manifold symbolism, is that life's securities and creativities do not lie in what we can do for ourselves and on our own, but in what we can do with what has already been done and is still being done for us, initiatives from beyond ourselves that we are free to count on and react to. We were designed to belong and to be at home in God's creation in a very special way: as finite creatures with capacities for participation in the divine love and goodness and joy (without ceasing to be creatures). It is a given in our existence (though not as gravity is given) that we have unique identities, not to invent or contrive but to acknowledge and to realize. Freedom is not a prize; it is a gift (a gift that can be lost or distorted but need not be). Maturity is less an achievement than the development of potentialities that we did not create. We are, indeed, achievers, inventors, creators—but always and only within a matrix of unearned gifts. Locked in a power struggle, our concerns focus on what is ours, what we have earned, achieved, what may have come to us by "luck" but that still is ours to dispense and to dispose. Rescued from such engrossments, we can ask a different question: How much of what we are or can be is, in reality, a bounty—not as mere circumstance but as gift, for which we are responsible and might even be thankful—to earthly givers and also to the Ultimate Giver?

This notion of the giftedness of what is most truly good and meaningful in the *humanum* is everywhere in high religion, and the Bible has some special words for it, the chief of which are *chesed* ("loving kindness") and *charis* ("Grace"). They have many cognates: creation, law, God's will, the kingdom of God, mercy, forgiveness, salvation. They have their analogs in all living religions, and it is no accident that the Greek translation of the Hebrew Bible has its Hebrew terms for "grace" (*chen* and *chesed*) turn up as *charis,* or that *charis* in the New Testament is a term with rich undertones and overtones of its Jewish background. In its ordinary usage, in hellenistic Greek, *charis* connotes warm, openhearted hospitality—the sort of thoughtful love that makes for feelings of at-homeness.

Grace, then, may be considered as power of a different sort: sovereignty manifest as benign order in creation (natural process) and as freedom in the *humanum* (viz., that cluster of human options to be humane without dominating or feeling victimized). Grace and lovingkindness have their source in God and their manifestations in human affairs. Grace is not, therefore, vacuous. As a term, it points to a special sort of giftedness about which we all know something: the giftedness of life itself and of our freedom to participate in our own divine design and character. But grace must be accepted as and for what it is, as gift, as bounty—else one is drawn into the absurd power games of merited grace, which is a contradiction in terms and where tragedy begins.

To speak of grace is to call attention to that wondrous spectrum in life where good things come from beyond and where everything is altered from circumstance to value, where one turns away from merits and demerits, away from pride and avarice, away from what the medieval called *accidie*—spiritual apathy. For the givens that are uniquely human cannot be self-created or merited or contrived. In friendship what matters and what lasts has the quality of gift, beyond the protocols of etiquette. In therapy, it is the thoughtful love of the therapist that plays the crucial role. In learning and teaching, there are reactive prerequisites, but the miracle of insight *happens* and is of grace. We love as we have been loved, not just by fellow humans but by the God who is Love Unbounded. Gratitude is the sort of action that is prompted by our acceptance of the gifts of grace as gifts (to paraphrase Tillich by a bit). Thus, grace begets gratitude and gratitude is the least easily corrupted virtue of them all. And this belongs to the essence of true religion: this reconciliation of God's alienated world to God's gracious sovereignty, through grace, in grace, for grace. Religion, in any such sense as this, is neither rival to science nor substitute, but a complementarity. It is a radically different orientation toward existence, with less interest in causality and process than in origins, ends, and meanings. It is about human energies let loose to be both more humane and more reverent than calculating and manipulative, energies devoted gratefully (and graciously) to the elevations of truly human interests, the chief of which is the divine glory.

Where grace abounds, there is a strange indifference to strict proportionality and a heightened concern for what is fitting, appropriate, truly helpful. Where it is justice that is at stake, our calculations must be exact with all relevant circumstances known and weighed by a knowledgeable and fair-minded judge. But this is rarely possible, which is why the whole system of justice comes so easily under the suspicion of haphazardness. In a state of grace, interpersonal strategies are less coercive and more persuasive. Under coercion, persons are bound to feel degraded; under persuasion, they feel more human, which is to say, with their dignity and freedom acknowledged and honored. There is, as Jung might say, something synchronous about grace: In it there is a certain spontaneity and gracious happenstance that enlarges life's horizons without being bound into the causal nexus.

This, in practice, confounds all systems based on merit and strict order. Life in the power syndrome looks always at the bottom line of advantage or disadvantage. The notion of relying on what we have not merited, of being more thankful than proud, is bound to disturb those whose ideal is self-sufficiency. Yet our experiences of grace are of a righteousness not our own that enhances our humanity, and this is at least in part what the New Testament means by "The kingdom of God and his righteousness." In trying to explain this special sort of righteousness (more gracious than merely just), Jesus ran into a blank wall of incomprehension, even among his disciples. Consequently, he resorted to strange stories called parables, every one of which points to the gratuity of God's dealings with his people and, by consequence, to the centrality of grace. Grace, in the parables, is love raised to a higher power by a higher power. There is that prodigal son and his gracious father and the straight-arrow brother who kept tabs on who got what! There is even a story about equal pay for unequal work, which is mind-blowing if taken seriously—as it rarely is. There is an ironic tale about an outcast (a Samaritan, and it is ironic to see how eagerly highly advantaged people prefer to identify themselves with him) who was more gracious than those who were, so to say, professionally gracious. All the parables are variations on this contrast between the order of merit and the domain of grace with its emphasis on love beyond demand. In this domain, our talents are recognized as given, and so also are our capacities, along with our friendships and unearned experiences of caring love and joy. But sometimes our grumblings about how much less we have been given than we deserved proceed to spoil our thankfulness for what we have been given and what we can do with that. This is a sure sign that our avarice exceeds our gratitude and that we are still tempted to seek redress more in power than in grace.

Science is intelligence in service of order (order that is given as structure rather than as consensus). Religion is faith in service of the *humanum* (of freedom that is of grace). Religion must rely on science for its understandings of what is given in creation. Science must rely on religion for its understanding of the whence of that givenness and to what ends. And since the same persons are, or may be, both scientific and religious in full integrity, the problem is not one of subordination from either side but of their shared awareness of the *humanum's* place in the orders of creation and freedom. This is the way beyond alienation to reconciliation.

Religion, which looks to God's uncreated grace as his essence and to the effects of created grace as the essence of the *humanum,* is a real alternative to all forms of idolatry, magic, self-salvation. Grace is the self-disclosed quality of the Mystery of which we have spoken. We cannot define or manipulate this Mystery but we can, by grace, live in it and die gracefully, since life itself is tinctured with grace, and death need not be graceless. Our experiences of grace are often unobtrusive. They come when they come; they are accepted as our gratitude allows. How else would one account for one's talents in their full measure? How else are our aptitudes stretched beyond their mediocrity? How else do we recognize how much we have been given, and how we may accept such unbidden disclosures? Grace is not a strategy; it is a *habitus* that is never taken for granted by the sensitive. It is as a swimmer, depending upon the water's buoyancy, uses his or her energies for getting on rather than on getting out. Grace is energy without alienation.

The gifts of grace are more than episodic. They are intimations of the essential goodness of the Ultimate Reality upon which we must depend and can depend, gratefully. Grace looks outward, from self to others, to the world, to God—to the more and more humane, the more and more creative, more productive, more serene. One of the central concerns of high religion has always been the *ars moriendi* (the art of meaningful life even with death in view), and if it has seemed to you that my vision of life in grace is more passive than activist, you must remember the prayer that my old friend Reinhold Niebuhr taught us: for courage and zeal to do all that ever can be done; for fortitude and grace to face what cannot be changed; for wisdom and honesty to know which is which, and when.

The crucial question in most of the social action I have known—for seven decades now, for I started as a child with the causes of world peace and desegregation and women's rights—is the one about motives and perseverance. When the struggle for justice is self-serving, its tactics will be opportunistic and its commitments will falter, as much with success as with failure. This is why gratitude is more trustworthy as a fuel for effectual goodness, since gratitude in response to grace ripens into generosity and zest. The Rule of Grace is, therefore, the sort of liberation that will benefit more people in the longer run—for living as if we truly were at home in God's family and, as a spiritual consequence, more wholly dedicated to God's good causes in his world. To live by grace, to live gracefully, is possible as one discerns, accepts, and responds to uncreated grace, freely given. For this, in turn, opens the way to dignity without pride, to maturity without smugness, to equanimity with élan.

What if our universe *is* open—to the transcendent, to the Ultimate Intention that designs both order and freedom for the *humanum's* good? What if there is an ascending order of knowledge and insight—from nature to the human to the holy, to the whole? Would it not then be the human destiny truly to be at home in such an order of freedom, not pyramidal nor yet random, but peaceable and productive in a way that the power syndrome cannot achieve and cannot quite prevent? This would be a bolster to our confidence in that power of grace that we have seen in high religion, over the ages and still now, as in the Psalmist's claim for the human prospect when it is faced as a work of grace:

> Surely goodness (*tobe*) and mercy (*chesed*) [both terms synonyms for "grace"] shall follow me all the days of my life and I shall dwell [shall be at home and dwell in peace] in the house of the Lord, forever (Psalm 23:6).

Endnotes

Preface

1   Albert C. Outler, *John Wesley.* In the *Library of Christian Thought* series (New York: Oxford University Press, 1964).

2   Albert C. Outler, ed. *The Works of John Wesley,* volumes 1–4 (Nashville: Abingdon, 1984–1987).

3   Albert C. Outler, *Psychotherapy and the Christian Message* (New York: Harper and Brothers, 1954).

Chapter 2—Forty Years Later: Some Personal Reflections on Religion and Mental Health

1   David E. Roberts, *Psychotherapy and a Christian View of Man* (New York: Charles Scribner's Sons, 1950).

2   See especially, Rollo May, *The Art of Counseling* (Nashville: Abingdon Press, 1978). The first edition of this book appeared in 1939. It was followed by *The Springs of Creative Living: a Study of Human Nature and God* (Nashville: Abingdon Press, 1940).

Chapter 3—The *Humanum:* Crux and Crunch in Contemporary Theology

1   At the time of this presentation, Bernard Lonergan was receiving widening critical acclaim for his book, *Insight: a Study of Human Understanding* (New York: Philosophical Library, 1970). In the early 1970s, Perkins theologians hosted a conference on Lonergan's thought, a conference in which Outler played a major role. After that conference, Outler's enthusiasm for Lonergan's contributions softened somewhat, but he continued to consider Transcendental Thomism crucial to the development of theology in this century.

Chapter 4—The Christian Clue

1   Irenaeus' thinking on this subject is scattered throughout his seminal work on Christian apologetics, the *Adversus haereses*

(*Against All Heresies*). An excellent discussion of his view, centered in his distinction between the "image" and the "likeness" of God (a distinction difficult to justify exegetically but impossible to avoid theologically) can be found in Maurice Wiles' *The Christian Fathers* (New York: Oxford University Press, 1982).

Chapter 7—Wesleyan Patterns of Pastoral Care

1   Rupert E. Davies, ed., *The Methodist Societies: History, Nature, and Design,* vol. 9 of *The Works of John Wesley* (Nashville, 1989), 77–78.

2   Outler is excerpting here from "The Order for the Ordination of Elders" of the Methodist *Book of Discipline.* It is not clear from his manuscript and attending file from which edition of the *Discipline* he is quoting. The cited words are those that the bishop says to persons presented for ordination as elders. They are read after the Epistle and the Gospel lessons, and before the questions that bishops have asked their ordinands since the time of Wesley.

Chapter 9—The Pastor as a Professional Person

1   During the period in which Outler was consolidating his own thinking on pastoral psychology, Paul Pruyser of the Menninger Institute was working on several projects aimed at prodding hospital chaplains in particular to bring their own unique contributions to bear on discussions about patient treatment and to rely less on the psychological jargon of their secular colleagues. Probably the most influential of Pruyser's writings on this subject, for clergy at least, was a little book published by Abingdon Press in 1975, entitled *The Minister as Diagnostician.*

2   James M. Lapsley, *Salvation and Health: the Interlocking Processes of Life* (Philadelphia: Westminster Press, 1972).

Chapter 10—The Good Shepherd: Changing Perspectives (1)

1   A fresh translation of this crucial letter, by M. Eugene Boring, is available in his commentary on *The Book of Revelation,* in the *Interpretation: A Bible Commentary for Teaching and Preaching* series (Louisville: John Knox Press, 1989), 14–15.

2 Outler's citation from Chrysostom is from a quotation in H. Richard Niebuhr and Daniel D. Williams, eds., *The Ministry in Historical Perspective* (New York: Harper and Brothers, 1956), 67–68.

3 Ambrose (340–397), *On the Duties of Clergy. A Select Library of the Nicene and Post-Nicene Fathers of the Christian Church (NPNF)*. H. Wace and P. Schaff, eds., 2d series, vol. 10, (New York: Christian, 1887–1892), 1–91.

4 Outler uses for this citation from Augustine a passage quoted in John T. McNeill, *A History of the Cure of Souls* (New York: Harper and Brothers, 1951), 100.

5 John T. McNeill, *The Celtic Penitentials and Their Influence on Continental Christianity* (Paris: E. Campion, 1923).

Chapter 11—Changing Images of the Good Shepherd (2)

1 Huldrich Zwingli (1484–1531), *Der Hirt* (Basil: C. Detloff, 1844).

2 George Herbert, *The Country Parson* (London: Henry Washbourne, 1832).

3 Jeremy Taylor (1613–1667), *The Rule and Exercises of Holy Dying* (London: Bell and Daldy, 1857).

4 Gilbert Burnet, *A Discourse of the Pastoral Care* (1692) (London: W. Bacques, 1818).

5 Richard Baxter, *The Reformed Pastor* (1656), William Brown, ed. (Carlisle, Pa.: Banner of Truth, 1979).

Chapter 12—Changing Images of the Good Shepherd (3)

1 Gregory the Great (540–604), *The Book of Pastoral Rule.* NPNF, 2d series, vol. 12.

Chapter 13—The Rise of Modern Psychotherapy and Alliances with Pastoral Care

1 Carl Rogers, *On Becoming a Person* (Boston: Houghton Mifflin, 1961).

2 Sigmund Freud, *Civilization and Its Discontents. The Standard Edition of the Complete Psychological Works of Sigmund Freud (SE).* Volume XXI, trans. James Strachey (London: Hogarth Press, 1953).

3 Carl Jung, *Modern Man in Search of a Soul* (London: Kegan Paul, 1933).

4 Erich Fromm, *Escape from Freedom* and *The Sane Society* (New York: Holt, Rinehart and Winston, 1941, 1955).

5 Paul Pruyser, *A Dynamic Psychology of Religion* (New York: Harper and Brothers, 1968).

Chapter 14—From Couch to Carpet: Vienna to Esalen

1 The most complete translation of the textbook of Emil Kraepelin to which Outler is referring is by A. Ross Diefendorf, *Clinical Psychiatry: a Textbook for Students and Physicians* (New York: Macmillan, 1915).

2 Richard Krafft-Ebing, *Psychopathia Sexualis: a Medicoforensic Study*, trans. F. J. Rabman (Brooklyn, N.Y.: Physicians' and Surgeons' Book Co., 1922).

3 Sigmund Freud, *The Interpretation of Dreams*. SE, vols. 4, 5, 1953.

Chapter 15—Of Human Bondage

1 Jean-Jacques Rousseau, *Social Contract*, trans. Henry J. Tozer (London: Allen and Unwin, 1924).

2 *Julius Caesar*, act I, sc. 2, line 134.

Chapter 17—A Gospel for the Guiltless

1 Arthur Miller, *Death of a Salesman* (New York: Viking Press, 1949).

Chapter 21—The Pastor and the Hallowing of Life: The Hallowing of the World

1 Donne, *Devotions*, XVII.

2 Richard Lovelace, "To Althea: From Prison," stanza 4.

3 Lord Acton, Letter to Bishop Mandell Creighton, 1887.

4 Edward Fitzgerald, "The Rubáiyát of Omar Khayyám," st. 13.

Chapter 22—Psychotherapy and Christian Faith

1 *Declaration on Human Freedom*, in *The Documents of Vatican II*, Walter M. Abbot, ed. (American Press: Geoffrey Chapman, 1966), 675–96.

2 See especially Van A. Harvey, *The Historian and the Believer* (New York: Macmillan, 1969).

Chapter 23—Psychotherapy and the Christian Message Revisited

1   Carl Jung, *Modern Man in Search of a Soul* (London: Kegan Paul, 1933).
2   Carl Jung, *Answer to Job. Collected Works (CW),* vol. 11 (Princeton: Princeton University Press, 1952).
3   Carl Jung, *Aion: Researches into the Phenomenology of the Self,* trans. R. F. C. Hull. *CW* 9, ii.
4   Carl Jung, *Memories, Dreams, and Reflections,* trans. Richard and Clara Winston (New York: Vantage Books, 1965).

Index

Freud, Sigmund 34–36, 39, 48,
117, 141, 168–169, 171,
177–182, 185–186, 188,
190, 208, 263–264,
272–273, 275–278, 280,
282–283
Civilization and Its Discontents 171, 254, 278
influence waning 278
Lust-Unlust Prinzip 218
myth of total depravity 185
The Interpretation of Dreams
179
Freudian revolution
essence of 179
Freudianism 265, 278
Fromm, Erich 141, 180, 182,
208, 272
*Escape to Freedom, The Sane
Society* 171
Fuller, Thomas 150–151
fundamentalism 121, 166, 176,
208–209
funerals 235
futuristic theology 210

G

Galilei 165, 166
Gaul 133
Gelasius 139
Genesis 190
Genesis myth 44, 76, 185, 289
George I of Hanover 150
Germany 157
Gestalt therapy 75, 180–182
Gladden, Washington
The Christian Pastor 117
Gnosticism 57, 129, 164, 223,
273, 278, 281
Goethe 279

good shepherd
a kind of cynic 199
art of shepherding 248
definition of 116, 128
effect of Social Gospel on 158
function in early church 132
imagery of 115
in Eastern Orthodoxy 137
joy and courage of 131
gospel songs
forensic image of sin in 207
grace 80, 109, 117, 154,
197, 213, 224, 232–233,
250, 262, 286, 294, 298
as used by Jung 284
Great Depression 86
Great Western schism 152
Greece 39
Greek 142
Gregory
Liber Regulae Pastorales 117
Pastoral Rules 153
Gregory of Nyssa 65
Grosseteste, Bishop 142
group dynamics
theory and practice of 107
guilt 192, 204, 206, 275

H

haecceity 62, 264
Hall, James 151, 270
Hallowe'en 222
Hardy, Thomas 292
Harms, Klaus 178
Harris, Tom 124
Hartshorne, Hugh 22, 164–165
Hartt, Julian 16
Hebrew prophets 256, 290
hedonism 293

Institute of Human Relations
162
Ireland 153
Irenaeus 131, 133, 164
notion of the Fall 62
Isidorian Decretals 139
isomorphism 267
Israel 39
Isthmus Institute in Dallas,
Texas 286
Italy 145
Ivanhoe 186

J

Jackson, Hughlings 239
Jacob of Voragine 142
Jansenists 154
Jaspers, Karl 264, 287
Jerusalem 132
Jesuits 154
Jesus
clue to mystery of humanity
53
his strange effects on us 66,
91
how he understood himself 66
image of God 212
reversed definition of power
292
John XXIII 124
Jonah 24
Judaism
wary of occult 280
Jung, Carl 19, 34, 39, 180,
264, 270, 272, 276–284,
295
Aion 276
Answer to Job 276, 278, 280
concept of grace 284
*Memories, Dreams, Reflec-
tions* 278

*Modern Man in Search of a
Soul* 171
parental influence on religious
views 278–279, 284
Jung Institute 39
Jungian psychotherapy 278
justification by faith 45
justification, doctrine of 144
Justin Martyr 131, 133

K

Kähler, Martin 86
kairos 125, 227, 229, 230
Kant, Immanuel 36, 166, 175,
182, 219, 281–283, 290
Critique of Pure Reason 281
kerygma 63, 83–85, 88, 91
about Jesus 86
Kierkegaard, Søren 279
kingdom of God 29, 67, 86,
126, 139, 209, 253, 293,
295
hunger for 252
kingdom of heaven. *See* kingdom
of God
Koch 178
Koestler, Arthur 50, 264
koinonia 90, 131, 137, 155
Kraepelin, Emil
Textbook of Psychiatry 179
Krafft-Ebing, Richard
Psychopathia Sexualis 179

L

LaMettrie 175
Lapsley, James 170
Salvation and Health 125
Lateran IV 263
Latin
language of Christendom 142

Murray, Grace   97
Mystery   40, 80, 116, 214,
   221, 229, 243, 245, 287,
   291, 296
mysticism   144, 209, 236, 245,
   266, 284
   Christian   242, 284
   Jewish   284
   Jungian   284
   nature   251
myth   38, 277–278, 282

N

narcissism   193, 227
   pastoral   249
nationalism   144
natural order   165
naturalism   121, 168, 174, 179,
   183, 281
   Christian   174
nature   165
   not concerned with individuals   79
Nazarenes   224
neo-Freudians   275
neoclassical theism   165
Nestorianism   58, 60, 88
New England   155
Newton, Sir Isaac   174
   Principia Mathematica   166
Nicea   57, 87, 263
Niebuhr, Reinhold   27, 45, 158,
   170–171, 272, 297
Nietzsche, Friedrich Wilhelm
   254, 275, 281
Ninety-five Theses. See Luther,
   Martin
noble savages   184
North America   145
nous   61, 88

O

Oates   172
obscurantism   169, 288
Occam   264
occasion   228–230, 235
   hallowing of   236
   negative   232–235
occultism   280
Oden, Thomas   172, 181
Ogden   165
oikoumene   131, 134
ordination   135, 247
   meaning of   225
   to ministry or marriage   139
Origen   131, 133, 164
original sin   157, 184, 190,
   194, 197
Orthodoxy   137
Orwell, George   290
ousia   57–58, 60, 64–65, 73,
   77, 79, 85, 87–88, 90–91
   of God is love   78

P

Pacific School of Religion
   Berkeley, California   42
Paine, Thomas   141
Palmer, Phoebe   156
Pannenberg, Wolfhart   58
pantheism   245
papacy
   England rejected   149
Paracelsus   283
parallelism   267
paranormal experience   243
parapsychology   239
Pareto   263
parson   120, 159
Pascal, Blaise   288
   Provincial Letters   154

Pasteur, Louis 178
pastoral care 271
  in Reformed tradition 148
  theology of 166
  theology of in America 157
pastoral care movement 35,
  160–162, 169
  has been conservative 252
  monasticizing tendency in 169
  weaknesses in 209
pastoral counseling 247
pastoral ministry
  and celebration 231
  essential tasks of 217,
  230–231
  fisherman not shepherds 142
  how it evolved in Roman
    Catholic Church 152–155
  in Anglican tradition 149–150
  in Middle Ages 120, 138, 141
  sensitive to gifts 243
  shift from Catholic to Protes-
    tant models 147
  to the ill 234
pastoral psychology 274
pastoral theology 116, 197,
  242, 247
  not a different kind of theology
    115
Pavlov, Ivan Petrovich 263
Peale 124
Pelagianism 126, 238, 273
Penfield, Wilder 174
penitential offices 139
  Celtic 139
Pentateuch 219
Pentecost 244
pentecostalism 137, 209
perichoresis 69
Pericles 290

Perkins School of Theology 6,
  11, 19, 82, 112, 286
Perkins, William 151
Perls, Fritz 180–181
personality theory 267
pessimism 193, 196
Petrine supremacy 131
Pfister, Oskar 19
Phanke, Walter 265
philanthropy 136
physeis 85
physis 58–61, 91
Piaget, Jean 182
Pierre de Berulle 155
pietism 134, 152, 156–158,
  177, 181, 252, 281
Plato 46, 65, 122, 182, 283,
  290
Platonism 163–165, 173, 262
  Christian 168, 173, 263,
    273
  humanness in the ideal 62
Pliny's "Letter to Trajan" 129
Pope, Alexander 47
Potter, Bishop John 108
preaching 145, 249
prevenient grace 15, 103, 154,
  214
pride 191
priesthood of all believers 120,
  131
progress 37
prosopon 59
Protestant Principle 145
Protestant Revolt
  Rome's reaction to 152
Protestantism 145–146, 158
  classical soteriology of 205
  in America 157
  liberal 159

World War I   86
worship   221, 243
Wrede   85

X

Ximénez   153

Y

Yale University   6, 10, 22,
27, 39, 54, 162, 239,
261, 276

Institute of Human Relations
261
Yellowlees, Henry   34
yoga   243

Z

Zahrndt   86
Zwingli
Der Hirt   146